WHAT IS HISTORY, NOW?

WHAT IS HISTORY, NOW?

How the past and present speak to each other

EDITED BY HELEN CARR AND SUZANNAH LIPSCOMB

WEIDENFELD & NICOLSON

First published in Great Britain in 2021 by Weidenfeld & Nicolson,
an imprint of The Orion Publishing Group Ltd
Carmelite House, 50 Victoria Embankment
London EC4Y 0DZ

An Hachette UK Company

1 3 5 7 9 10 8 6 4 2

Typeset by Input Data Services Ltd, Somerset

Printed and bound in Great Britain by Clays Ltd, Elcograf S.p.A.

MIX
Paper from
responsible sources
FSC
www.fsc.org FSC® C104740

www.weidenfeldandnicolson.co.uk
www.orionbooks.co.uk

For our children

CONTENTS

FOREWORD

Helen Carr

History consists of a corpus of ascertained facts. The facts are available to the historian in documents, inscriptions and so on, like fish on the fishmonger's slab. The historian collects them, takes them home, and cooks and serves them in whatever style appeals to him.

E.H. Carr, What is History? (1961)

In 1961, Edward Hallett Carr gave a series of lectures at the University of Cambridge which he called *What is History?* His leading intention was to demonstrate that, like 'fish on the fishmonger's slab', facts are served as the historian wishes to serve them and that history is by and large interpretive. This theory was so popular, groundbreaking and revolutionary in its time, that *What is History?* was compiled into a book that quickly became a key text for generations of history students and historians thereafter. Carr's work was so popular it was republished as a Penguin Classic in 2018. I am a historian who has been influenced by Carr's key text but his influence on me perhaps goes a little further, for E.H. Carr was my great-grandfather.

My memories of history and the learning of history were enhanced by the omnipresent familial legacy of E.H. Carr, nicknamed 'the Prof' but known affectionately as 'Ted'. He died six years before I was born, but his energy has lived on within our family and encouraged my insatiable interest in history, prompting an imagined dialogue with my great-grandfather, one of our greatest and most influential historians and thinkers. I am fortunate enough to observe the work he has carefully and thoughtfully created take its place on the grand stage of History, and I share with his son (my grandfather) John the hope that it will 'stimulate further study and understanding of the future way forward in the world'. This collection of voices is inspired by *What is History?* and serves as a tribute to Carr's timeless work but it is also an olive branch to those who have felt pushed out or marginalised from history and the way we talk about it. *What is History, Now?* argues loudly that history belongs to us all and by making space for all histories, we can perhaps begin to understand a much deeper, broader past.

Helen Carr
Cambridge, March 2021

Prologue: Ways in

Helen Carr and Suzannah Lipscomb

Mary Queen of Scots was beheaded on 8 February 1587 at Fotheringhay Castle in Northamptonshire. She laid her head upon a
block and, after a couple of awkward and bloody attempts, her
head was struck from her body. This macabre fact about Mary
Queen of Scots is the first history fact I, Helen, remember from
probably the age of four or five as I ambled about the ruins of
Fotheringhay Castle on a day out with my father. For some reason,
it gripped me. Apparently I forced him to return to Fotheringhay
regularly to ascertain the exact location of the beheading (the
centre of the Great Hall, for those who want to know).

Saturdays in my childhood were mostly spent like this. These
adventures – trips to castles, houses, churches, cathedrals, monuments, ancient stones – were how I became fascinated with
the past. I sought out history elsewhere. In nature: wondering
how old is the oldest tree and was it around at the same time
as Henry VIII? In movies: I watched *Braveheart* far too young
and thought it was magical. And in landscape and myth: I grew
up nearby the Avebury Stones, the little sister of Stonehenge.

3

Here, I dreamed about Merlin and wondered where Excalibur was now.

This type of history excited me far more than the history that was offered at school, which I found strangely disappointing. School history didn't fit with my version of history. My history was more than facts and dates; it was the *feeling* of the past, the myth, the magic, the stuff we didn't know. All of this was my way into history.

For reasons of adoption or possibly short memories, the histories that came down to me, Suzannah, as a child were all on one side of my family. Tracing the patrimonial line takes the family back to Richard Lipscomb, baptised in Portsmouth at the parish church in September 1668, who later drowned in the harbour, having possibly fallen off the pier when drunk. (Late last year, a distant Lipscomb relative sent me a portrait of him. Wearing a white wig over a shaved head – you can detect the faintest shadow of his natural hairline – and dressed in a modest, matching coat and waistcoat of brown wool over a linen shirt with cravat or frills made of very fine, transparent lawn, he looks likely to have been a moderately wealthy merchant – someone rich enough to have his portrait painted, but not by a painter who could do hands.) I have a well-used wooden chopping board, with ears of wheat and the initials 'J.T. Lipscomb A.D. 1851' in relief carving around the rim, which must have belonged to his grandson, John Thomas Lipscomb. Then there's a line of Fredericks, including poor Rev. Frederick Bell Lipscomb who, at the age of forty-six, had been paying a visit to a fellow clergyman in a neighbouring village and was returning home on his bicycle 'when,' a local newspaper tells me, 'a pony, then being harnessed in the stable of

4

a public house,' suddenly rushed into the road and collided with him. Frederick Bell was violently thrown to the ground and never regained consciousness. He left a widow and five children. One of those was my great-grandfather, who, like many of his era, spent most of his distinguished career in India, as a doctor in the Royal Army Medical Corps. He was one of the first medics into the liberated concentration camp at Belsen. He died eight years before I was born, and I am writing this at his desk.

These family histories were one reason why the past seemed so alluring to me growing up. I didn't realise until much later that the pursuit of genealogy invariably means losing track of the women; as far as family trees are concerned, they birth sons and die. But the fables about these almost tangible relatives gave me an odd, indefinable thrill. They made the past seem both remote and, quite literally, familiar. This was my way into history.

As we write, history is hot stuff. It is the focus of hot-off-the-press news, the subject of heated debate – or, at least, so we're led to believe – and some people express fears that it's being stolen. But how hot are we on what history actually is?

In March 2021, the *Daily Telegraph* ran a piece with the headline, '"Soviet" universities are fictionalising history'. It reported that Universities Minister Michelle Donelan had said, 'The so-called decolonisation of the curriculum is, in effect, censoring history. As a history student, I'm a vehement protector and champion of safeguarding our history. It otherwise becomes fiction, if you start editing it, taking bits out that we view as stains.' She went on, 'most of the narrative that is coming out . . . is about removing elements of history, about whitewashing it, and pretending it never happened, which I just think is naive, and almost irresponsible.' She compared such behaviour to practices in China and the Soviet Union.

The idea of removing the troubling bits from history is itself very troubling; that universities might be fictionalising or censoring history should alarm anyone. But is that what is happening? 'Decolonising the curriculum' involves considering histories of race, empire and slavery; not perpetuating imperialist attitudes; and attending to historical experiences beyond those of the (usually) white colonisers. It is about diversifying the voices included in 'history' rather than censoring them, about examining the 'stains' on history rather than taking bits out. As Priyamvada Gopal writes, it is instead about putting 'the "offensive" bits BACK IN'. In other words, it means almost exactly the opposite of what Donelan seems to think it means. But it is Donelan's insistence that what she said was 'as a history student' and a 'champion of safeguarding our history' that requires our special attention. It suggests we need to think more about what history is.

In the early 2020s in the UK, what history is has felt confused. In June 2020, when a statue of slave trader Edward Colston was pulled down in Bristol and a movement gathered once again to dethrone imperialist Cecil Rhodes from his place outside Oriel College, Oxford, the prime minister tweeted 'We cannot now try to edit or censor our past.' This was also the attitude of Oliver Dowden, secretary of state for culture, when he wrote to the Museum of the Home in Hackney, London, that month. The museum had recently changed its name from that of slave trader Robert Geffrye and was holding a public consultation on relocating a statue of Geffrye from above the entrance. Dowden cautioned the museum's trustees, 'We cannot pretend to have a different history.' Two months later, the culture secretary interposed himself again, writing to inform organisations such as the Imperial War Museum, Historic Royal Palaces and the British Museum that 'the government does not support the removal of statues' (in fact, the government is, at the time of writing, seeking to pass legislation that would make damaging a statue or monument punishable by up to ten years in gaol, double the minimum sentence for rape). 'Removing difficult and contentious parts' of the historic environment, he warned, 'risks harming our understanding of our collective past.' Both the prime minister and the culture secretary were echoing art historian and former director of the V&A, Sir Roy Strong, who in 2016 had responded to an earlier iteration of the Rhodes Must Fall protests by stating, 'Once you start rewriting history on that scale, there won't be a statue or a historic house standing . . . The past is the past. You can't rewrite history.'

Concerns about rewriting history seem also to have been at the forefront of Charles Moore's mind when, in September 2020, he reacted to news that the National Trust had published a report on the colonial connections of its properties, including links to the transatlantic slave trade. In the *Spectator*, Moore called it a 'shameful manifesto'. He was not commenting on the shamefulness of past behaviour, rather he was concerned that this critique of the past would make the British feel ashamed: that a critical examination of the past would taint the present. Yet, the reverse is true: it is when we persist in viewing the tainted past uncritically that we continue to sully the present.

Donelan, Johnson, Dowden, Strong and Moore think that removing statues of slave traders and colonisers and reconsidering the history that is taught in universities or presented in heritage sites constitutes a 'rewriting' of history. This they consider, in the words of *1066 And All That*, a Bad Thing – a kind of erasure of the past. But this is surely to go through the looking glass. Advocating an end to commemorating those who authorised and benefitted from the colonisation, oppression and enslavement of other humans, while encouraging us to pay attention to the stories of those who were colonised, oppressed and enslaved is the very antithesis of erasing the past: it's about refusing to accept a censored version of history that glorifies certain people and erases others. Neither is rewriting history necessarily the bogeyman they fear it to be. Rewriting history, as Charlotte Lydia Riley argues eloquently in this book, is the definition of what historians do and have always done. (Robert Gildea, emeritus professor of modern history at the University of Oxford, argues that those who state, 'You can't rewrite history,' simply mean 'You mustn't rewrite the history we have already written.') History can, of course, be rewritten to advance a political narrative or to expunge parts of history – but it can also be rewritten to direct our gaze to troubling bits of history that have, until now, been hidden. In this latter form, it is the equivalent of wisely changing one's mind when faced with new evidence or a new perspective. And, in fact, if we're looking for examples of the more pernicious rewriting of history, we need look no further than the erection of many statues themselves. Of monuments to slaveholders and Confederate leaders put up long after the American Civil War and during the era of the segregating Jim Crow laws, historian Julian Hayter remarks that they 'were designed to tell a story. They were designed to rewrite history, to essentially justify the rise of racial apartheid and segregation.' By contrast, he says, taking them down is a way of correcting this rewriting – of rewriting the rewriting, if you will. Which is to say, as one of our contributors, Alex von Tunzelmann, argues in her book, *Fallen Idols*,

> Statues . . . are not really about history at all, but are about how we see ourselves reflected in history: pride versus shame, good versus bad, heroes versus villains. Statues are not a record of history but of historical memory. They reflected what somebody at some point thought we should think.

Our memory of history and what we choose to acknowledge about the past matters because, *pace* Sir Roy Strong, the past, to quote William Faulkner, is not past. Which stories we tell about history, who we celebrate and the ideas and values they embody determine the world we live in today.

What this whole debate makes clear is that we need to think long and hard about what history is now, and what it means to write it, and rewrite it. And it turns out that in working out how to do that, we can take some pointers from history itself: from E.H. Carr writing sixty years ago.

The central idea in *What is History?* came to Carr while he was still an undergraduate in Classics at Cambridge. He realised that Herodotus's account of the Persian Wars in the fifth century BC was shaped by his attitude to the Peloponnesian War (431 BC), which was being fought as Herodotus wrote. Carr called this a 'fascinating revelation . . . it gave me my first understanding of what history was about'. For Carr, Herodotus demonstrated that historians do not draw on objective facts, but their experience of them; 'our picture of Greece in the fifth century BC is defective not primarily because so many of the bits have been lost, but because it is, by and large, the picture formed by a tiny group of people in the city of Athens.' This argument formed the backbone of *What is History?*

Accepting that historians cannot help but be subjective, however, was not the concrete way of doing history. Nineteenth-century historians approached the past as if they were Olympian gods: they believed they could write objective history, a dispassionate, linear timeline of accepted events, as made famous by the scholar Leopold von Ranke in the 1830s, who wanted 'simply to show how it really was'. This approach was, according to Carr, a 'preposterous fallacy'. Carr explained that while we can formulate a subjective understanding of the past, we simply cannot know it, exactly as it was, from the facts presented to us.

'What is a historical fact? This is a crucial question into which we must look a little more closely.' So Carr begins his interrogation of facts by analysing how the 'fact' is prepared and presented by the historian who studies it. He does so by dividing facts into two categories: facts of the past and facts of the present. A fact of the past, such as 'the Battle of Hastings was fought in 1066', is indisputable but basic. A fact of the present is a fact an historian has chosen to be a fact. In an analogy you'll see oft-repeated in this book, Carr wrote: 'by and large, the historian will get the kind of facts he wants. History means interpretation.' The truth was and still is that facts can be changed or manipulated to benefit those relaying them. 'Alternative facts' are not a new phenomenon. During Carr's lifetime, both the Stalinist regime and the British government destroyed documents, altered evidence and distorted history. It is this misrepresentation and misuse of fact, deliberate or accidental, that Carr also interrogates in

What is History? He encourages any student of history, above all things, to be discerning.

However, Carr did not always wave the flag of subjectivity. During the Cold War in the early 1950s the global political atmosphere was particularly partisan, pushing him to embrace objectivity as he sought a 'rational liberal outlook on the world'. Carr's attempt at liberalism had no place in the Cold War era and his refusal to 'pick a side' prompted accusations that he was an apologist for Stalin. According to George Orwell, he even held Soviet sympathies, having praised the USSR for their successes. Carr's decision to end his *History of Soviet Russia* at 1929, before Stalin exercised his major atrocities, also invited suspicion and criticism. His biographer, Jonathan Haslam, even believes that the Trevelyan Lectures would have been very different had they been delivered by Carr a decade earlier. With the world no longer in a position of immense nuclear anxiety, Carr no longer felt the need to protect liberalism and, according to Haslam, he 'felt free to attack it and did so with vigour'.

Despite Carr's political contentions in the 1950s, *What is History?* does not reflect his politics a decade later. It should therefore be judged on its own merits, as it is throughout this volume. History, Carr said, is a process that needs consistent interrogation and reinterpretation, for there is 'a continuous process of interaction between the historian and his [or her] facts'. This book continues that process.

It is not the first to revisit *What is History?* In 1985, the magazine *History Today* ran a series of articles from leading historians on different branches of history, and the problems involved in studying, researching and writing these. A selection edited by Juliet Gardiner was published by Macmillan as *What is History*

11

Today? The chapters were called things like 'What is military history?', 'What is the history of science?', 'What is Third World history?', 'What is diplomatic history?' Under each topic, four or five historians provided a short version of an answer. Aside from the editor and the five women who contributed to the chapter 'What is women's history?', only one other female historian appears, alongside sixty-three male historians. There was only one non-white contributor.

In 2002, David Cannadine published *What is History Now?* with Palgrave Macmillan. In it, ten distinguished academic historians (including Richard J. Evans, Linda Colley, Felipe Fernández-Armesto and Miri Rubin, who also contributes to this book) each responded to questions in the format: 'What is social history now?' 'What is political history now?' and 'What is intellectual history now?' Reviews described it as 'a must-have text for today's history students' and 'invaluable to graduate students and scholars', and that was its intended audience. But we think the conversation is bigger than the academy. It isn't just about those, like us, who have had the luxury of studying history. There is much too much at stake for that.

Sixty years on from *What is History?* E.H. Carr's questions about how we investigate and interrogate the past remain. Sixty years on, it is crucial as well as timely to reinvestigate, reinterrogate and reinterpret our understanding of the past. Not the past of the select few, but the past of the many, in order to demonstrate, share – shout from the rooftops – that history belongs to us all.

The two of us each have, at home, a ruler of rulers: a list of monarchs of Britain from AD 43 to 1952 on a 30cm rule. It's the sort of thing one buys for a history lover. But, in fact, it elides 'British'

with 'English' – it doesn't provide a list of the monarchs of Scotland – and it omits the contested queens Matilda and Jane. It's a
good example of how history, as a discipline, can seem to offer
us access to a straight and comprehensive inventory of empirical,
objective, historical facts, when the past was actually far more
convoluted, contentious and confusing. As the essays in this
collection show, we now know that not only does the writing of
history always involve selection and interpretation, but what was
included in the archives from which historians can derive their
facts was also subject to selection. The evidence we have is partial, and the archive has its own silences and erasures. As Dame
Hilary Mantel explained it in her 2017 BBC Reith Lectures,

> history is not the past – it is the method we have evolved of
> organising our ignorance of the past. It's the record of what's
> left on the record . . . It's what's left in the sieve when the
> centuries have run through it . . .

But what if time ground down the people of the past to such fine
dust that we catch nothing of them in history's sieve? Trying to
write the history of people whose stories did not make it into the
archives presents huge challenges for historians. How does one
write about silence?

The problem of silences in the archives is especially pressing if
we recognise that history is not only constructed in the present –
our understanding of it also constructs the sort of present we live
in. We live with the legacies of the past. Carr recognised that history was an 'unending dialogue between the past and the present'.
Histories of racism and sexism, for example, determine what survived in the archives and what stories they can tell. Archives testify

to the nature of power in the past, and if we want the nature of who has power in the present to be more equitably distributed than it has historically been, then we need to understand the process by which certain peoples have been excluded from history. Seeking to tell their stories is a way of seeking redress – not for the dead, who remain dead, but in the interests of the living. An old-fashioned Olympian view of history would have thought that determining the questions we ask of the past by the realities of the present was to risk anachronism and partisanship, but Carr demonstrated to us that, consciously or unconsciously, we always ask questions from the point of view of the present. Some of those who have written for this book research the histories of women, histories of Black and Indigenous people, histories of those with disabilities, histories of those who are queer – because we think all those people matter in the present.

There are many ways into history, none are right or wrong, better or worse.

Some people enjoy history by reading novels, imagining a world of windswept historical hunks and damsels in distress – this romantic trope has indeed been perpetuated by some wonderful fiction and fiction is an important part of enjoying history. Mantel's *Wolf Hall* has demonstrated the power of fiction in telling the story of the past. 'Freedom!': the simple word from Mel Gibson covered in blue woad is a household one that instantly speaks of the fight for Scottish independence in the late thirteenth century. Yes, *Braveheart* was full of anachronisms, but it was also passionate and exciting. For some, it was a way in. Watching *Gladiator* or visiting the Colosseum is no more or less valid a way into ancient history than reading Edward Gibbon's six-volume *History of the*

Decline and Fall of the Roman Empire: the former could actually lead to the latter should an interest be piqued. Yet, some people feel that history is not for everyone, or not for them; they find it 'boring' or 'they just could not get on with all those dates'. This is understandable. Many feel their way into history has been this 'ruler history' – as if history must always be austere, straight, hard, and scholarly. One colour, one gender. This book intends to prove the opposite: that history can be flexible, malleable, colourful and without bias – that history is, above all, interpretation. This is why this volume hosts a multiplicity of voices. Shortly before his death, Carr had prepared material for a second edition of *What is History?* In it he hoped that the study of history could create 'an optimistic, at . . . any rate a saner and more balanced outlook on the future'. This book attempts to provide a balanced outlook by offering a collective one. We have deliberately included a range of diverse voices: both academic and non-academic; people at different stages of their career, leading scholars and also new voices, discussing history in a variety of forms.

This book is for everyone intrigued and perturbed by the recent debates about how and whose history should be commemorated; everyone who feels alienated from the stories that have been told – and equally fascinated by those that have been omitted from history; and everyone who wants to educate themselves about the past.

In the last sixty years there has been an upsurge in the public interest in history. Through movies, television, fiction and the media, history has become popularised and consumed as recreation. In the last years, history has dominated the print media, podcasts, talk shows, news headlines, programmes and personal conversations. People have asked: can history be erased? How do we talk about the past? Can we impose our values on those who lived hundreds – even thousands – of years before us? In answer to these ubiquitous questions and following the enormous global upheaval of COVID-19, we believe that it is time to return to the 'dialogue' and to Carr's question: what is history, now?

The essays in this volume explore some of the ways in which people approach the past – through films, literature and their own family histories. Contributors examine different approaches to the study of history – the history of religion, racism, the environment, emotions, and mythologies of the past – and the different ways one can tell history – narratively, immersively, and through the 'stuff' of the past. They address marginalised histories that were not part of the mainstream narrative in 1961: the history of women, Black history, queer histories, the history of people with disabilities and Indigenous histories, and they also consider the revision or 'rewriting' of history, including the question of how we write the history of empire today, why our histories must be global, and why that means paying particular heed to Asia.

This book is designed to offer a way in, proving that history is for everybody and inviting you, the reader, to enter and share in the many ways in which history can be enjoyed and interpreted. It is for everyone who is questioning how to look at the past, how to think about the present, and how to act in the future.

Chapter 1

Why global history matters

Peter Frankopan

Historians do not agree about what 'global history' means. For some, it means widening the geographic lens through which the past is normally examined. Traditionally, studying history at school and at university has meant beginning with the Greeks and the Romans, moving swiftly to the Middle Ages before taking in the Tudors, the Civil War, French Revolution and Napoleonic Wars before reaching the First and the Second World Wars. In recent years, that has started to change, with a welcome initiative to also think about parts of the world that are not in Europe, and which were not impacted by the centuries of European colonisation.

In that sense, 'global history' can be like a blank canvas that enables historians to think and write about parts of the world that have been too long ignored by the mainstream of historical scholarship – whose focus has been heavily dominated by the history of 'the West'. Looking at the histories of the peoples of the Pacific, for example, at the Indigenous cultures of the Americas before (or after) 1492, or at pre-colonial Africa, fits into this broad description and is individually and collectively important in helping create a wider and more exciting overall view of the past by opening up regions and subjects that have been poorly served by historians in the past.

So, for example, while most historians of the fifteenth and six-teenth centuries write about the Tudors, the Reformation and new ideas about politics that changed Europe, few spare a thought, let alone monographs, about the Songhay Empire that was one of the largest states in African history in the same period. Likewise, while much attention is paid to social change in Europe in the eighteenth century, to the Enlightenment, to colonialism or to the origins and impact of the industrial revolution, few write about what was happening with empires elsewhere – such as the military confrontation between Burmese and Thai forces that brought down the Siamese kingdom and led to the sack of Ayutthaya, one of the most destructive moments in South East Asian history.

Other historians, though, think of 'global history' as a means of providing greater global texture and context even to events, episodes and periods from the past that can be and sometimes already are well covered by modern scholarship by opening up a perspective that is not only more inclusive but more balanced and instructive. For example, few scholars who write about the Middle Ages – a term that means more for those who work on Europe but has little or no meaning for other regions – discuss diplomatic contacts between the Ethiopian emperor Wedem Arad (ወደም አራድ) and the pope as well as with royal rulers in Europe at the start of the fourteenth century, or comment on the proposed alliance between the Mongol court and the King of England against the Mamluks of Egypt, which included a Christian Bishop sent from what is now western China to not only meet King Edward I but to celebrate Mass with him.

Likewise, the story of the age of revolutions that takes in the Declaration of Independence in America in 1776 and the storming of the Bastille in 1789 often overlooks what happened in Haiti, where former slaves took power and liberated the island from its colonial masters. Or there are the accounts of the First World War that almost always fail to note that 140,000 Chinese people (almost exclusively men) served on the Western Front in Europe, let alone explain the significance of military conflict in Africa and the Middle East, or what the dramatic consequences were of the post-war settlements for South and East Asia. Or there are the roles played by significant populations during the Second World War which go unrecorded and undiscussed – thereby distorting how we think about the past. For example, almost as many Kazakhs as British soldiers died fighting against German forces, while five times more Kazakh civilians died during the war than British. From a British perspective, this was and is a footnote; to Kazakhs at the time and today, anything but.

Others, though, think of 'global history' as needing and demanding more structure than simply filling in the blanks that have been left untouched. In this understanding, global history is about telling a global story, about linking narratives that do not just create new silos that are independent of each other as stand-alone topics. Rather, the aim is – or should be – to join up the dots by finding, highlighting and demonstrating connections that link peoples, regions and even continents together.

This can be fruitful to chart the spread of goods, technologies, religions, languages and even of art, to present a story that sees borrowings and continuities as being important – regardless of whether they spread through violence and conquest or through adoption and peaceful competition and development. Networks like the Silk Roads, maritime connections that linked the Pacific and Indian Oceans with the Red Sea, Gulf and Mediterranean, or zones like the South Pacific, or South Western and Central America along with the Caribbean, can be helpful in framing ideas of how connections worked at practical and local levels by focusing on logistical issues like transportation, infrastructure, tax and taxation, as well as on the impact of local, regional and intercontinental relations, the development of cultural ties or changing ideas about the divine.

This approach helps to explain how societies borrowed and learned from each other and can provide an important corrective to insular ideas about the past by showing how those living hundreds, and even thousands of years ago, were aware of each other in a world that was more 'globalised' than we sometimes think. Pottery from North Africa found in the most northern parts of Scotland dating to nearly two millennia ago, amphora bringing wine from the eastern Mediterranean fifteen hundred years ago that have been found off the coast of Plymouth, or coins minted in Central Asia with Arabic inscriptions found in central England, speak of a complex, intensive and connected world that requires us to broaden our own horizons when we think about the past.

It is possible too, of course, to break down connections by looking at a single idea, product or foodstuff to show the impact that they have had. Indeed, some outstanding histories have been published in recent years that chart how concepts of the supernatural beliefs developed and spread from South Asia as far as Northern Europe, or how cotton, or potatoes or bananas have had impacts on social and political change and even on life expectancy when introduced to new regions and peoples.

And of course, global history does not need to be told through the prism of commercial exchange. Some of the most exciting work being done today in the field of global history is about genetics and linguistics, while contemporary interest in climate change and in disease, and especially in epidemics and pandemics, is prompting more attention to be paid to problems that were recognisable to previous generations as well as to the present day.

Some historians, however, are less enamoured by the idea of 'global history', seeing the label as simplistic and even misleading, implying ideas about what it means to be global and globalised in a past where such terms did not mean the same as they do today. It is hard to argue with this critique, or to take issue with the associated problem of 'periodisation' when it comes to history. Labels like 'antiquity', 'the Middle Ages' or 'early modern' are not entirely unproblematic for historians of the West; but they are meaningless for vast parts of the world. Moreover, because historians tend to specialise in one period, even those who are able and willing to cast their eyes over wider regions, working on 'global history' can create as many problems as it solves by leaving chronological boundaries in place while taking down those of geography.

Some have concerns too that global history can too often be 'top-down', looking at rulers, their courts and senior officials, at elite culture and diplomatic exchange, rather than taking in fuller cross-sections of society and using methodologies that are familiar for those working in more specialised fields. Other prisms that are second nature to many historians, for example those of gender, have also lagged behind in recent years, but questions about how to read gender within and as part of global history have started to be posed more regularly. There are occasional mutterings too that a large proportion of those who work on global themes are men – something that is itself revealing about wider problems of the role that gender plays not just in the study of history but for historians themselves.

Perhaps the single greatest problem about global history, however, revolves around something more basic even than frames of reference – and in fact is centred on the most simple element of being a historian: technical expertise. Being able to deal with complex sources requires training, patience and experience. Written sources are not documents that can be stripped of their data; they need to be understood. The identity, background and motivation of a text's author – whether they are lawyers, poets, traders or children – need to be understood. This requires language skills to be able to understand not only what the words mean, but their meaning and their context.

And that in turn means understanding different literary registers, ranging from high-flown poems delivered to praise a ruler, to bureaucratic documents that record the mechanics and logistics of the state. It means being able to read and understand diplomatic missives, private letters and diaries written by those who were eyewitnesses or even protagonists at events in the past. It means understanding the audience and reception of texts, whether they are narrative histories or ships' logs recording a vessel's cargo, draught, speed and position.

It also means being able to understand and represent voices that are not heard, either because they are not represented in historical records, or because of the shortcomings of the materials available – which in itself requires awareness of what kinds of sources survive and why. How, for example, are we to capture the thoughts and fears of the many millions of slaves who were transported across the Atlantic? How do we build pictures of rural and agricultural populations a thousand years ago when so much of the evidence was written in towns, about towns and for people who lived in towns and cities? How do we use chance discoveries to be more than haphazard anecdotes, but present them to provide insights about the past? While we know how people wrote, how do we know how they spoke, joked and used slang in distant time periods? How do we incorporate less formal documents, including those written or composed by those who were not members of the bureaucratic or commercial elites? One good example (one of my favourites) is a piece of birch bark found in Novgorod in Russia, dating to the thirteenth century, that shows a young boy's schoolwork revealing him learning to form letters and to write, perhaps as practice, or perhaps while day-dreaming during class or at home. The boy – who we know was named Onfim – has drawn a picture of an animal alongside which he has jotted 'I am a beast.'

Being able to navigate the primary sources is a vital part of being able to work on global pasts. But so too are other technical skills, for in addition to written materials are a myriad of other resources which also require knowledge and training to be able to work with. These include archaeological finds of coins, lead seals, stratigraphic layers in houses that show evidence of fires; or city walls, irrigation channels and grave goods. All such kinds of historical materials need to be understood in terms of what they can help illuminate, but also in terms of their meaning and their limitations. For example, without understanding the age profile of coin hoards, the metallic composition of the coins themselves, their dating and the context for their discovery, it is possible to create as many, if not more, problems than one solves.

Likewise, a vast array of new kinds of materials that are transforming the study of history requires historians to keep on acquiring and refining technical skills, often in the fields of maths and statistical analysis, as well as of physical and biological sciences. Contrary to popular assumptions that little or nothing new can be found about the past, the opposite is the case, with an explosion of new kinds of data and new methods that are making the early twenty-first century a revolutionary and transformative moment in the way in which we are able to look at and understand the past.

For example, projects using satellite imagery taken to try to keep an eye on Soviet military installations in Central Asia during the Cold War and, latterly, on the movements of Taliban forces have become goldmines of material by showing outlines of caravanserais (or resting points) for overland commercial traders that had not previously been identified on the ground. New light detection and ranging technology (LIDAR) has revolutionised what we know about the size of settlements in Guatemala during the Maya era, revealing tens of thousands of structures beneath a rainforest that has grown over them for a thousand years or more.

Advances in climate science too have provided extraordinary new insights into the past, through inspection of late sediment, fossilised pollen, or through the investigation of ice cores that reveal information not only about temperature changes, but about past global volcanic activity and even about the smelting of metals, for example in the centuries after the fall of the Roman Empire, or during the period of the Black Death – both of which show empirical, measurable falls in productivity that in turn prompt new questions about the nature and the implications of these major transformations.

Seen in this way, 'global history' is a rabbit hole down which it is possible to disappear very quickly. There are pitfalls and traps wherever one looks; a requirement for more and more knowledge and for higher engagement with new tools and skills at every turn; and to top it all, is the centrality of being able to assess, analyse and form the evidence into a coherent and balanced piece of work, whether as an academic article or scholarly monograph, or a book or a piece in a magazine written for a wider audience.

If that sounds difficult, it is because it is. As any historian will tell you, writing history is very different to writing 'good history', whether global or otherwise. Some criticisms of the concept of global history centre on the assumption that there can be a tendency, if not a pressure, to over-simplification, to sweeping statements and to broad brushstrokes that do not paint a picture in enough detail. That can only be mitigated by working as closely with the sources as possible – whether they relate to written works, to material culture or to new scientific data – and then thinking through how to understand and use them properly. Getting the basics right is crucial: learning how to read and use sources of different kinds and then relying on one's judgement to interpret them as best as possible is what matters.

This can be helped, as it happens, by working alongside another new trend of history that has emerged, in part as a reaction to global history. 'Micro-history' looks at smaller topics or compressed timescales to build up finely detailed pictures that are both revealing and exciting because of the depth of attention that can be paid in this way. That narrowness of focus can be just as difficult, if not harder, than the *longue durée* (or the 'long view'), as Fernand Braudel called the expansive approach to history. But essentially, the best way to write global history is

25

to build up from scores of micro-histories to weave a tapestry not only from local, highly detailed sources, but from the scholarly studies that have brought them together too.

Having set out what global history means and what some of the challenges are, the next question is why it is needed in the first place. What, if anything, is wrong with reading about the familiar topics of the past in familiar ways? Why do we need new interpretations at all? And why does being more open-minded about history make a difference – and to whom?

As E.H. Carr wrote so presciently, historians are always products of their times. It is often difficult to be aware of biases and of the influences of one's own contexts, audience and reception. However, in a globalised and interlinked world that we live in today, it is more important than ever to be thinking more inclusively about the past.

One reason for this is the unbalanced and skewed views of events, periods and people that build up with layers of assumptions and unasked questions. The fact that it can take more than a hundred years to take down statues of slave traders and to finally rename buildings celebrating their 'achievements' is not only revealing as to a casual acceptance of history, but to the fundamental failure to ask questions about what those achievements were in the first place. It is only now, centuries after some of the great museums of the world began their collections, that questions about the origins, circumstances of acquisition and sometimes downright theft of the items in their collections are being asked. That too speaks not only of a lack of curiosity at the time – as well as over the intervening centuries, decades and years – but also of a lack of critical thinking to consider how the fabric of the past has been woven.

There are many answers to questions surrounding what should be done with the famous bronze statues stolen in a raid from Benin in 1897, plunder taken from the imperial palace in Beijing in 1860, or many of the greatest works of classical antiquity that are to be found not in Italy and Greece, or in places like Albania, Libya and Lebanon and other places that were part of the Roman and Greek world, but on display far away in the great museums of the world. And it is important too to note that these are not only issues for Europeans to face up to – as there are parallel questions relating to all parts of the world, whether in South Asia, the Americas or in Africa, where artworks, wealth and the past have been removed, forcibly taken away and in some cases deliberately damaged. European museums hold incomparable treasures from all over the world; but all successful states and empires took artefacts and goods (as well as men and women) from those they conquered.

All empires are extractive but it can be easy to slump into a self-regarding Eurocentrism that sees European empires as 'different' to empires built in other parts of the world. The scale of extraction, certainly, was greater and longer from the early modern period as Europeans established themselves all around the world, partly because of new technologies that enabled quicker and very substantial acquisition and removal of goods. But the Inca used the same model of hierarchies, persecution, and violence to dominate other Indigenous peoples in the Americas, as did the Arabs in Central Asia and North Africa, as did the Bantu during their expansions in Africa. Restitution does not stop at Point Zero, in other words, but requires the intellectual journey to be completed in full – ultimately going back to understand human history fully, and not just cherry-picking starting points that are invariably based on the arrival and activities of Europeans in other parts of the world.

Nevertheless, one outcome of the debate around restitution has been a focus on how cultural objects have been treated, looted, and re-appropriated to rewrite histories of the past and of the present. This has led to some pioneering institutions such as the Getty Center in Los Angeles calling for cultural clearing to be classified as a war crime: destroying or removing and even selling objects does not just damage materials that are often beautiful or valuable, but demeans, distorts and twists history itself. This was what motivated the so-called Islamic State to take sledgehammers and dynamite to pre-Islamic monuments in Iraq and Syria: to erase a past that did not suit a single-minded, intolerant narrative.

This underscores the significance of global histories, for the effect of leaving out cultures, peoples, regions and periods that are not part of the mainstream does more than leave a gap in the picture. It erases histories too. By focusing so heavily on Europe, huge parts of the global population have had the pasts of their ancestors at least implicitly deemed as secondary. But, furthermore, this too has the effect of leaving a void that not surprisingly leads to a lack of respect, a lack of dignity and a lack of equality.

One of the reasons why the Black Lives Matter campaign became so significant globally was not only because of the brutal murder of George Floyd, one of many Black people killed by the police in the US, or because of a spontaneous protest at institutional racism across many parts of society, but also because it brought to the forefront the painful truth that history and historians have failed to deal with the realities of the past.

Even dealing with the question of race and civil rights, as many schools and universities are now seeking to do, does not address the problem fully, any more than the origins and horrors of the slave trade do. Global history can help with that by re-centring multiple foci – above all on the 'global south', that is to say the parts of Latin America, Africa, Asia and Oceania that have been poorly served by the mainstream of historical scholarship, by the lack of funding and resources in many locations that had an obvious and direct impact on pupils and students, teachers and professors, libraries and online capability – particularly in places that are not Anglophone and work in Indigenous languages.

So in the globalised world of the twenty-first century, we should be keenly aware of these imbalances, and be working much harder to try to address them – through exchange programmes, capacity building, engaging with the needs of local scholars, supporting their research through collaborations where appropriate and ensuring their work gets read and voices get heard. And perhaps most important of all, it is vital for schools and universities to provide space to integrate studies of and from these regions into our own curricula.

This should be as obvious to historians today as it was to some writing more than two thousand years ago. Once, wrote the Greek author Polybius in the third century BC, 'the world's history had consisted, so to speak, of a series of unrelated episodes'. But the world had changed, he went on. Now it was clear that 'history has become an organic whole: the affairs of Italy and Africa are connected with those of Asia and Greece, and all events bear a relationship and contribute to a single end'. That sounds like global history to me.

Writing about the past is not an easy thing to do. Writing

about it well is even harder. E.H. Carr wrote in *What is History?* about the relationship between the historian and 'facts'. That relationship is considerably more complex today because of the sheer range of new materials that can and indeed should be considered when writing about history. But what has always been the hardest thing to do is to write about silences – about gaps, about lacunae where it is hard to know what happened, when, where and why.

When it comes to global history – in whichever interpretation – the issue is that in many cases those gaps have often not been left because of the absence of material such as texts, art, music, archaeological finds, inscriptions or archaeobotanical evidence. Rather, they have remained so untouched because of a lack of interest, combined with a lack of initiative to capture pasts that have received less attention. History today is in danger of becoming a circular story where more and more is known about fewer and fewer topics. Global history can help correct some of those faults.

In some cases, certainly, there are still considerable barriers. Oral traditions can be brittle, and as languages die out – as they are doing at an unprecedented rate – then histories are lost forever. Likewise, academic freedoms are not uniform around the world and there are countries where there are significant limitations of expression not only for scholars but for minorities, sometimes even very substantial minorities, whose pasts are deemed so threatening as to require silencing or deliberate distortion. As George Orwell put it in *1984*, 'who controls the past controls the future; who controls the present controls the past'.

We can sometimes think that these words of wisdom – and warning – apply only to totalitarian and authoritarian states;

and there is no question that Orwell was thinking about the Soviet Union in the immediate aftermath of the Second World War when he wrote them. But this message is essential for us all. History should be about broadening horizons, widening perspectives, giving greater context to help us understand others, and to better understand ourselves. If we fail to do that, history becomes something closer to the fairy tales that are read to children: stories that are above all both familiar and exciting. Rather than return to those, how much more rewarding, equitable and invigorating to be like the hero at the start of *Peter and the Wolf*, and open the gate and stride into the big green meadows to explore what lies beyond the backyard he has played in for too long.

Selected Further Reading

David Abulafia, *The Boundless Sea: A Human History of the Oceans* (London: Allen Lane, 2019)

Peter Frankopan, *The Silk Roads: A New History of the World* (London: Bloomsbury, 2015)

Toby Green, *A Fistful of Shells: West Africa from the Rise of the Slave Trade to the Age of Revolution* (London: Allen Lane, 2019)

Ramachandra Guha, *Environmentalism: A Global History* (New York: Longman, 2000)

Pekka Hämäläinen, *The Comanche Empire* (New Haven, London: Yale University Press, 2008)

Julia Lovell, *Maoism: A Global History* (London: Bodley Head, 2019)

Olivette Otele, *African Europeans: An Untold History* (London: Hurst & Company, 2020)

Eugene Rogan, *The Arabs: A History* (London: Allen Lane, 2009)

Camilla Townsend, *Fifth Sun: A New History of the Aztecs* (New York, Oxford: Oxford University Press, 2019)

Chapter 2

Why history deserves to be at the movies

Alex von Tunzelmann

In *What is History?*, E.H. Carr was concerned with the academic study of history. Yet the way most adults regularly encounter history is through popular culture. History has been at the movies since the movies began. The Australian production *The Story of the Kelly Gang* (1906), considered the first feature film, was a historical drama. Equally, historical films have been controversial for as long as they have existed. *The Story of the Kelly Gang* was banned in parts of Australia the year after its original release. *The Australasian* reported at the time: 'It is felt that a representation of the different scenes in the careers of the outlaws should not be exhibited in the district where they spent their lives, and in which some crimes represented in the entertainment were committed.' Despite, or perhaps in part because of the ban, the film was a great success.

Historical films and, since the advent of television, TV shows have proved enduringly popular. Yet the anxiety felt by the Australian authorities in 1907 has endured, too. In 2020, a casual observer might have thought the British government would have had its hands full with Brexit and the coronavirus pandemic. Still, it found time to attack Netflix's *The Crown*, a historical drama about the life of the Queen and the Royal Family. *The Crown* broadcast its fourth season in 2020, reaching the ticklish territory of the 1980s, including the relationship between Prince Charles and Diana, Princess of Wales. The backlash made the front pages of tabloid newspapers, with friends of Prince Charles calling the show 'trolling on a Hollywood budget'. The culture secretary, Oliver Dowden, said he would ask Netflix to put a 'health warning' on the show stating that it was fiction. 'Without this, I fear a generation of viewers who did not live through these events may mistake fiction for fact,' he said. Culture minister John Whittingdale raised the question of regulating Netflix, which is based in the Netherlands. The *Mail on Sunday* reported in horror on 28 November that *The Crown* 'has already been watched by more people than tuned in for Charles's real-life wedding to Princess Diana'. Historians might amuse themselves debating which broadcast was the more effective work of fiction.

The Crown does, of course, say upfront that it is fiction. It is billed as historical drama, not documentary, and the lavish production design could not easily be mistaken for candid footage. The people in it are well-known actors and the conversations, especially private ones, are self-evidently dramatised. These are the conventions by which we learn to recognise fiction on screen. Yet in the 2020s, as in 1907, fears persist that audiences will not be able to understand it as such: that historical drama is not harmless fun but a perversion of history, and may be dangerous. It may create hyperreality, a state originally defined by Jean Baudrillard, in which one cannot tell reality from a simulation of reality. This is what critics of historical drama fear: the prospect of reality itself coming apart at the seams, making it impossible to tell what is real and what is fake.

The claims that some people – by implication, less intelligent people – will be bamboozled by historical fictions are usually made without much evidence beyond the anecdotal. One example for which we do have useful data is Oliver Stone's blockbuster action thriller *JFK* (1991). Covering an investigation into John F. Kennedy's assassination, *JFK* does everything in its power to subvert the historical record and persuade its audience that Kennedy was not murdered by Lee Harvey Oswald acting alone, but by a high-level conspiracy. Stone deliberately discarded many of the conventions of historical screen fiction used by shows like *The Crown*, shooting and editing his film in a 'documentary' style, chopping in bits of real-life footage and reconstruction. The case he presents, though, is completely fabricated. Unreliable witnesses are reinvented as credible. A whistleblower who confirms the extent of the conspiracy is created out of thin air. A discredited ballistics study is presented as decisive. The underlying thesis of the movie, that the conspiracy goes all the way to the top of the government, is based on a famous hoax called *The Report from Iron Mountain* – published in 1967, and revealed by its own author in 1972 to have been a spoof. Nonetheless, the film can come across as authoritative: it is incredibly well made, tightly scripted and brilliantly acted, and was nominated for eight Oscars.

There was anxiety at the time of its release that *JFK* would convince everyone who saw it that it was the truth, though it was fictionalised well beyond the limits of popular conspiracy theories. Pollsters Gallup tracked the percentage of Americans who believe Lee Harvey Oswald acted alone versus those who believe in a conspiracy between 1963 and 2013. This means there are figures not just for the time when the film was released in 1991, but comparable data from over half a century. What they show is that the film made little difference. In 1983, 74 per cent of Americans believed in a conspiracy. In 1992, after the film's release, the figure went up slightly to 77 per cent. The following year, it fell back to 75 per cent. A far more significant change can be seen between 1966, when 50 per cent believed in a conspiracy, and 1976, when 81 per cent did. This can probably be attributed to the 1976 House Select Committee on Assassinations, which concluded – controversially and, frankly, irresponsibly – that there had been some sort of conspiracy, though there was no clear evidence in favour of any of the options. Most historians take the view that Oswald acted alone. Clearly, most Americans disagree, but that cannot be blamed on Oliver Stone's movie. Public views of history seem to have been influenced far more strongly by politicians than by filmmakers.

One positive effect of *JFK* for historians was that, following its release, Congress ordered all remaining archives on the assassination to be opened. Ninety-nine per cent of them now have been, and there is still no convincing evidence for any of the conspiracy theories. Again, this documentary work, enabled by politicians and carried out by historians, appears to have had more impact on public opinion than the film: by 2013, belief in a conspiracy had fallen again to 61 per cent.

In the case of *JFK*, then, a smash-hit historical film which set out to influence public views hardly did so at all, and any effect it had was short-lived. There are subtler effects that historical films may have on public consciousness, though. *Braveheart*, Mel Gibson's 1995 epic about the Scottish patriot William Wallace, is often linked to the rise of Scottish nationalism. Professor Sally Morgan, who researches the political use of Scottish cinema in the 1990s, has argued that the film's aesthetic and themes influenced independence campaigners: 'I think Scotland was kind of ready for this image of itself as this wild, empire defying, Celtic tribesman that needed to be apart from England.' After Scotland voted for devolution in 1997, Alex Salmond, then first minister, announced: 'Scotland looked forward to this with a brave heart' – prompting cheers from the crowd.

Historically speaking, *Braveheart* is just as much of a fabrication as *JFK*, getting pretty much every date and detail wrong all the way down to the inappropriate woad and anachronistic kilts. Among a veritable feast of porky pies, it fully invents a storyline about Wallace impregnating Edward II's wife Isabella in around 1304. This is definitely not true: in 1304 Isabella was nine years old, had not yet married Edward, and lived in France. It is certainly possible to demonstrate, as Professor Morgan does, that the film's theme and tropes had a cultural impact in Scotland. It is not clear that it *drove* support for Scottish nationalism so much as playing to existing supporters. There is no evidence that it actually convinced significant numbers of people of any of its absurd historical contentions.

After they have left school, most people do not encounter history much except as fiction – unless they make a conscious choice to watch history documentaries, read historical non-fiction, visit museums and so on. Notably, the moral panic about historical film and television is rarely extended now to plays or novels, though playwrights and authors muck around with the facts just as much as filmmakers. The distortions in Shakespeare's history plays are well documented, yet audiences are trusted to watch them without disclaimers. In Colson Whitehead's novel, *The Underground Railroad* (2016), the railroad is reimagined literally, with subterranean trains smuggling slaves out of Georgia. George Saunders' *Lincoln in the Bardo* (2017) is told through carefully footnoted historical references mixed with the brilliantly imagined voices of ghosts. Far from being criticised, these books were widely praised for their creative, subversive takes on history: the former won a Pulitzer Prize and National Book Award, while the latter won the Booker Prize.

Perhaps there is less anxiety about theatre and literature because they are presumed to be aimed at a cultural elite, whereas all manner of people might watch films or television. When historical novels were the most cutting-edge popular medium, they too often caused controversy. Leo Tolstoy's distortions of history came under fire from all sides when he published *War and Peace* in 1869. 'It is lucky that Count Tolstoy does not possess a powerful talent,' wrote the radical critic Nikolai Shelgunov, disgusted by his romanticised historical portrait of the Russian aristocracy. 'If he did possess the talent either of Shakespeare or Byron, no curse would suffice to condemn him.' Similarly, many historical films that are now considered classics provoked angry reactions on their release. The family of Auda abu Tayi were deeply offended by his cartoonish portrayal by Anthony Quinn in *Lawrence of Arabia* (1962) and tried unsuccessfully to sue the film's producers. The daughter of Henry Hook VC was so upset by her father, a teetotaller with an exemplary record, being rewritten as an alcoholic malingerer in *Zulu* (1964) that she walked out of the premiere. The reason that film and television productions now carry a disclaimer – 'All characters appearing in this motion picture are fictitious. Any resemblance to actual persons, living or dead, is purely coincidental' – is that Princess Irina Yusupova successfully sued MGM over a character based on her in *Rasputin and the Empress* (1932).

Some historical films and TV shows are notably faithful to their subjects, and a few even manage to be so without sacrificing creativity. *Ran* (1985), Akira Kurosawa's extraordinary synthesis of *King Lear* and the story of sixteenth-century Japanese daimyo Mori Motonari, sublimely fictionalises its story without losing its grip on the historical context. *The Madness of King George* (1994) is a simultaneously illuminating and deeply moving dramatisation of George III's health problems. *The Right Stuff* (1983), based on Tom Wolfe's book about the Space Race, humanises a complicated story and makes it both gripping and informative. A generation of filmgoers will probably never forget the searing horror of some all too accurate scenes in *Twelve Years a Slave* (2013), Steve Mc-Queen's adaptation of the story of Solomon Northup.

Yet there are also, of course, plenty of historical films and TV shows that do not stick to the historical record, and some of them have sinister intent. Propaganda films are funded by official civil or military bodies to spread political messages, and often abuse history in any way that suits that purpose. Historical dramas such as *Jud Süß* and *Die Rothschilds* (both 1940) were produced by Nazi Germany to encourage anti-Semitism. On the other side, both Joseph Stalin and Winston Churchill were tremendous film fans, and both were involved in the making of historical films. Stalin often intervened in the production process, reading scripts and judging final cuts before release. Churchill even tried his hand at becoming a historical screenwriter: he wrote a fictionalised biopic of George V for Alexander Korda in the 1930s, though sadly it was never filmed.

Returning to *The Crown*, though, the concerns about it do not stem from it being propaganda. They relate to a much more common complaint that commercial film and television productions change the past to make their stories more exciting for their audiences. Outraged articles in the *Guardian* and *The Times* listed such inaccuracies as 'Princess Margaret ridiculed Princess Diana for not being able to curtsey' and 'The Queen was repeatedly shown wrongly dressed for Trooping the Colour.' In comparison to the whoppers told by many other historical dramas, these look distinctly minor. The whole premise of *Amadeus* (1984) is an entirely fictitious claim that Mozart was murdered by his rival, Salieri. *Anonymous* (2011) not only claims that the Earl of Oxford wrote Shakespeare's plays, but that Shakespeare himself was illiterate – and that the Virgin Queen, Elizabeth I, secretly gave birth to dozens of bastards. In *U-571* (2000), the capture of Enigma machines by British sailors is credited instead to a crew of plucky Americans, led by rock star Jon Bon Jovi. *Apocalypto* (2006) moves the date of the Mayan collapse by six hundred years so that it can elbow in a scene of Spanish conquistadors arriving at the end.

In response to a newspaper piece accusing *The Crown* of errors, the historian Greg Jenner tweeted: 'They're not "errors", they're creative choices – the kind that every dramatist has to make because there's no such thing as an accurate history drama.' Plenty of filmmakers take a playful attitude to history, often to wonderful effect. *Monty Python and the Holy Grail* (1975), for instance, does not aim for historical truth: its purpose is to make Arthurian jokes. Films like *A Lion in Winter* (1968) or *The Death of Stalin* (2017) are not supposed to be documentary retellings, but instead are imaginative, darkly comic extrapolations from

40

historical situations – and much more fun for it. A 1995 screen version of *Richard III* is set in the 1930s: when Richard (Ian McKellen) screams 'A horse! A horse! My kingdom for a horse!', it is because his jeep has broken down.

Historical fantasies blend themes, settings or stories from history with pure imagination. In *X-Men: First Class* (2011), a gang of superhero mutants avert the Cuban Missile Crisis. *Pirates of the Caribbean* (2003–17) embellishes Caribbean history with ghosts and sea-monsters. *Game of Thrones* (2011–19) goes even further into fiction, mashing up bits of the Wars of the Roses, the story of El Cid, the Black Dinner and countless other ancient, medieval and early modern gobbets with dragons and ice zombies.

With these huge variations in tone, intent and scope, it is not clear how any official body could even begin to regulate historical fiction. How would anyone draft clear rules that would rein in *The Crown*, while permitting full artistic freedom to *Chernobyl*, *Band of Brothers*, *Peaky Blinders* and *Blackadder*? If the specific concern regarding *The Crown* is that some of those who are fictionalised in it are still alive, then libel laws already offer protection to living people. The expense and publicity entailed in using the courts may put potential claimants off. Equally, though, the ruinous cost of fighting, let alone losing, a libel suit is a strong deterrent to film producers tempted to disparage their subjects.

Government regulation of historical fiction would inevitably violate freedom of expression. Since parts of Australia banned *The Story of the Kelly Gang*, various countries have censored historical films and TV shows for their inaccuracies, or for accuracies that they do not like, or for offending national sensibilities. Britain, France, Spain, Germany and Finland all banned

Battleship Potemkin (1925). Nazi Germany banned *The Great Dictator* (1940). Thailand banned *The King and I* (1956). Norway banned *Monty Python's Life of Brian* (1979). Italy banned *Lion of the Desert* (1981). Iran banned *300* (2006). Russia banned *The Death of Stalin*. Banning a film is, of course, the best marketing campaign for it: *The Death of Stalin* is estimated to have been illegally downloaded in Russia 1.5 million times. It would not be surprising if the British government's interventions over *The Crown* have resulted in many more people watching it to see what the fuss is about.

Some countries have even tried screening films to historians before their release. A Bollywood epic about the fourteenth-century Queen Padmavati, who many historians are not even convinced existed, provoked riots in 2017. It was banned in several Indian states; the filmmakers challenged the bans at the Supreme Court, and won. The Indian Central Board of Film Certification showed it to five historians, who suggested various changes. These were implemented, and included changing its title from *Padmavati* to *Padmaavat* – the latter being the name of an epic poem about the queen, thus supposedly making it clear that the film was based on fiction rather than reality.

This was a way to resolve the controversy around one particular film, but submitting all historical fiction to a judging panel of historians with editorial powers would place intolerable limits on freedom of expression. It is not even practical – by their very nature, historians do not agree with each other all the time. Who chooses which historians are qualified to judge which films? What if filmmakers challenge that and bring in their own historians? Most of all, though, it misses the point: historical fiction is not history, but fiction.

There is a better way to address how we tell fact from fiction, and that is to encourage and teach critical thinking at all levels. Here is where the study of history can come in. If history is taught as long lists of kings and dates to be swallowed and regurgitated, then students might win a pub quiz one day. If history is taught instead as a process of questioning and research, of sifting through information and making informed judgements about reliable or unreliable sources, of contextualising, synthesising and understanding – then that equips students with an extraordinarily powerful range of tools to navigate the modern world.

There are much greater threats to our grip on reality out there than a few dodgy history flicks. The internet, modern political propaganda, and increasingly atomised, polarised media make our lives information-heavy. At the same time, many of the traditional filters on that information – such as taboos against overt political lying, or the practice of rigorous fact-checking at newspapers – have collapsed. We need to learn to survive in this environment, and the discipline of history can help us. Rather than patronising audiences by loftily instructing them that fiction is fiction, we should be thinking about how to empower everyone to ask questions and look for answers.

Historical movies – even bad historical movies – can help here too. In fact, they already do. Publishers know that, in the wake of a successful historical drama, sales of history books on the subject will go up. Once someone's imagination has been captured, they often want to know more and seek out the real story. Historians may have wrung their hands at the inaccuracies in *Braveheart*. Nonetheless, in the decade between 1985 and 1995, there were three books on William Wallace published; in the decade after *Braveheart* was released, 1995–2005, there were twenty-seven. Museums have long been responding to public interest as driven by fiction, too. The Hollywood film *Troy* (2004) is all over the place from a historical perspective. At one point, an ancient Trojan marketplace is shown populated with llamas: native to the Andes, and not seen in Eurasia until long after Christopher Columbus first landed in the Americas. Yet the film's inventions were part of the draw when it formed an exhibit in the British Museum's excellent *Troy: Myth and Reality* exhibition in 2019–20. It is unlikely that the Titanic Belfast museum would exist at all if it had not been for the international smash hit *Titanic* (1997), which is heavily referenced in its 'Myths and Legends' gallery.

While some people would be horrified by the thought of historical movies being shown in history lessons, they can (if appropriately contextualised) help teach practical critical thinking. Some schools and universities run clubs and optional courses where students are shown a historical film, research the real story, and discuss the differences between the two. Similarly, when historical films are released, historians usually get to write angry pieces about them in newspapers. Sometimes, this even provokes a wider debate. For instance, while some attacked the film *Selma* (2014) for being too hard on Lyndon Johnson's attitude to Martin Luther King and civil rights, others fiercely defended it as an accurate depiction. These academic discussions would not have anything like the public impact they do if there was no movie to spark media interest.

Of course there are historical films that promote damaging falsehoods, attempt to influence their audiences politically, and cause great offence. This is also true, though, of plenty of material that is billed as historical fact. There are bestselling historical books and documentaries which claim to be 'non-fiction' and yet promote absurd conspiracy theories that Jesus of Nazareth founded the Merovingian dynasty, that 'ancient aliens' built the pyramids, or that the Royal Family are giant lizards. Sickeningly, there is a whole industry of Holocaust denial. 'I am way more comfortable with *The Crown* than I am seeing the stories written [in news media] about my family, my wife, or myself,' said Prince Harry, Duke of Sussex, in 2021. *The Crown*, he said, 'is obviously fiction, take it how you will,' but lies about his family are 're-ported on as fact, because you are supposedly news. I have a real issue with that.' Historians can and do refute false claims when they arise, but there are not enough historians to address every claim in the world. The only way to begin to tackle this is to give everyone the skills to judge for themselves. Historical fiction is at least billed as fiction, and provides an opportunity for historians to demonstrate how that process of judgement can work.

This is not to say that filmmakers have no responsibility for what they put on screen. They can be criticised, and frequently are. Ultimately, though, their job is not to serve up historical ac-curacy – it is to make the best film or TV show they can, whether that means artistically, commercially or both. Those who insist on judging any historical drama only on whether it ticks a series of accuracy boxes may be missing some of the fun. It is good for historians to be at the movies, but neither they nor politicians own history: it is part of everyone's cultural heritage, and people may relate to it however they choose.

When it comes to historical drama, the evidence suggests that people are quite good at telling fact from fiction. Far from posing a threat, history on screen can be a democratising force:

it can promote a real interest in and engagement with the past. Many historians, museum creators and archaeologists today will admit that their love of history was sparked by watching films like the Indiana Jones series or *The Mummy* in childhood. E.H. Carr wrote of 'the historian's need of imaginative understanding for the minds of the people with whom he is dealing': historical fictions can be a route to thinking oneself into different times, places and mindsets.

If politicians are genuinely concerned about the public understanding of history, they can support that by funding public events, museums, festivals and research, making the study and discussion of history more accessible to a wider audience. The more they enable critical thinking, the less they will have to worry that the general public are merely grubs, unquestioningly chewing up and absorbing anything that is fed to them.

Of course, if you are a politician, there is a downside to empowering the public to ask questions and seek answers. One day, they may turn those skills back on you.

Selected Further Reading

Mike Chopra-Gant, *Cinema and History: The Telling of Stories* (London: Wallflower Press, 2008)

Rachel Dwyer, *Bollywood's India: Hindi Cinema as a Guide to Contemporary India* (London: Reaktion Books, 2014)

Andrew B.R. Elliott, *Remaking the Middle Ages: The Methods of Cinema and History in Portraying the Medieval World* (Jefferson: McFarland & Co, 2010)

Leen Engelen and Roel Vande Winkel, eds. *Perspectives on European Film and History* (Ghent: Academia Press, 2007)

Claire Monk and Amy Sargeant, eds. *British Historical Cinema* (London: Routledge, 2002)

Jeffrey Richards, *Hollywood's Ancient Worlds* (London: Continuum Books, 2008)

Robert A. Rosenstone, *History on Film/Film on History* (3rd ed., London: Routledge, 2018)

Robert A. Rosenstone and Constantin Parvulescu, eds. *A Companion to the Historical Film* (Oxford: Wiley-Blackwell, 2013)

Viola Shafik, *Arab Cinema: History and Cultural Identity* (Cairo: American University in Cairo Press, 2007)

Jonathan Stubbs, *Historical Film: A Critical Introduction* (London: Bloomsbury, 2013)

Robert Brent Toplin, *History by Hollywood: The Use and Abuse of the American Past* (Chicago: University of Illinois Press, 1996)

Alex von Tunzelmann, *Reel History: The World According to the Movies* (London: Atlantic Books, 2015)

Chapter 3

Can and should we queer the past?

Justin Bengry

The past is a queer place. Its inhabitants are deceptive. They tease us with seemingly familiar appearances and promises of kinship. But don't let them trick you. People in the past are not always as they seem. They are not necessarily like you and me. These are queer people indeed.

But what is queer about them and what exactly is 'queer'? Is it an insult hurled around playgrounds or accompanying kicks and punches? Is it a term of self-description, assertively and proudly recovered from homophobic abuse and misuse? Or is it just a new way to say LGBT, an umbrella that catches all kinds of lesbian, gay, bisexual and transgender people, and perhaps others too? Queer is a *queer* word, with its own history and its own problems and possibilities. It's also a useful way of thinking about the past.

From the mid-nineteenth century, 'queer' was already associated with difference, strangeness and eccentricity. The *Oxford English Dictionary* linked it to homosexuality by 1922, even if that use of queer only became clearer to most people a few decades later. Historian Matt Cook reminds us that because queer doesn't mean 'opposite to' straight, it challenges us to think about the messiness of both homosexuality *and* hetero-sexuality. People in the past, after all, rarely fit so neatly into these categories as we might like them to do. The 1930s urban bohemian is not the same as the 1960s victim of homophobic abuse. Neither necessarily resembles the 1990s sexual theorist or political radical, nor our contemporaries in the 2020s who may reject binary categories of gender and sexual identity altogether. All of these people have described themselves or were described by others as queer.

But isn't all of this actually just 'gay' history? If we look to the past for examples of men who desired and had sex with other men – still the most recorded and studied amongst LGBT people – are they best described as 'gay'? Sometimes. We don't always know. Too often we can only incompletely reconstruct parts of their lives from the imperfect observations of others who likewise grappled to understand them. Observers studied their behaviours and mannerisms, only sometimes knowing who they desired or had sex with, or why they did so. Sometimes we have their own words, but these are rarely unequivocal or unmediated by courts and police, families and friends, the Church or doctors. They rarely present unambiguously clear evidence of self-identified 'gay' people telling me about lives that look like my own as a gay man in twenty-first-century London. Their stories are more interesting because of it.

Stories that seem to show us examples of sexualities beyond heterosexuality, particularly those that pre-date living memory, gay liberation and subsequent activism, are for me more rightly part of 'queer' rather than 'gay' history. These histories, and the sources that describe them, so often hinge on perceptions of difference, strangeness and eccentricity; they demonstrate history's multiple threads of possibility that we may not be able (nor want) to disentangle.

Of course, we historians do not all agree. Many argue that 'gay' is a perfectly sufficient term to recover past expressions of same-sex desire as a category of human experience that cuts across time and perhaps even place. Historian John Boswell, for example, identified 'gay people' since antiquity, defining them as anyone who exhibited a 'conscious preference' for members of their own gender. There are gay people in the past, historians have asserted, men and women who loved and desired members of their own sex just as some of us do today. And even if they did not use the term gay – and these historians rightly remind us that most people in the past did not have the word queer either – it is our task to honour them by welcoming them into our shared gay or even LGBT histories and communities. In this telling of history, our gay forebears may range from a twentieth-century suffragette to a Victorian poet ruminating on beautiful youths and 'Greek' love, from a seventeenth-century labourer accused of sodomy to a medieval king and his favourites. These 'gay' ancestors, some historians argue, share with us a common bond much stronger than other experiences and understandings of selfhood that might separate us.

This isn't an entirely unreasonable proposition, nor one without its own important historical context. From the 1970s and 1980s, with the onset of gay liberation, the growth of academic research into histories of same-sex love and desire, and continuing violence and systemic homophobia, it was crucially important to recover a shared 'gay' past. For centuries our histories had been obscured, neglected and destroyed. Diaries were written in code; letters and love mementoes were destroyed. Self-described gay people worked tirelessly to recover that past in order to have a history, use it to claim space in the present, and demand better for the future. 'Gay' was, and remains for many, a deeply political word, and recovering gay history was, and is, vitally important.

Half a century later, the words lesbian and gay in particular have become such familiar terms of identity that they can no longer sustain the task of describing experiences in the past that may differ radically from our lives today and in the recent past. They start from an assumption of similarity or even sameness, which serves to reconstitute the past in our own image. Can these terms ever accommodate people in the past who understood their desires and sexualities differently from us, if they even understood themselves to have sexualities?

Other terms have their own histories, opportunities and challenges. Bisexuality labours under some of the same burdens, but usefully suggests greater fluidity of sexual desires. Transgender describes expressions of gender identity that depart from one's gender as assigned at birth. Transgender scholar Susan Stryker describes it as 'the movement across a socially imposed boundary away from an unchosen starting place – rather than any particular destination or mode of transition'. Transgender may include, but is not the same as, transsexual, another more specifically twentieth-century identity which, like gay and lesbian, does important work but may likewise not be suited to describing the queer past. Transgender, or trans, much like queer, however, offers space to think about dissimilarity, variability and historical possibility.

So why might we now want to *queer* the past, rather than

51

seek out our forebears and assign them identities that map on to contemporary understandings of lesbian and gay, bi and trans? To answer this question we need to think not only about what we mean by queer history (noun), of which we have ample evidence, but also what we want to do *to queer* (verb) the past.

To queer the past is to let people in history define themselves in often complex and unfamiliar ways, or to accept that even if they did define themselves, we may never know how. They may seem to exhibit identities that appear universal or to live and love in ways that cut across categories. We may find that they have other ways of organising their desires or even deny the need for categories altogether. To queer the past is to knowingly hold these possibilities in suspension even as we may also recover and relabel people in the past for our own uses. It is a conversation between us and them about the resonances we may feel with their lives without demanding from them a direct line of kinship and exclusive ownership. Queering the past is an act that happens in the present.

Queer people

From the 1980s some gay people and other gender and sexual non-conformists began to harness and redirect the venom of the word 'queer', reclaiming it from those who had spat the word at them or hurled it with fists and kicks. It was a rallying cry, a challenge to social norms, and a declaration of difference soon taken up by queer theorists as a useful way to question the power, inevitability and boundaries of binary labels, categories and identities. Others would use it to position themselves against what they identified as the assimilationist tendencies of gay politics and identities that had lost their political relevance and urgency. Today, some of us might identify as queer to question gender and sexual identity labels, to move between them, or to deny these labels altogether. For others, queer is just a new label to replace 'gay' or 'lesbian' as they become increasingly dated and burdened by the weight of a half-century of use. This history of queer is familiar and embedded in LGBTQ histories of the twentieth century. It is linear, progressing from homophobic violence and repression to activism, liberation, and radical reimagining of self. In short, it's not a particularly *queer* story.

If we resist our need to contain 'queer' within an easy narrative of post-war repression, recovery and resistance, we find evidence of its use as a term of self-description already as early as the 1930s in Britain. Writing to his friend Billy in 1934, Cyril 'Coeur de Leon' describes his wife and two-year-old daughter, even as he admits hoping to have an affair with Billy. In his own words, Cyril has 'only been queer since I came to London' but 'I still like girls occasionally'. He contrasts queer with 'normal', complaining that queers are 'temperamental and dissatisfied'. Cyril was arrested in a raid of the Caravan Club in Endell Street, London, a club that a complaint described as 'only frequented by sexual perverts, lesbians and sodomites'. So, while Cyril's use of queer is not unrelated to ours, it's also different: it is tied to urban space and opportunity; it might be temporary or situationally specific; it leaves space for opposite-sex attraction; it isn't a political identity. The letter shows us that queer in the 1930s included same-sex attraction but could also be a more expansive term of sexual difference.

Cyril's story offers us insights into the value of a specifically 'queer' history. It is easy enough to avoid describing Cyril as gay when he so clearly names himself as queer. Historian Matt Houl-brook warns us, however, that the meaning of queer was 'never self-evident, stable, or singular'. For Cyril, queerness wasn't just a matter of his attraction to men, but also his flamboyance, ef-feminacy, and relationship to the city. And 'normal' men at this time weren't always clearly differentiated from 'queer' men, at least in terms of who they had sex with. So, if queerness for Cyril and his contemporaries was never entirely defined by sexual de-sires, where does that leave us? The past and the present bump into each other. Gay and bisexual men today might find kinship with Cyril, feeling resonances across nearly a century. We may recognise in his experiences of the sexual opportunities of the city something familiar and seek to recover him as one of our own. But we cannot erase the complexity of his life, the context of his experience and the flux of his identity. Is Cyril queer be-cause of his attraction to Billy, his movement away from his wife geographically and sexually, his self-presentation and discovery of London's bohemian haunts? Cyril and his queerness can only be understood in his own historical moment even as he may seem to reach toward ours.

Two hundred years before Cyril was arrested, other raids by other authorities in the eighteenth and nineteenth centuries iden-tified notorious gathering places used by 'mollies' within walking distance of Endell Street. To some historians these mollies are familiar, just as Cyril is familiar: they are effeminate gay men from another era. Their cross-dressing and female names such as Miss Muff and Princess Seraphina suggest continuities to twentieth-century gay drag culture. Historian Rictor Norton, for example, describes a molly 'gay subculture' that existed in taverns, gin houses and coffee houses until the early nineteenth century. The most popular was Mother Clap's in Holborn, owned by John and his wife Margaret Clap. Mollies socialised there, sang bawdy songs, danced and had sex, though molly houses weren't houses of commercial prostitution. Mollies also performed the female roles in rituals of marriage and giving birth in addition to their own customs. A molly taking a 'maiden', or female, name might receive a glass of gin in the face as a kind of baptism into this community.

But are these mollies our gay kin? Were they simply gay men in drag camping it up in the eighteenth century until state homophobia destroyed their subculture? When Mother Clap's was raided in 1726 forty men were arrested. Clap herself was charged with keeping a disorderly house for sodomites and put in the pillory at Smithfield Market. She was met with such abuse that she fainted several times and probably died in prison. Another dozen mollies were tried, pilloried and imprisoned. Three were executed for sodomy. The line of kinship from these mollies to gay men who continue to live under punitive laws, including capital punishment, for homosexual offences might seem clear. It is felt strongly by some gay men today. But need this be the only story? Do gay men alone own the mollies' histories?

What if, instead of prioritising mollies' sexual activities, we focus on their gender expressions, their behaviour, and the lengths they went to take on female identities? Female names, clothing, mannerisms and rituals might indicate a desire to take the sacred rites of marriage and childbirth and show them up. So far, so camp. But the mollies' investment in these female rituals and the effort and risk taken to perform them may suggest something beyond sexual opportunity and sexual subcultures. Reflecting on mollies' disruptive gender behaviours, at odds with the expectations of eighteenth-century men, opens up trans possibility. Using today's language, we might ask if the mollies' gender deviated from the gender they were assigned at birth. Were the mollies transgender?

'Thinking queer', as advocated by Matt Houlbrook, by 'suspending both contemporary identity categories and binary understandings of difference and normality' about the mollies allows us to hold both of these possibilities in suspension, or neither. We can recognise the resonances they have both for many gay men and also transwomen today, without necessarily having to impose either label or any modern category onto them. While individual historians may choose to emphasise one understanding of the mollies over another, the cumulative work of scholars over time should present a picture less definitive and more complex – more queer – than what may dominate in any one story. As a gay man and a queer historian, I'm OK with that.

The lives of women who loved women have likewise attracted the interest of lesbian historians looking for their own sapphic ancestors. Lauded by some as the 'first modern lesbian', the Yorkshire diarist and landowner Anne Lister (1791–1840) is the most famous of these in part because of her extensive diaries that recorded sexual exploits with other women in code. At Easter 1834 Lister took Holy Communion and exchanged rings with Ann Walker, after which they considered themselves married. For many lesbians today the lines of kinship are self-evident.

Conflict erupted in 2018 in York about how to label Lister on a plaque on Holy Trinity Church, the location of her and Walker's union. Initially describing Lister as a 'gender-nonconforming en-trepreneur', the plaque was replaced with another describing the 'lesbian and diarist' after complaints that her sexuality had been erased. Some historians have long been uncomfortable, however, with too readily applying the identity of lesbian to women so distant from us, or whose lives don't conform neatly to modern lesbian identities, even as they may resonate for many lesbian women today. Queer historians might argue that Lister could be both lesbian and gender-nonconforming; sexuality and gender identity are not mutually exclusive.

Medievalist Judith Bennett has suggested the term 'lesbian-like' to include a range of women and also allow for greater acknowledgement of *possibility* in the past for women to love, live with and organise their lives around other women. They need not have had sex. Bennett reminds us that in a millennium of medieval records we might only have a dozen cases that record genital contact between women. Some historians have therefore found it more useful to consider the greater possibilities that some women had to experience same-sex love and desire. This opens further questions. Are medieval single women or nuns 'lesbian-like'?

Perhaps even that imperfect term, despite being modified and comparative, is still too burdened, too close to suggestions of a stable lesbian identity across time, to do justice to what women in the past felt and experienced. Queer, however, may be sufficiently expansive and inclusive to open up possibilities for thinking differently about female desires or the possibility of female desires. For me, queer gives us a way to think about both medieval, and other, women's distance from and their proximity to lesbians today, how they may be 'lesbian-like' or 'lesbian-*un*like'. At the same time, I appreciate the particular threat that women's and lesbian history faces, underrepresented in scholarship, underfunded in research, and understudied in schools and universities. There is a legitimate fear that 'queer' erases women from LGBT histories.

Perhaps the queerest story to come out of medieval Europe is that of a person arrested as a prostitute off Cheapside in the City of London not far from St Paul's Cathedral in December 1394. Caught having sex with a man called John Britby over a stall in Soper's Lane, both were taken before the authorities for questioning. Eleanor Rykener, they learned, had been christened John and was legally a man. She had been trained by other women how to dress and to attract male clients. She served at an inn and worked as a cross-dressed prostitute in Burford, and she learned to be an embroideress in Oxford. Identified initially in the mid-1990s by David Lorenzo Boyd and Ruth Mazo Karras as a 'male transvestite prostitute', Eleanor today resonates with us more strongly as a transwoman. Her story of deliberate self-presentation, the expense and the effort she made to create a female identity and her seeming recognition by contemporaries offer evidence of transness or at least trans possibility more than six centuries ago. But is Eleanor Rykener part of queer history only because we might subsume trans history under this larger queerer umbrella?

Eleanor's life is more complicated still. Under interrogation she revealed that she lived as both a woman and a man. And, as a man, John Rykener had sex with women, including numerous nuns and married women. As a woman, Eleanor more readily had sex with male priests because they paid her more than others. John's life complicates our understanding of Rykener as a transwoman because he seems to express a genuine sense of authenticity when living as John. But Eleanor seems likewise authentic, even if economically strategic. How are historians to grapple with multiple identities that are as disruptive to sexual and gender norms today as in the fourteenth century? Instead of using 'he' to describe John and 'she' to describe Eleanor, as

I have done, is it better to honour Rykener's exceptional life of deliberate gender crossing by using 'they'? Or should we more deliberately use disruptive gender-neutral pronouns like 'hir' as Karras has more recently done? Queer history usefully poses these questions, but stubbornly refuses to give us definitive answers. Finally, we cannot even be sure that Rykener existed at all. Historian Jeremy Goldberg believes that Rykener is in fact a clever fiction created by London clerks lampooning King Richard II, whose own sexual incongruities came under scrutiny in his conflicts with the City of London. Whether we see Rykener as a gay man, transwoman, transvestite or fictional character, we might at least agree that this is a queer person indeed.

Queering history

If we now have sufficient evidence of queer people across history – people like Cyril, Miss Muff, Anne Lister and Rykener who defy simple labels of LGB or T – does that in and of itself sufficiently *queer* history? One of the most exciting opportunities of queer history is not only to find examples of similarity and difference in the past, whether forebears or examples of human diversity, but also to think about how history can be done differently. How do histories of labour, class, capitalism, colonialism and more change when we think about them queerly? How do our understandings of these concepts change when we not only recognise the place of queer people in the past but consider how these concepts might be understood differently or inflected when considered alongside queerness?

Looking to the mines and steelworks of northern England in the first half of the twentieth century, historian Helen Smith has challenged long-held understandings of the exclusively hetero-sexual industrial working-class culture of this region. She finds that labels like gay and straight swiftly become inadequate terms of identity there. Many industrial working men who understood themselves as 'normal', men who had girlfriends or wives and possibly children, also had sex with other men without a sense of disruption to their senses of self, their positions in their communities or their roles in their families. So long as they demonstrated the qualities of good 'character' – hard-working, reliable breadwinners – and so long as they didn't disrupt their communities or families, sexual activity with other men could be accommodated within local understandings of 'normal' mas-culine behaviour. Many of these men were no doubt aware via the media of 'homosexuals', men tried for 'gross' and 'indecent' offences, and some of them might even have recognised in such stories familiar and shared desires for other men. Many others, however, found no such kinship. They went about their lives in-vested in their communities and families, satisfied with their lives and living out their days. These men appear outwardly to us in the historical record as assertively heterosexual or straight, but it's not so simple. Are these otherwise 'normal' men 'really gay', 'mostly straight', 'bisexual'?

Previous historians might have understood these men as gay victims of a homophobic post-war society that constrained their life possibilities and opportunities to express their authentic selves. Thinking queer also presents the possibility that hetero-sexuality is not so monolithic, constraining and limiting. Queer is as useful for understanding 'gay' men in the past as it is for understanding their 'straight' neighbours and co-workers, and it challenges us to question the division between them. Thinking queer we might ask: how rigid were industrial working-class sexual cultures in practice? Did 'sexuality' matter for organising one's desires? And was the heterosexual–homosexual binary even meaningful for these men and their communities? Understanding class through queer history means thinking about histories of class differently, and, in the case of northern England, recognising that working-class experiences of manhood allowed for homoerotic possibility.

Further examining labour, same-sex spaces and colonialism opens up other possibilities for queer understandings to help us rethink other seemingly straightforward histories. In the early twentieth-century South African gold mines, Black African men formed what sociologist T. Dunbar Moodie labels 'mine marriages'. A younger man would act as a *tinkonkana* or 'wife' to an older male 'husband' or *xibonda* of the mines, cooking and cleaning for him, and also having sex. But this wasn't just a matter of more powerful men finding sexual release with those of lower status in a men-only environment. Older *xibondas* also believed that these couplings protected them from contracting venereal disease from female sex workers in town. The usefulness of these same-sex 'mine marriages' went further for their partners. Younger *tinkonkanas*, yet to set up households with a female wife or buy cattle to ensure their position back home, used the position of 'wife' in the mines to earn money and build up resources to create a stable, heterosexual home. Early historians of the 'mine marriages' have been criticised by gay and queer activists including Zackie Achmat for describing them in such utilitarian ways, lacking emotional investment or desire, in effect erasing queerness from them. I sympathise with this critique and it seems these relationships offered much: they satisfied sexual desires, encouraged emotional investment, organised economic exchange, offered a sense of safety from venereal disease, and all the while also facilitated future heterosexual stability and masculine position. Surely these are queer relationships in several ways.

Queer history

Across history there are people whose sexual desires and behaviours, gender presentation or identity mark them out for historians. In some cases we have specific historical or local words to describe them. Recently, lesbian, gay and bisexual dominate in place of words such as homosexual, homophile or more quaintly homosexualist; before transgender and trans came into use transsexual and transvestite were more common; earlier terms that combined gender and sexual identity to understand difference included sexual invert, third sex, third gender, intermediate sex, uranian; women who loved women might call themselves or be called dyke, butch, femme, sapphist, tribade; some men who desired men might be described as queens or queans, mollies, sodomites or buggers, pederasts; and there is any combination of homo, mary, pervert, pansy, nancy, poof, fairy, bent, and other terms used jokingly by insiders or viciously by our enemies. And these lists don't include words that describe intersex conditions, or specific terms like hijra, joya or berdache with origins in other cultures and describing particular relationships with gender and sexuality. These are all distinct words, with specific meanings, and few describe precisely the same person or situation.

'Queer' tries to accommodate many of these and other words, and it can be useful too where none of them adequately captures the expression of identity or desire that we might see or find recorded in the past. 'Queer' leaves open the possibility that these words might be right for some people, and that they are wrong for others. It also expands our understandings of history to think about how people in the past might have resonated across multiple labels and categories, for themselves and for us, and where the practice of doing history must constantly be rethought and reimagined.

Queer history matters because it offers us possibilities of kinship, people whose lives feel so very familiar across the centuries. Having a history matters. Queer history gives us a past even as it simultaneously frustrates us with the unfamiliarity and unknowability of past lives. We can never really know how most people in the past understood their own lives and desires. Queer history gives us ancestors and aliens in the very same people. That the past is ultimately so full of possibility *must* challenge us to reconsider our own times. Queer history, I believe, teaches us much about the present, about the incredible variety, diversity and changeability of gender and sexualities today by recognising how radically unfamiliar – or queer – the past always was.

Can and should we queer the past? Or is history – with all its ambiguity, misleading familiarity and unknowable possibility – already queer?

Selected Further Reading

Books

John Boswell, *Christianity, Social Tolerance, and Homosexuality: Gay People in Western Europe from the Beginning of the Christian Era to the Fourteenth Century* (Chicago: University of Chicago Press, 1980)

Matt Cook, *Queer Domesticities: Homosexuality and Home Life in Twentieth-Century London* (London: Palgrave Macmillan, 2014)

Matt Houlbrook, *Queer London: Perils and Pleasures in the Sexual Metropolis, 1918–1957* (Chicago: University of Chicago Press, 2005)

Rictor Norton, *Mother Clap's Molly House: The Gay Subculture in England, 1700–1830* (London, Gay Men's Press, 1992)

Alison Oram and Annmarie Turnbull, *The Lesbian History Sourcebook: Love and Sex Between Women in Britain from 1780 to 1970* (London: Routledge, 2001)

Helen Smith, *Masculinity, Class and Same-Sex Desire in Industrial England, 1895–1957* (London: Palgrave Macmillan, 2015)

Susan Stryker, *Transgender History* (New York: Seal Press, 2008)

Chapters and articles

Zackie Achmat, '"Apostles of Civilised Vice": "Immoral Practices" and "Unnatural Vice" in South African Prisons and Compounds, 1890–1920', *Social Dynamics* 19, no. 2 (1993), 92–110

Judith M. Bennett, '"Lesbian-like" and the Social History of Lesbianisms', *Journal of the History of Sexuality* 9, no. 1 (2000), 1–24

David Lorenzo Boyd and Ruth Mazo Karras, 'The interrogation of a male transvestite prostitute in fourteenth-century London', *GLQ: A journal of Lesbian and Gay Studies* 1, no. 4 (1995), 459–65

Anna Clark, 'Anne Lister's Construction of Lesbian Identity', *Journal of the History of Sexuality* 7, no. 1 (1996), 23–50

Jeremy Goldberg, 'John Rykener, Richard II and the Governance of London', *Leeds Studies in English* 45 (2014), 49–70

Matt Houlbrook, 'Thinking Queer: The Social and the Sexual in Interwar Britain', *British Queer History: New Approaches and Perspectives*, ed. Lewis Brian (Manchester, New York: Manchester University Press, 2013), 134–64

Ruth Mazo Karras and Tom Linkinen, 'John/Eleanor Rykener Revisited', *Founding Feminisms in Medieval Studies: Essays in Honor of E. Jane Burns*, ed. Laine E. Doggett and Daniel E. O'Sullivan (Cambridge: DS Brewer, 2016), 111–21

T. Dunbar Moodie, 'Migrancy and Male Sexuality on the South African Gold Mines', *Journal of Southern African Studies* 14, no. 2 (1988), 228–56

Chapter 4

What is vernacular history?

Sarah Churchwell

There is no more significant pointer to the character of a society
than the kind of history it writes or fails to write.

E.H. Carr, *What is History?*

In January 1922, an article in *Scientific American* entitled
'Reading Between the Lines' revealed some of the new techniques
for invisible ink that had been employed during the First World
War, the *'sympathetic, mysterious, or magic inks'* (original
emphasis) used to conceal secret messages within 'an ordinary
business document'. The article reproduced such a letter, 'seized
in course of transmission' from a French spy, showing how 'the
correct treatment' had caused the 'real message' to appear between the lines.

The practice of using invisible ink to communicate secret messages between the lines of official correspondence is an ancient
one, stretching back to the Greeks and Romans; by the early
nineteenth century, 'reading between the lines' had become a vernacular phrase for deciphering subtext, interpreting implication

and connotation beyond the literal or explicit meanings of any communication. As the *Scientific American* writer suggests, such meanings will often appear deeper or more profound than the superficial or official communication – 'the real message' revealed by means of an appropriate interpretive method. In this case, that requires being alert to the indirect or tacit meanings embedded in metaphors like 'reading between the lines'. The 'real' or total meaning of any historical event can only prove fugitive, and requires sympathetic ink to reveal its fragile traces, by which I mean sympathetic readings that appreciate how mysterious and magical the relationship between language and meaning can be, as elusive as it is communicative. This applies no less to historical chronicles than to any other kind of textual or documentary narrative: reading between the lines requires inference as well as interpretation.

What any culture chooses to make official and takes as a given about itself and its history is as telling as what it fails to notice or repudiates; reading between the lines reveals that there is meaning in the gaps in our histories as well as in the printed pages. British history, if judged by the publishing marketplace, might be thought to consist of only three epochs: the Tudors, the First World War and the Second World War. Popular American history is also disproportionately dominated by three pivotal events: the landing of the *Mayflower* in 1620; Revolution and the nation's founding in the late eighteenth century; and the Civil War of 1861–5. These popular fixations bespeak a bellicose transatlantic society with an embarrassingly narrow attention span. They also speak to a kind of compulsion to repeat events that have become central to a culture's sense of its own identity – a compulsion to mythologise.

WHAT IS HISTORY, NOW?

Myth-making is never far from any act of communal storytelling, from folk tales to tall tales to urban myths and conspiracy
theories, and there is far more myth in even our official history
than we like to admit. The story of 'the British at Dunkirk'
during the Second World War is representative. It is historically
true, insofar as the British forces were at Dunkirk and their
paradoxically successful retreat was a consequential moment
in the British public's understanding of the war. But as it has
been told and retold over time, in shorthand references in journalism and politicians' speeches, in novels and films, 'Dunkirk'
has transformed into a fiction – a myth – about how the plucky
British turned defeat into victory. That myth, in turn, became a
self-fulfilling prophecy, as the British public's feeling of triumph
in the aftermath of a crushing defeat at Dunkirk enabled the in-
cident to function as a victory in collective memory and national
identity, and helped define later events like the British exit from
the European Union eighty years later. A good rule of thumb is
to assume that self-serving history is probably mythical, because
the truth is not usually so flattering.* Some historical myths are
politically malicious as well as self-serving. The big lie that the
Germans were 'stabbed in the back by Jews' after the First World

---

* Another rule of thumb is that language is just as prone to false histories
and urban myths as are historical events, including 'rule of thumb'. In the
second half of the twentieth century a folk etymology developed around
the phrase, attributing it to a supposed tradition in English common law
that said a man could only beat his wife with a stick no bigger round than
his thumb. There is negligible evidence of such a rule in English common
law; but there are nineteenth-century instances in American law of a judge
citing the supposedly ancient 'thumb standard' to excuse men accused
of domestic violence – a perfect example of the ways in which historical
myths can shape legal and political reality.

War helped Hitler take power, while the face-saving myth that the American Confederacy was a noble 'Lost Cause' maintained white governance in the United States even after slavery was abolished, and eventually led to the Black Lives Matter movement and political protests in 2020.

There are two obvious ways to resist such mythologising impulses. One is to write history about everything else, filling in the gaps, which is what the majority of professional historians do. But the other is to work at dismantling the mythologies, to resist received wisdoms and construct alternative histories. Doing that requires different kinds of reading and archival practices than have been customary in the historical profession – it involves reading for the gaps, for what's been left out or unsaid, reading between the lines of official historiography, to resist the dominant mythologising impulses that determine which history matters.

Such meanings, and their origins, can be forgotten as easily as the metaphorical origins of the phrase 'between the lines' itself. Reading between the lines reminds us that the significance we seek may lurk elsewhere, deflected from the obvious events or actors that clamour for our attention. Most history comes to us through language, the vast majority of it in the form of stories. But orthodox approaches to history – the so-called 'great man' accounts, the events-driven narratives of politics, diplomacy, trade, faith, conflict – encourage the reader to join in the mutual pretence that language is transparent and stable (in addition to the pretence that only 'great men', as determined by other men like them, matter).

A more 'literary' way of reading historical documents would entail paying close attention to the working of language, recognising that even the most ordinary and vernacular words and phrases – like 'reading between the lines' – carry histories and sympathies embedded within them. It reminds us that all history is shaped through language and story, neither of which is as straightforward as conventional approaches to history might have us believe. This is not to accuse historians of naivety: good historians are alert to bias, ambiguity, subjectivity and miscommunication in the documents they study and the stories they tell. But it is to say that history as a field has yet to fully shake off the legacy of positivism, the belief that evidence can – or should – speak for itself. It was this belief, fundamentally, that E.H. Carr set out to challenge, when he noted that historians speak for their evidence while purporting to let it speak for itself. Carr encouraged us to think harder about the people doing the speaking, and how they choose which evidence to speak about. Extending that logic would mean thinking harder about the words they use to do their speaking, as well. It means approaching history in a testing spirit, looking for the meanings that lurk between the lines, knowing that those meanings require sensitivity to feelings and beliefs, to the complexity of human motives and intentions, as well as to the ostensible facts.

As a literary scholar, I was trained to resist the idea that language ever speaks for itself: or rather, that it ever only speaks for itself. Language speaks for so much more than itself: it speaks entire histories every time we use it, whether we're aware of it or not, as in the example of reading between the lines. As Heidegger famously said, we don't speak language, language speaks us: we understand ourselves and our world through a historical language into which we are inserted when we learn to speak, that shapes our minds and all of our ideas, including our ideas of history. And language is simply not a stable – 'positive' – medium, whether we admit it or not. Miscommunication is a constant in human life, while the realism of historical writing is an inherited convention its practitioners too rarely question. Approaching historical questions with a literary sensibility makes me reach for metaphors like reading between the lines, and the idea that we need 'sympathetic ink' to infer deeper, richer meanings than the ones printed on the surface of our histories or documents. The language of the past is as full of metaphors and implicit and vernacular meanings as our language today, and being not only sensitive to those meanings, but actively curious about them, can open up entire new avenues of historical discovery.

For one thing, the meanings of words evolve – sometimes drastically – over time. When Jane Austen writes in 1815 of Emma Woodhouse's astonishment at finding herself in a carriage with 'Mr Elton actually making violent love to her', she does not mean that Mr Elton has sexually assaulted Emma or that they suddenly engaged in wild sexual intercourse; she means that he is verbally pressuring her, what today we'd call 'hitting on her' or 'chatting her up'. Social conventions or political pressures may also determine what was made explicit or left implicit in historical language uses. Some ambiguities are deliberate, to avoid repercussion or allow room for political, social or legal manoeuvring, as when an illegal gathering, for example, uses deliberately innocuous language to disguise its true intent – a disguise that might fool not only contemporary authorities but later historians. When American white supremacists in the Deep South wanted to advertise a lynching – something they did with horrific regularity in the early decades of the twentieth century – they used codes such as 'extralegal justice' to gather a mob without using the incriminating word 'lynch'. 'Extralegal justice' is a comparatively straightforward instance, translating directly into vigilante violence. But what of historical vernacular expressions that mean more than one thing, like the phrase 'working girl'? Does a 'working girl' in a nineteenth-century newspaper refer to a sex worker, or simply a girl with a job? A cultural history of working girls might set out to answer that question, to understand what was collectively understood by the phrase, and what its implications suggest about the ideas relating to gender, sex, age, class and paid labour of the society that used it.

Other vernacular codes offer shorthand ways to express complex historical, political or ideological ideas: what does a society that says it believes in the 'American Dream' mean by this phrase? Is that meaning consistent over time, or does it evolve – and does its ambiguity ever cause consequential misunderstandings? Coded meanings may arise through simple pragmatic considerations of money or space, or from the fun of an in-joke. Where once telegrams necessitated the use of highly abridged language that requires experience to decipher, future students may similarly struggle to decode the abbreviations and images of SMS messages today, and need historical context to learn that a small picture of an aubergine was a ribald joke, or how 'eye tests' became a shorthand in Britain during the 2020 coronavirus pandemic thanks to the flimsy excuse of an unpopular government adviser.

As all of these examples suggest, historical and linguistic meanings can very rapidly be lost in transmission. Recovering those meanings, and following the threads they create, are increasingly central to my own work, which blends literary and historical approaches into a kind of vernacular history, which itself is a type of cultural history. Broadly construed, cultural history collects and examines the stories we tell ourselves, asking what the stories we choose to tell ourselves tells us about ourselves. What values do we reveal through the tales, objects and figures we revere or revile, conserve or forget? What do our habits and interests – in food or music, for mourning or recreation, in books or statuary – say about us? If any culture is a system of beliefs, values and ideas, then cultural history tries to read those value systems, to understand a culture's mentality: seeking pointers to the character of a society, as Carr put it.

Some of the best cultural histories begin with the most apparently overlooked or insignificant subjects, refocusing our attention on the history of sleep, or the footnote, or camouflage, or the female victims of Jack the Ripper instead of the homicidal man – 'flipping the script', reversing expectations, reframing foreground and background. Any object, however negligible it seems, can connect myriad histories: a cultural history of the paperclip, invented in 1899 by a Norwegian engineer, might stretch back to the history of paper, forward to mobile phone SIM cards, and include the wearing of paperclips as a symbol of resistance against Nazi occupation in Norway during the Second World War. A cultural history of salt would include histories of engineering and the spice route and might discuss the folk tale that inspired *King Lear*. A cultural history of valentines might begin in the third century of the Roman Empire, trace the emergence of the doctrine of courtly love in the Middle Ages and Renaissance, spend some time in Prohibition-era Chicago as Al Capone guns down seven gangsters in 1929, and then move to the modern greeting card industry. It would need to understand how fact and fiction blend throughout this tale, how an early Christian martyr led by improbable but actual steps to cartoons of chubby angels carrying hearts pierced with arrows.

Cultural history is one of the oldest forms of historical inquiry, and also one of the newest. As an academic discipline in the West, it is largely a post-war phenomenon; but as an area of human interest, it is as central to any concept of history (or culture) as it is fundamental to storytelling – so much so that it was not identified as a subdiscipline in Anglo-American culture until the 1980s or so. Cultural history as we practise it today first emerged in France and Germany in the late eighteenth century, and (in my view, at least) it's no coincidence that some of the earliest and most influential examples of cultural history as we know it first emerged through a study of folk histories and vernacular language. The Grimm brothers, philologists who collected folktales and folksongs, were classic exemplars, understanding German language and culture through stories and songs, dance and ritual, seeing in them not merely amusement but also instruction, explanation, and transmission of cultural traditions.

Vernacular history, closely related to folk history, is a species of cultural history, concerning the ways in which popular patterns of remembering and forgetting are transmitted and sustained through popular – vernacular – traditions and languages. Initially, for scholars 'vernacular history' described those 'unofficial' histories that began to appear in medieval vernacular languages – Old French, Italian, Anglo-Norman – across Europe during the twelfth and thirteenth centuries, when Latin was still the official institutional language of Church, law and history.

Today 'vernacular history' is similarly used to describe histories written in vernacular languages by Indigenous peoples around the world, to explore questions of ancestry, heritage, identity and region.

Vernacular history can also be understood in a more expansive way, however, to think about the vernacular in all its senses: the colloquial and informal; the Indigenous and local; the idiomatic and customary; the popular as opposed to the official; and especially pertaining to, or interested in, matters of language, dialect and style. Such vernacular history can pursue any of these lines of inquiry, but it will be especially interested in the idiomatic and axiomatic, local and popular understandings of history, and how such popular histories relate to vernacular languages and expressions. As its name suggests, vernacular history will be attentive to the voices of ordinary people – not only what they said, but how they said it – while recognising how irrecoverable many of those voices remain, lost in the gaps, only to be inferred from between the lines, if at all. Just as in any conversation, intonations, contexts and cues can point to richer arrays of implied meanings, including the feelings and emotions that are revealed in and through those vernacular styles. Paying attention to systems of feeling, as well as of fact, vernacular history lets us read the traces of the irrational and the unconscious in the archive. It recognises that beliefs partially, but imperfectly, influence what people do, and that they do not always act rationally; it understands that miscommunication is as endemic, but also as meaningful, as communication, and one of the (many) reasons that myths entangle with history.

Popular memory is created through language and narrative – history, but also fiction, film, television, games, song – as well as through rituals and performances, among which we might include not only ceremonies of commemoration and celebration, but other tribal cultural encounters with deep histories, such as professional sports. Supporters of Scotland's Celtic football team, for example, understand their loyalties in profoundly historical terms – but that history is vernacular. Memorialisation projects can be formal and state-sanctioned, but they are also often local and informal, particularly when the memory of a collective trauma such as state terror, or mob violence, is being preserved. These are historical interventions – the creation of vernacular histories – that work to fill in the gaps of the histories the official culture has failed to write.

Often such vernacular histories are resistant, or in outright opposition, to institutional histories. It is not always the case that vernacular histories are mythical while institutional histories are trustworthy; on the contrary, there are countless examples of official state interests distorting, suppressing or destroying historical evidence of state-sanctioned wrongdoing, or erasing or criminalising political resistance, while vernacular histories keep the memory of marginalised events alive. Resisting such distortions of the record requires reading between the lines and against the grain of official historiography, learning to read for the unspoken and suppressed, but tacitly discernible. When an official account declares 'the illegal uprising was suppressed and the criminals arrested', vernacular history may offer a markedly different version of that event, allowing us to recover or infer histories that the state or the socially dominant have disavowed or overlooked.

That said, vernacular histories are far more likely to be mythical than resistant – which arguably makes them more, not less, meaningful. Just as a Freudian slip may accidentally reveal more than its speaker intended, so can history be revealed through cultural slips, less mistakes than the slipstreams of thoughts, ideas, and feelings captured in a culture's narratives and expressions across time, and especially in its myths and legends. We are no freer of myths in our society than cavemen carving pictures of gods and monsters to explain the coming of fire. Our myths take different forms, but they still create bogus history to fill a vacuum in knowledge or claim spurious evidentiary truth – as in the analogy I just drew to cavemen, a mythical cartoon to which our society has recourse whenever it wants to claim that a given human behaviour is 'hard-wired', a metaphor that makes us cavemen and computers at the same time. Our past as hunter-gatherers is used to explain everything from gender-reveal parties to Communism: in the absence of any evidence, such invocations are myths, not history.

In a society where opinion holds as much sway as demonstrable fact, myth takes hold, and these myths shape our history in ways we are too slow to understand, rendering us susceptible to manipulation. History is always political; when it is deliberately falsified by political interests it becomes propaganda. Studying the interplay between myth and history lets us see this process more clearly, and learn how to dismantle it; it lets us trace the myths that are emerging in our own moment and try to impede their growth. We give our myths different names – conspiracy theories, fake news, urban legends, hoaxes, moral panics – but they are myths all the same, and we use them to justify our choices no less than an ancient general sacrificing a daughter to ensure he wasn't late for the war he had already decided to start.

All cultural history involves a kind of archaeology of Indigenous vernaculars. New digital methods are particularly adept at this kind of archaeological recovery, helping us locate and map the uses of various vernaculars – expressions, ideas, understandings – in the mass grave of the digital archive, enabling us to reconstruct entire worlds that may overturn received ideas about what those worlds thought, how they spoke, or what they believed. In 1963, Richard Hofstadter identified what he called the 'paranoid style' in American culture, a 'way of seeing the world and expressing oneself' that recurred at points of crisis throughout its history. While some American historians objected to this way of reading the nation's history, arguing that it pathologised or psychologised American politics, Hofstadter's essay can also be seen as a landmark work of vernacular, rather than political, history. The paranoid style offered a metaphor for reading the American vernacular, what Philip Roth later called 'the indigenous American berserk' – a way of understanding a collective mindset that threads through enclaves in American life, understanding that cultures, like individuals, can be revealed through their idiomatic styles. These styles will not simply replicate dominant values, but may also register resistance, subversion or rejection, as well as pathologies, the disruptions and failures of its value systems.

This is why, as Carr noted, what histories a culture *fails* to tell about itself are as significant as the ones it does: registering such failures, listening for the unsaid, lets us tell a different kind of history. Paying attention to apocryphal histories is another form of reading between the lines, a way of capturing the fugitive histories that Carr urged us to remember. The apocryphal legends woven around our facts shape human history as much as, if not more than, the canonical stories – which often reach far fewer people than the apocryphal accounts do.

But it's really in the dialogue between canonical and apocryphal accounts that we can begin to capture the fullness of meaning around a given experience or event. As the old adage reminds us, our interest in trees mustn't distract us from the forest. Where an environmental history of forests might look at ecological change and human agency, at practices of farming and cultivation, a vernacular history of forests might begin with dryads and wood nymphs, tracing how laurel came to tell of victory and yew of immortality, the healing properties of aspen, or why silver birch was favoured for witches' brooms. It might tell tales of boys raised by wolves, or girls led astray by them. It might discuss campfires and Boy Scouts, or Paul Bunyan and his ox, or the 'forest primeval' of poetic Arcadia. It might tell aboriginal tales of how the world was made, or describe the Bodhi tree under which the Buddha found Enlightenment.

Or it might focus on Robin Hood, a mythical but instantly recognisable figure who symbolises his culture's ideas of the forest – the wilderness against which civilisation is measured, the refuge of outlaws and outcasts, but also the space in which social freedom is imagined. The story of Robin Hood is not merely a legend to be consigned to the pages of children's books; it developed in response to specific historical events and ruptures, registering a culture's reaction to those events. The legend of Robin Hood countered the fact of Norman conquest with myths of Saxon liberty; during battles over constitutional monarchy it offered visions of popular resistance to tyranny; its later versions, including Hollywood films, with their marked nostalgic longings for a lost rural past, respond to the encroachments of enclosure and modern industrial economies. Looked at this way, our vernacular histories serve as records of communal reactions or emotions, of how a given event or episode was construed by the people who experienced it.

As all of these examples suggest, the facts of history are shaped by myths and fictions, and vernacular history offers a way of thinking through that complex exchange. Consider a more conventionally 'historical' event, and certainly a factual one, in all its magnitude and consequence: the American Civil War. An orthodox history would write of origins and causes, plantations and slaves, politicians and statesmen, battles and stratagems, generals plotting and troops trudging through mud and carnage, presidential assassination, and finally the achievement of a Pyrrhic peace.

But a different history of the Civil War could be told through the myths and fictions that wove themselves around this momentous event, bringing in other perspectives that make clear, for example, how actively involved women were in shaping the moral debate over slavery. Rather than reading the telegrams of generals and the memoranda of government secretaries, it might begin with the 1850 publication of *Uncle Tom's Cabin,* and the legend of Abraham Lincoln greeting its author, Harriet Beecher Stowe, with the words: 'So you're the little woman who wrote the book that made this great war!' It's one of the most popular anecdotes in American history, and thoroughly debunked, but like most axiomatic legends it contains profound cultural truths. The immense popularity of *Uncle Tom's Cabin,* which Stowe conceived as a deliberate, polemical, moral intervention into the question of slavery, had as much to do with instigating the Civil War as any other proximate cause; the novel successfully shifted the sympathies of white middle-class northerners, and especially northern women, to the abolitionist cause, helping to normalise what until then had been seen by many white Americans as a radical political position.

In fact, a serious cultural history of the Civil War could be told entirely through America's favourite historical fictions, beginning with Stowe and, perhaps, the novels of Sir Walter Scott, who gave to the slaveholding South its myths of feudalism and loyal serfs, its cavaliers and knights, its gallantry and clans. It would take in the novels of Mark Twain, who created the vernacular tradition in America, especially the story of Huckleberry Finn, and his crisis of conscience over slavery. It would draw on historiography such as Gary Wills's 1992 *Lincoln at Gettysburg: The Words that Remade America*, which argues that Lincoln's Gettysburg Address changed the American political vernacular, and Jill Lepore's 'How Longfellow Woke the Dead', which shows that Henry Wadsworth Longfellow's 1861 poem 'Paul Revere's Ride' concerns the Civil War more than the American Revolution.

This cultural history would pivot on a book published in 1866 called *The Lost Cause*, which purported to be history but was entirely mendacious, up to and including the claim that slavery was a northern invention foisted upon the innocent South. *The Lost Cause* bequeathed to American historiography a mythical narrative of the nobility of the South in defeat and the Confederacy as a 'just cause' that fought a civil war in defence against 'northern aggression', rather than out of a ruthless determination to maintain slavery at any cost – a nonsense that is easily disproved but took hold across both vernacular and academic American histories over the course of the next century.

Our putative history would then take us, via Thomas W. Dixon's bestselling 1905 novel *The Clansman*, to D.W. Griffith's 1915 film adaptation of it called *The Birth of a Nation*, which single-handedly inspired the rebirth of the Ku Klux Klan. It would then be a short step from Margaret Mitchell's *Gone with the Wind* (1936), the most popular novel in the world for a century, via resistant revisions like Alice Randall's *The Wind Done Gone* (2001), to Donald Trump declaring in 2019 that the 1939 film *Gone with the Wind* was better than *Parasite*, the first South Korean film to win the Academy Award for Best Picture, and to HBO's decision to historically contextualise *Gone with the Wind* on its streaming service after the Black Lives Matter protests of 2020. That very need – to restore factual context to a deeply influential myth – bespeaks the power of cultural fictions, which had far outstripped the historical facts. Our history would end as a mob stormed the US Capitol building on 6 January 2021, waving Confederate flags and carrying nooses, shouting about fake news and conspiracy theories that swirl around an apocryphal figure called 'Q' – thus demonstrating beyond any reasonable doubt how profoundly history can be shaped by the symbols and myths of the vernacular.

Selected Further Reading

Sarah Bakewell, *At the Existentialist Café: Freedom, Being, and Apricot Cocktails* (London: Chatto, 2016)

Sarah Churchwell, *Behold, America: A History of America First and the American Dream* (London: Bloomsbury, 2018)

Saidiya Hartman, *Wayward Lives, Beautiful Experiments:*

Intimate Histories of Social Upheaval (New York: W.W. Norton, 2019)

Jill Lepore, 'How Longfellow Woke the Dead', *The American Scholar* (Spring 2011) https://theamericanscholar.org/how-longfellow-woke-the-dead/

Peter Martin, *The Dictionary Wars: The American Fight Over the English Language* (Princeton: Princeton University Press, 2019)

Lucasta Miller, *The Brontë Myth* (London: Vintage, 2001)

James Shapiro, *Contested Will: Who Wrote Shakespeare?* (London: Faber & Faber, 2010)

James Sharpe, *Remember Remember: A Cultural History of Guy Fawkes Day* (Cambridge, MA: Harvard University Press, 2006)

Linda Simon, *Lost Girls: The Invention of the Flapper* (Chicago: University of Chicago Press, 2017)

Garry Wills, *Lincoln at Gettysburg: The Words that Remade America* (New York: Simon & Schuster, 1992)

Chapter 5

How can we write the history of empire?

Maya Jasanoff

The word 'empire', to English-language readers, probably con-
notes one empire in particular – the British, the largest in world
history, which at its height encompassed about a quarter of the
earth's surface – and perhaps one emperor above all, the evil
Palpatine of the *Star Wars* franchise (who speaks, of course, with
a British accent). Yet taken together, empires are the oldest and
most durable form of polity in history. From the Mesopotamian
Empire of the Akkadians some four thousand years ago to the
global empire of the British, less than a hundred, a large portion
of the people who have ever lived, and most of the places ever
populated, have at some point been subjects of an imperial power.
Much of the history of the world is a history of empires, in the
very basic sense that empires were the containers for lots of things
historians study, from queens, kings and battles, to articulations
of cultural difference and processes of environmental change.

A working definition of 'empire' refers to a state of some
geographical extent, with some centralised authority, and some
degree of ethnic, linguistic and/or religious diversity. Beyond

that, however, empires have come in vast and various forms.

An atlas of the world from the year of E.H. Carr's birth, 1892, might double as an encyclopaedia of imperial kinds. The Eurasian heartlands were dominated by the vast land empires of China and Russia, while two more, the Ottoman and Austro-Hungarian Empires, stretched from Arabia to the Alps. In India and the Indian Ocean, a handful of trading posts established by the English East India Company in the seventeenth century had swelled into a British Empire encompassing the entire subcontinent plus an arc of colonies from Aden to Singapore. In the East Indies (present-day Indonesia), the Netherlands had likewise established colonial rule on the back of Dutch East India Company factories. The Meiji Emperor of Japan, the 122nd in a line of succession dating back to the sixth century, would soon preside over surging colonial expansion in Korea and China. In western Africa, the Portuguese, French and British governed colonies from which they had formerly trafficked slaves across the Atlantic; in southern Africa and the Congo Free State, administered by King Leopold II of Belgium, resource extraction powered a violent new wave of European incursion. White-settler colonialism, which had transformed the Americas after 1500, was still being pursued by the French in Algeria and the British in the Antipodes. In the Americas themselves, alongside the plantation colonies of the Caribbean – such as Cuba and Jamaica – foreign investors held such a large stake in the economies of some Latin American countries as to render Argentina, for instance, part of a British 'informal' empire. Then there was the United States, itself a continental, settler-colonial empire (though it rejected the name), which would scoop up Spain's overseas colonies in the Spanish-American War of 1898.

The late nineteenth century marked the apogee of what Eric Hobsbawm has called the 'age of empires'. It was also the age in which 'imperial history' as a field of study came into being. This is often said to have been launched as a modern academic subject by John Robert Seeley (1834–95), Regius Professor of History at Cambridge, who published a series of lectures in 1883 called *The Expansion of England*. Seeley wrote when British imperial hegemony was at its height, and his work reflected the prejudices of a white, male, middle-class Liberal. He is best known for the line 'We seem, as it were, to have conquered and peopled half the world in a fit of absence of mind' – by which he meant his students and readers should learn more about the empire, and embrace their role as agents of a civilising mission.

The ethnocentrism of Seeley's era persisted long enough for Carr to complain in *his* Cambridge lectures, *What is History?* (1961), about an exam paper 'called with magnificent nineteenth-century *panache* "The Expansion of Europe"' for which students weren't required 'to know anything even of countries . . . like China or Persia except what happened when the Europeans attempted to take them over'. (The paper's title was not changed until 2009.) But the millennia-long history of empires was hurtling to an end. By the end of the First World War, the emperor of China and tsar of Russia had been deposed, and the German, Austro-Hungarian and Ottoman Empires dissolved. The Second World War ended the empires of Italy and Japan, and accelerated the dissolution of others: the United States recognised Philippine independence in 1946, Britain withdrew from India and Pakistan in 1947, the Dutch from Indonesia in 1949, France from Indochina in 1954. In 1960, British prime minister Harold Macmillan told the apartheid South African Parliament that 'the wind of change is blowing through this continent, and whether we like it or not, this growth of national consciousness is a political fact'. Within a decade, more than twenty British colonies in Africa and elsewhere had become independent, as had French Algeria and Belgian Congo; Portugal largely dissolved its empire in the 1970s. A map of the British Empire in the year of Carr's death, 1982, would show little beyond a scattering of small islands, the most economically significant of which, Hong Kong, would be returned to China in 1997. The collapse of the Soviet Union and break-up of Yugoslavia in the 1990s continued the fragment-ation, bringing the number of independent nation-states from a few dozen, at the turn of the twentieth century, to approaching two hundred at the start of the twenty-first.

Anybody writing about empires today thus does so from a unique vantage point: this is (so far) the first century since an-tiquity with no formal empires.* How can we write the history of empire now that self-declared empires are history?

The first wave of scholars to take up this question were pion-eers in the field of 'post-colonial studies'. Post-colonial studies developed a complex, culturally grounded understanding of imperial power. Influenced by theorists including Frantz Fanon and Michel Foucault, Edward Said's seminal study *Orientalism* (1978) showed how imperial power was responsible for producing cultural knowledge. Critics including Stuart Hall, Gayatri Spivak and Dipesh Chakrabarty explored the construction of race and

---

* The Emperor of Japan is the only head of state with that title, and holds no political power.

ideas of difference, diasporic identity, hybridity, and the Euro-centrism of ostensibly 'universal' ideals. Meanwhile, historians such as C. A. Bayly situated European imperialism in the context of Asian empires, while the fields of Atlantic, Indian Ocean and Pacific history emerged as arenas for comparative and connec-tive study. Scholars of empire in recent decades have continued to recover and analyse the experiences of the colonised, modes of resistance, and the mutual entanglements of metropole and colony.

As a first answer to the question 'What is history?' Carr pro-posed that it was 'a continuous process of interaction between the historian and [their] facts, an unending dialogue between the present and the past'. In the 2020s, the most dynamic area of research about empire concerns the age of decolonisation, circa 1945 to 1980. At once distant enough for various classified doc-uments to have been released and recent enough for survivors to offer first-hand testimony, the events of those decades have pow-erfully engaged the attention of a rising generation of empire's descendants. And uncovering the 'facts' has been as challenging as it is revelatory.

Carr could not have known it, but at precisely the same time he was suggesting that 'facts are really not at all like fish on the fishmonger's slab. They are like fish swimming about in a vast and sometimes inaccessible ocean', his compatriots were busily trawling the records of empire to rid them of any compromising catch. As one colony after another neared independence, depart-ing British administrators deliberately destroyed any archives that 'might embarrass H[er] M[ajesty's] G[overnment] or other governments' (as a 1961 Colonial Office cable put it) if left in the wrong hands. 'Blue smoke from half a dozen little fires rose from the yards and balconies of government buildings . . . as British officials conducted a real burning of papers,' reported a journalist covering the withdrawal from Palestine in 1948. In Kuala Lumpur, twelve days before Malaysia became independent in 1957, British soldiers loaded trucks with boxes of records to be driven down to Singapore and 'destroyed in the Navy's splendid incinerator'. The governor of Trinidad was advised that, since 'it would perhaps be a little unfortunate to celebrate Independence Day with smoke', he might consider packing files into weighted crates and dumping them into the sea. Officials in Uganda came up with a codename for the culling process: they called it Operation Legacy.

None of these materials, obviously, made it into the eighteen volumes of *British Documents of the End of Empire* (published starting in 1992), a seemingly authoritative compilation of British administrative paperwork during colonial transfers of power. But in the late 1990s, historians researching the 1950s Mau Mau Emergency in Kenya grew increasingly suspicious about apparent gaps in archival records – especially as oral testimony detailed a horrific story: that the British had set up an elaborate system of detention camps, in which they subjected suspected rebels to grotesque abuse. Only in 2011, as part of a lawsuit brought against the British government by Kenyan victims of this torture, was the documentary evidence brought to light. It emerged that, nine days before Kenya's independence in 1963, four crates of sensitive papers had been hustled onto a plane in Nairobi and flown to the UK, where they were whisked off into hiding. They, together with tens of thousands more colonial documents, ended up stashed behind the razor wire of a top-secret intelligence facility on the outskirts of Milton Keynes, 'lost' to historians.

An inventory of these so-called 'migrated archives' has now revealed at least 170,000 files related to British decolonisation that were deliberately hidden from public view. Not only do these papers upend a picture of independence as something peaceably 'given' or 'granted' by benevolent imperialists. The history of their hiding (and the destruction of so many others) exposes how, long after the formal end of empire, the power structures that sustained it have restricted historians' ability to access the 'facts'. The Mau Mau case also shows how prone historians – to say nothing of politicians, courts and the general public – may still be to what Carr called the 'fetishism of the archive', endowing state-produced documents with an authority denied to the oral testimony of colonial subjects.

New research on the end of the British Empire radically redraws a history that has, till recently, been filtered through nationalist lenses. It largely remains to be seen what similarly probing studies will reveal about the ends of other European empires in the twentieth century, but one thing is likely: there will be further difficult reckonings to come.

The history of empires has traditionally been framed in terms of 'rise' and 'fall'. One problem with this model is that it smoothes imperial history into a sine curve, when in practice imperial power often jerked and stuttered in the face of resistance. Another is that it obscures the many ways empires have abutted, overlapped, and been built on top of one another – sometimes literally, as one can see in the buildings, plazas and streets of imperial capitals like Istanbul, Cairo, Delhi or Mexico City. Most histories of empire concentrate on single empires, or single regions within empires. Recovering the connections between and across empires – their layerings and lineages – can help break down normative assumptions, and provide a clearer sense of how imperial power endures.

Emulation and assimilation were key components of Britain's global ascent. While English theorists of the seventeenth century were eager to distinguish their kind of Atlantic colonialism – Protestant, commercial and 'free' – from the absolutist Catholic empires of France, Spain and Portugal, in practice the distinctions were blurrier. The English snatched what they could of Spain's wealth, using piracy; learned how to cultivate the Caribbean's major cash crop, sugar, from the Dutch in Brazil; and followed Portugal to become the largest transatlantic slave trader of the eighteenth century. While eighteenth- and nineteenth-century Britons contrasted their rule in Asia against Indigenous 'Oriental despotism', the East India Company deliberately adopted Mughal practices and rituals. Fully half of British domains by 1900 – from Nigeria to the Persian Gulf to Malaya – were not even colonies but 'protectorates', where imperial rule was disguised under the nominal authority of Indigenous sovereigns. ('Spheres of Interference,' quipped the authors of 1066 and All That, 'were necessary in all Countries inhabited by their own natives.')

Behind the actions of modern European empires hovered the example of ancient Rome, sometimes like a halo, sometimes like a ghost. The word 'empire' entered English via Norman French, which derived it in turn from Latin imperium. 'Kaiser' and 'Tsar' both come from 'Caesar' – a title Mehmed the Conqueror also adopted when he captured Constantinople in 1453. Victorian British imperialists heralded the making of a Pax Britannica, erected marble statues of themselves swathed in togas, and turned study of the Classics into a prerequisite for imperial service.

Candidates for the Victorian Indian Civil Service were expected on their qualifying exams to be able to translate Edmund Burke into Latin, render John Ruskin into Greek and decline a Sanskrit noun. Getting tested in Indian vernacular languages or modern history came later.

To be sure, ancient history also offered disquieting reminders of imperial vulnerability. It was not lost on some that the greatest area of overlap between the Roman and British Empires was Britain itself. The novelist Joseph Conrad opened his powerful critique of colonialism, *Heart of Darkness* (1899), by imagining a Roman soldier sailing up the Thames into the 'savage' hinterland of pre-colonial Britannia: 'This, too,' the narrator reflects, 'has been one of the dark places of the earth.' That Edward Gibbon published the first volume of *The Decline and Fall of the Roman Empire* in 1776, the year of the American Declaration of Independence, was a coincidence. That Rudyard Kipling published his poem 'Recessional', invoking the ruins of empires past, on the occasion of Queen Victoria's Diamond Jubilee in 1897, was a caution.

Turn-of-the-century anxieties about imperial decline led some British thinkers to recognise that their best hope for sustained power lay in tighter relations with the United States. Some advocated the formation of a 'Greater Britain' that would federate English-speaking settler colonies and potentially include the United States. (Cecil Rhodes endowed his eponymous scholarships to further this aim.) The journalist W.T. Stead went further, arguing in 1902 that Britain faced a choice: merge with the United States outright and 'continue for all time to be an integral part of the greatest of all World Powers' – or retain its independence and be reduced 'to the status of an English-speaking Belgium'.

In the event, by the Second World War it was the United States that dictated the terms of the Anglo-American relationship, and one of them was for Britain to divest itself of an empire. By then, however, empire had become an '-ism'. In *Imperialism: A Study* (1902), the economist J.A. Hobson argued that imperialism was the process whereby capitalists invested in profitable overseas markets, shortchanging workers at home. The idea was taken up by Lenin in his *Imperialism: The Highest Stage of Capitalism* (1917), to revolutionary effect. Whether or not one buys Hobson's or Lenin's thesis, the premise that imperial expansion is driven more by economic imperatives than ideological or geopolitical ones has gone on to inform a great deal of historical scholarship, some of it hugely influential. In *Capitalism and Slavery* (1944), for instance, Eric Williams (future prime minister of Trinidad and Tobago) argued that the abolition of slavery in the British Empire owed more to the decline in the profitability of sugar than to the campaigns of much-touted humanitarian agitators. In a widely cited article called 'The Imperialism of Free Trade' (1953), historians Ronald Robinson and John Gallagher described a nineteenth-century British 'informal empire' rooted in foreign investment, and proposed that informal empire turned into 'formal' conquest when assets (such as the Suez Canal) had to be defended.

'Empires', then, can be marked on a map. 'Imperialism', by contrast, involves a set of coercive relationships that may exist even in the absence of direct rule. Seen in this light, it might be more accurate to recast the 'fall' of Western European empires in the twentieth century as another set of overlays, this time by American power. To be sure, the United States long pointedly rejected any notion of itself as an empire, and imperialism itself, as contrary to 'freedom'. (So did the Soviet Union, which decried imperialism as the enemy of the global working class.) Yet the Cold War found the United States mouthing truisms about anti-imperial liberty as it fought a war in the former French Indochina, orchestrated political assassination in the former Belgian Congo, engaged in proxy conflict in the former Portuguese Angola, and meddled perniciously in nations across the Caribbean and Latin America. The invasions of Afghanistan in 2001 and Iraq in 2003 brought forth a flurry of debate in the American press about whether the United States should henceforth embrace a conception of itself as an empire. With soldiers on the ground in both regions for two decades (longer than the British Mandate in interwar Iraq), and some eight hundred American bases around the world (Russia, Britain and France have about forty between them), the question of whether America is an empire seems moot.

It took some foresight for Carr to ask in 1961 whether 'the world centre of gravity now resides, or will continue for long to reside, in the English-speaking world with its western European annex'. In 2021, only a myopic could deny that Anglo-American supremacy is faltering morally and materially. Though the US remains the largest global economy, China is on track to surpass it by the end of the decade, and has established expansive global interests by means such as its Belt and Road Initiative. Those who assert that China has no intention of converting its economic influence in Asia and Africa into political or military control might do well to consider the history of British informal imperialism, one of whose primary targets was China itself. (One could also look to China's internal affairs, with the Sinicisation of Tibet, genocide in Xinjiang and curtailment of Hong Kong's freedoms.) Meanwhile Vladimir Putin has pursued the restoration of 'Greater Russia' with the occupation of Crimea, among other ventures. Time will tell whether empire, in name, has really gone for good.

The twenty-first-century world may be largely post-colonial (with all due recognition to dependencies such as Puerto Rico, Greenland and French Polynesia). But to follow the lineages of empire is to arrive at a world which is by no means post-imperial. That, in turn, invests the question of how to write the history of empire with political and moral stakes.

Western histories of empire have long been bound up with ideas of 'progress'. That is partly because the historical profession coalesced in the nineteenth century alongside the consolidation of European imperial power.

Human civilisation developed in stages, proposed Enlightenment intellectuals. Nineteenth-century British historians looked at their own country and saw a place that had advanced from an agrarian society to an industrial one, from an autocratic monarchy to a constitutional one, from mercantilism to free trade. The purpose of British imperial rule, they held, was to teach colonial societies how to advance in turn. 'Every society may progress if it chooses, or can be shown how to do so,' pronounced the utilitarian James Mill in his *History of British India* (1817). His book, rife with chauvinistic judgements ('a man . . . may obtain more knowledge of India in one year in his closet in England, than he could obtain during the course of the longest life, by the use of his eyes and ears in India'), became a manual for colonial administrators well into the nineteenth century.

Portrayals of British imperialism as an engine of historical progress doubled as potent means of moral rationalisation. Early nineteenth-century historians turned the abolition of the transatlantic slave trade in 1807 into an exemplum of British virtue, trying to efface Britain's shameful past as the largest slave trader in the eighteenth-century world. Thomas Babington Macaulay wrote essays redeeming the reputations of the East India Company power-brokers Robert Clive and Warren Hastings, once castigated for their brutality and corruption. J.R. Seeley resolved the paradox inherent in a British Empire which trumpeted its commitment to 'liberty' while denying it to colonial subjects by setting up a racist distinction between white-majority colonies, which he judged mature enough for 'responsible' self-government, and Caribbean, African and Asian colonies, deemed to require further tutelage. As late as the Second World War, when anticolonial independence movements rattled the cage of imperial rule, the rise of European fascism fuelled fresh justifications for empire, British-style. 'Perhaps only in the shock of 1940,' mused the historian Herbert Butterfield (who famously condemned the 'Whig' devotion to progress narratives), 'did we realize to what a degree the British Empire had become an organization for the purpose of liberty.'

In the sole passage referring to empire in *What is History?*, E.H. Carr decried the way historians justified barbarous colonisation in Africa and Asia on the grounds that those regions were 'developed' in turn. Decades of post-colonial scholarship have helped complicate one-sided ideas about the virtues of imperial rule. Nevertheless, the old picture of the British Empire as a force for good in the world was dusted off in the aftermath of 9/11. Niall Ferguson, in his 2002 bestseller *Empire*, made the case that the British Empire, despite its faults, laid the foundations of a global order anchored in open markets and liberal values; in subsequent writings he urged the United States to lean into its role as Britain's successor. More recently, while Whitehall officials mused about forming a post-Brexit 'Empire 2.0' through trade deals, the Oxford theologian Nigel Biggar launched a multi-year research project devoted to producing a cost-benefit assessment of empire, and urged readers in a *Times* op-ed: 'Don't feel guilty about our colonial history.' Within twenty-four hours, 170 academics had signed a letter condemning 'crude cost/benefit analysis' for 'wilfully obscur[ing] the complexities which scholars of empire have carefully unpicked in recent decades'.

Another 'problem with weighing up pros and cons', historian Priya Satia has written, 'is that it presumes there is a point at which the story is over, the accounts are closed, and we can actually tot up the balance'. But the legacies of racism, expropriation and colonial violence endure. They are what students at the University of Cape Town protested in 2015 when they called for the removal of a statue of Cecil Rhodes and the 'decolonisation' of the curriculum, and what inspired related protests at Oxford and Harvard. They are what propelled Black Lives Matter protestors into the streets of cities around the world in the summer of 2020, after the murder of George Floyd in Minneapolis, pulling down the effigy of a slave trader in England; defacing a statue of King Leopold II in Belgium; rallying against institutional racism in France; decrying Aboriginal deaths in custody in Australia.

So what are some directions the history of empire might take in years to come? Here are a few suggestions. First, building on the contributions of post-colonial studies, historians ought to press ahead in uncovering sources and stories that imperial regimes had vested interests in keeping out of sight. This is especially acute with respect to the histories of decolonisation and state-sponsored violence. The present age of increasing economic inequality should also keep directing more historians' attention toward the imperial entanglements of race, money and power, which – as pointedly illustrated by the 'Legacies of British Slave-Ownership' project at University College London, which traces UK government payouts to individual slave-owners following the 1833 abolition of slavery – continue to shape the landscape of privilege within and between post-colonial nations.

A second proposal would be to pursue more comparative and connective studies of empire across time periods and regions. Imperial history has increasingly dovetailed with 'global' and 'transnational' history to explore the movement of people, things and ideas across geographical regions. But most imperial history (like most history) continues to be framed by the borders of single nations and empires, which risks injecting exceptionalism into our histories, and limiting our perspectives on widespread features of imperial rule, such as settler colonialism and coercive labour regimes. Similarly, the increasingly modern skew of historical research (toward the twentieth century in particular) – welcome in many ways though it is – can make it harder to identify precedents and longer-term patterns. Given the obvious limits to any single scholar's expertise and access to sources, studies of empire across space and time present a great arena for collaboration. Indeed, pursued mindfully, collaborative initiatives could even help combat another legacy of empire, namely a disproportionate concentration of resources and 'authority' in the well-endowed universities of former colonial metropoles.

And then there is the word 'we'. The membership of the historical profession has diversified massively since Carr's day, along with the kinds of histories scholars write. (Though it remains to be seen what will happen in the face of the – related? – contraction in the number of postgraduate positions and permanent jobs in the humanities.) So why is it that, despite at least thirty years of scholarship dedicated to examining the multifarious workings of imperial power, everywhere from the bedroom to the boardroom to the battlefield, British public discussion still so often reduces to simplistic debates about whether empire was 'good' or 'bad'? It is easy to point the finger at jargonistic academic prose. But it's far more accurate to highlight the persistent prejudices that allow students to complete their schooling with scant expo-sure to imperial history; television producers to keep tapping white, RP-accented males to present histories of empire; trade publishers to promote 'big' books by white men, about white men, to white men; and newspaper editors to serve up culture war polemics.

How 'we' write the history of empires is thus closely tied to the question of who gets to do so, and what kinds of histories make it into schoolrooms and public spaces, onto airwaves and screens. Given the manifest imprint of imperial history on the present world, the answer must be to interpret that 'we' as widely as possible. About one thing we can be certain. Historians will go on writing about the imperial past. History's heirs will keep finding ways to right it.

Selected Further Reading

David Anderson, 'Guilty Secrets: Deceit, Denial, and the Discovery of Kenya's "Migrated Archive"', *History Workshop Journal*, vol. 80, issue 1 (Autumn 2015)

C. A. Bayly, *The Birth of the Modern World, 1780–1914* (Oxford: Wiley-Blackwell, 2003)

Jane Burbank and Frederick Cooper, *Empires in World History: Power and the Politics of Difference* (Princeton: Princeton University Press, 2011)

Antoinette Burton, *The Trouble with Empire: Challenges to Modern British Imperialism* (Oxford: Oxford University Press, 2015)

John Darwin, *After Tamerlane: The Rise and Fall of Global Empires, 1400–2000* (London: Penguin, 2007)

Robert Gildea, *Empires of the Mind: The Colonial Past and the Politics of the Present* (Cambridge: Cambridge University Press, 2019)

Priyamvada Gopal, *Insurgent Empire: Anticolonial Resistance and British Dissent* (London: Verso, 2019)

Eric Hobsbawm, *The Age of Empire: 1875–1914* (New York: Pantheon Books, 1987)

Daniel Immerwahr, *How to Hide an Empire: A History of the Greater United States* (New York: Vintage, 2019)

Achille Mbembe, *Out of the Dark Night: Essays on Decolonization* (New York: Columbia University Press, 2021)

Priya Satia, *Time's Monster: How History Makes History* (London: Penguin, 2020)

Odd Arne Westad, *The Global Cold War: Third World Interventions and the Making of Our Times* (Cambridge: Cambridge University Press, 2005)

Chapter 6

Glorious memory

Dan Hicks

The first statues or memorials I remember were church monuments. The smooth cold feel of an alabaster dog curled at the feet of the recumbent effigy of a knight, gloved hands held at his chest in prayer. A waxy scrawl on soft paper as the crayon between my fingers revealed line by line the figures of a lord and lady from the monumental brass beneath, chain mail and pointed shoes, some Latin text below and a date, framed by a frottage of specks and dimples picked out from the limestone of the tomb in which the brass was set. The army of one hundred and thirteen kings, bishops and saints that adorn the West Front of Lichfield Cathedral – Moses with his tablets, Abel with a crook, Alfred with a harp, William with his sword, Eve with a distaff.

Later there were the museums. Jacob Epstein's two-ton bronze Lucifer which greets visitors climbing the stairs to enter Birmingham Art Gallery, his archangel's wings spread out behind him and his hands clenched like claws, installed, my father proudly assured me, to mark the defeat of fascism, as some kind of warning. The Art Deco lions that guard the British Museum's north entrance at

Montague Place, the outlines of their manes somehow recalling the headcloths of ancient Egyptian pharaohs, their front paws folded one onto another. Then a Barbara Hepworth somewhere, possibly while on holiday in Cornwall. A Henry Moore.

In the streets there were Queen Victorias and blokes on horseback. But from my time growing up in Birmingham two particular public sculptures stuck with me, both commemorations of the sacrifice and losses of war.

As a teenager, every day on my walk to school I would pass the First World War memorial outside Sutton Coldfield town hall. The strikingly realistic bronze figure of a serviceman in battledress stands on a sandstone plinth, his greatcoat buttoned up, a tin helmet on his head, the work of sculptor and medallist Francis Doyle-Jones. A gas mask holder and water bottle hang at his waist, and he is leaning forwards on his rifle with crossed hands, as if he just got off a train at the nearby railway station.

ERECTED TO THE GLORIOUS MEMORY

the plaque reads,

THEY DIED THAT WE MIGHT LIVE

Then there was that day when we came across a vast bronze sculpture on a pink granite plinth in Cannon Hill Park. Two British soldiers push a 15-pounder field gun forward into the void. Above them a female figure stands on a half globe, holding a wreath and a shield bearing the arms of the city of Birmingham, symbolising Peace. This New Sculpture work was made by Albert Toft, who later created four bronze allegorical figures for the city's Hall of Memory memorial for the First World War in Centenary Square: navy holding a ship's wheel, air force holding a propeller blade, women's services holding a book of remembrance, and army clutching the barrel of a machine gun.

TO THE GLORIOUS MEMORY

the plaque on the Cannon Hill monument reads,

OF THE SONS OF BIRMINGHAM
WHO FELL IN THE SOUTH AFRICAN WAR 1899–1902
AND TO PERPETUATE
THE EXAMPLE OF ALL WHO
SERVED IN THE WAR
THIS MEMORIAL IS ERECTED
BY THEIR FELLOW CITIZENS

To their glorious memory. To perpetuate their example. Both monuments were built through public subscription, erected in 1922 and 1906 respectively. In the case of Toft's memorial it was built with £2000 raised through the *Birmingham Daily Mail*. On Empire Day in May 1907 flags were flown on all Birmingham's public buildings, and a procession to the statue was organised by Roger Pocock's recently formed paramilitary body the Legion of Frontiersmen. Mounted police led the march, and then a military band, and then a detachment of the Naval Brigade who were drawing a gun that bore a wreath. 'After the placing of the wreath,' the *Times* correspondent reported, 'a short address was delivered by the chaplain, and the Last Post was sounded by the trumpeters of the Royal Warwick Garrison Artillery'.

Much later, when I moved to Bristol in the late 1990s, a third statue came into view. Community protests called for the removal of a memorial erected in 1895 to the seventeenth-century slaver Edward Colston. Was there some sense that the sculpture already contained within it some kernel of its future downfall, a generation later?

A monument is not a history book. But then again is a monument totally unlike a history book? Is reading a journal article always so different from reading a memorial plaque? The word 'memoirs' sounds strange to a modern ear when used in its archaic sense of the proceedings or transactions of a learned society, such as the *Memoirs of the Literary and Philosophical Society of Manchester* or the *Memoirs of the American Anthropological Association*. This is because it is conventional among historians to distinguish between memorialisation, museums and heritage on the one hand and academic writing on the other. Writing history takes place in libraries, archives and academic studies, sitting at desks or in armchairs, we imagine. Surely quite unlike casting a bronze image of a field gun, or erecting a statue in a public park, or marching with a military band to lay a wreath, or sending the call of 'thin brazen notes' from a lone bugle, as Robert Graves put it. The boundary between words and things sometimes breaks down, of course – a handwritten postcard landing on the doormat, the stack of books under my laptop for video calls. But what of the boundaries between words, things and memory?

Returning to E.H. Carr's 1961 text *What is History?* is instructive. While that book had very little to say about memory, it did describe the raising of a 'monument to a great man', the Foreign

Minister of the Weimar Republic Gustav Stresemann. But that monument was, Carr explained, a three-volume set of his papers published posthumously by his secretary. Carr used this example in his argument that history is always to a large degree an exercise in interpretation, not the neutral presentation of facts. He contrasted his sense of the selectivity of the historian with Lord Acton's positivist, 'common-sense' belief, expressed in 1896, in history as the gradual accumulation of knowledge. Carr traced a 'cult of facts' from Locke to Bertrand Russell via Acton and the scholar Leopold von Ranke, who believed in the naively optimistic idea that historians could describe historical reality *wie es eigentlich gewesen* (how it actually was). Carr borrowed aspects of social science to suggest that the interpretive historian is not so much discovering as always 'in a relation with' the facts.

Standing six decades on from Carr, just as Carr stood six decades from Acton, embracing a post-Rankean philosophy of history has perhaps never been more important. Some wish to turn the clock back to a late Victorian conception of history writing as national pride. In 2020 calls for the removal of statues erected to memorialise white supremacy were renewed in Bristol, London, Oxford, Cardiff and beyond, but politicians have called for such images to be 'retained and explained', and even 'maintained and acclaimed'. Calls to 'defend' statues and claims that they are being attacked in a 'culture war' have been the first line of defence for those wishing to stand against the recent advances of anti-racism, which seek to protect living, breathing human bodies rather than stone or metal effigies. Revisionist histories of the British Empire have been derided as unpatriotic. As I write, just this morning Cambridge historian Robert Tombs published an article in the *Spectator* bearing the title 'The Distortion of

British History', which claims that writing histories of slavery and empire are mere attempts to 'manufacture a guilt-laden history' that 'serves hidden political agendas'.

In underlining that 'the historian belongs not to the past but to the present', Carr criticised Hugh Trevor-Roper's claim that the historian 'ought to love the past'. Such a sentiment, Carr argued, was 'a symptom of loss of faith and interest in the present or future', which held back the potential of 'freeing oneself from the dead hand of the past'. But today the false choice between jingoism or guilt, hand in hand with the false claim that we require a 'balanced' account of 'race science' and colonial violence, is being presented in a British society very different from that of 1961. One part of these changes is that history-writing has expanded far beyond the book-lined studies of Oxbridge dons, through the seismic shifts in public history, Black history, local history, women's history, queer history, industrial history, Indigenous history, history written from across the global south, history told in new ways, asking new questions. These new public histories are led by communities from the grassroots, experienced through broadcast media on screens of all varieties, excavated by a new profession of archaeologists, encountered in museums, galleries, landscapes, historic sites, cities, coastlines; googled, tweeted, re-tweeted, snapped and shared – all at a scale unimaginable in 1961. And here, Carr's emphasis then on the relative 'softness' of history-writing in his critique of the ideology of hard facts, his effort to raise delicate relativism above outmoded realism, runs into a problem – a problem of materialism.

These new ecologies of history-writing take place in living landscapes, at sites of excavation, in the built environment, with objects or images, whether on display or in archives and storerooms. This is the terrain of the archaeologist rather than the historian, and the field in which I was trained – the archaeology of the modern and contemporary world – has emerged from almost nothing in 1961 to become a significant part of how we study the past. This is a problem when we revisit Carr because when it comes to material culture, Carr dismantled only one part of the empiricism of the late Victorian construction of history as a discipline. His book repeated the old idea of archaeology as one of 'the auxiliary sciences of history', along with 'epigraphy, numismatics, chronology, and so forth', each concerned with the production of 'so-called basic facts, which are the same for all historians, [and] commonly belong to the category of the raw materials of the historian rather than of history itself'. This idea belonged to the very worldview with which Carr was seeking to break.

Between 1897 and 1911, Swiss librarian Charles Martel drafted a new system of classification for the Library of Congress, where he was chief classifier in the catalogue division. In developing the new system Martel drew on a number of earlier schemes, especially that of *Expansive Classification* which Charles Ammi Cutter had developed and put into practice at the Boston Athenaeum, where he was head librarian, in 1880. Among the changes that Martel made to Cutter's scheme was a reorganisation of the subject of History. Cutter had organised the Class 'History (F)' into Periods, Countries and Allied Studies – the last of which included Chronology, Philosophy of History, 'Antiquities, Manners and Customs', Inscriptions, Numismatics, Chivalry, Knightly Orders, Heraldry, and Peerages and Nobility. In contrast Martel now gave over a whole Class (C) to what he called the *Auxiliary Sciences of History*, which included 'Archaeology' and

'Antiquities' alongside 'Diplomatics, Chronology, Numismatics, Epigraphy, Heraldry, Genealogy and Biography'. In doing so, he built a kind of division of labour, or hierarchy of facts, into the very arrangement of knowledge in libraries, writing the idea of the archaeologist as mere technician into the very card indexes themselves.

Such a view of the place of 'data' and interpretation, mapping archaeology and history onto realism and relativism, was current in Americanist historical archaeology in the fifties and sixties, most famously in Ivor Noël Hume's controversial definition of historical archaeology as 'the "handmaiden" to early American and colonial history' in 1964. But this is not just a view of interdisciplinarity that most would now reject; it is a category error that has been superseded by how we understand history and memory in the historic built environment in the 2020s.

On the morning of Friday 12 June 2020, five days after the grassroots removal of the statue of Edward Colston in Bristol, following a failed public consultation process over three decades, Prime Minister Boris Johnson tweeted 'We cannot now try to edit or censor our past. We cannot pretend to have a different history.'

Mr Johnson's comments defending a Victorian memorial to a Jacobean slaver remind us of the close relationships between late Victorian conceptions of history, late Victorian British colonialism and colonial nostalgia after Brexit. The vision of *wie es eigentlich gewesen* was set out in the introduction to Ranke's *Geschichte der romanischen und germanischen Völker (History of the Latin and Teutonic Nations)*. Written from Berlin in 1824, and entering its third edition in 1885 (translated into English in

1887) just as the Berlin Congress was carving up the continent of Africa between Europeans, Ranke's introduction set out a vision of Germanic-Roman cultural continuity from the Migration Period, through the Crusades, to contemporary European colonialism. The construction of such continuities took future-oriented forms as well. Statues were erected to naturalise colonial power, to celebrate empire, yes, but more than that, to make it endure, to give it deep roots, to build it into the very fabric of our cities. Statues like those of Colston in Bristol or Rhodes in Oxford worked with that lasting sense of childhood introductions to statues in churches, cathedrals and galleries. Images of inequality and white supremacy were brought onto the streets, rewiring the aesthetics of divinity for an ongoing colonial future.

And here we see the danger of treating objects as somehow more factual than documents. The contextualising impulse of Carr's interpretive historicism gives way to a particular kind of moral judgement. These were men of their times, we find ourselves saying; our ancestors not our contemporaries. And yet here they stand before us in the street.

Before you know it, the assertion is made that to remove a statue or change an interpretation would be to erase history, to silence the past. The demand is for the facts served up raw. Blink, and the solidity and apparent eternal permanence of the statue will have transformed into the idol as a historical fact. Historicism has often served to bolster conservative accounts of the past, of course. Hugh Trevor-Roper's injunction to love the past was absent from his later rather snooty critique of the idea of traditional Scottish material culture, which he depicted as nothing but a modern fabrication of bagpipe tartanry misrepresented as ancient custom. This deconstructionist falsification of belief, of identity, of the work of culture, came to form a kind of laissez-faire Tory postmodernism – in which the facts could be warped by those in a position to do so. Trevor-Roper expressed this in his valedictory lecture on leaving Oriel College, Oxford, to become Master of Peterhouse, Cambridge, in 1980:

> Objective science has its place in historical study, but it is a subordinate place: the heart of the subject is not in the method but in the motor, not in the technique but in the historian.

Think back to the two decades after Carr's book was published, when a very real attack on the material facts of British imperial violence took place, as the British Colonial Office ran a project known as Operation Legacy to destroy physical documents by burning or dumping at sea. Further classified documents of empire, some of which were held in a security facility at Hanslope Park in Buckinghamshire, still remain classified under provisions in the 1958 Public Records Act. Jump forward to May 2015; as an Oxford Union debate about Britain paying reparations to its former colonies is held, the bar manager puts up posters advertising a 'Colonial Comeback' cocktail. The ways in which colonialism persists can thus include denials, erasures and endurances, renaming drinks, erecting statues, those in control of the past seeking to intervene in the material world and the historic environment as if it were the fabric of time itself.

We might add the example of the 'cleaning' of the Parthenon marbles in 1938 – their vandalistic grinding-down with blunt copper chisels and carborundum until they achieved an imagined ideal of 'whiteness', an event that led Epstein to claim in a letter to *The Times* that the sculptures were at risk of being 'permanently ruined'. The physical record of the past, far from being a neutral physical record requiring mere documentation – what Carr mistook as 'basic facts' – is often interfered with. A statement is made, and made to last. And such statements can include ongoing violence rather than memory alone.

As a historian Carr shared with Ranke a self-image as working in a tradition that began with Herodotus and Thucydides, noting how *The Histories* begins by defining the historian's purpose as 'to preserve a memory of the deeds of the Greeks and the barbarians'. These foundational figures for the historian were of course largely concerned with narrating wars, whether Graeco-Persian or Peloponnesian. The 1700 years of inheritance that Ranke imagined was a charter myth for nineteenth-century ideas of European civilisation, of European peoples (*Völker*) and of European colonisation, but the militarist dimension of his history writing reached back seven hundred years further. Now echoes of that militarism are revealed to be with us still, as calls to remove racist statues are misrepresented as a 'culture war'.

At stake here is not just the fact that the distinction Carr drew between material evidence and interpretive choices left out the question of statues and monuments. A sculpture can operate like language – as a statement that must be interpreted. But it can also blend fact with memory and myth, in the same way as a memory can become intertwined with a photograph, the personal memory of seeing a photograph. Like a photograph, or like any archaeological ceramic sherd, or like E.H. Carr's sixty-year-old book on the desk in front of me taken from the library shelf and reread, a monument is not a fragment of time frozen as a 'basic fact', but a human endurance. What then of those statues built to be confused with facts? What can these confusions tell us? Some monuments are weaponised analogies. They set out to efface some people and erase their humanity while idolising others with graven materiality. But there's more than that.

Some historians write about the past as if they were erecting a monument. We all know these books. The prime minister's book about Winston Churchill is a prime example, or the lord president of the council's maladroit *The Victorians*. Monuments to position and privilege, to an exclusionary vision of civilisation. Some conduct research for a book of history as if violently looting a continent. Some give lectures as if not just silencing the past but speaking over its voices. Some venerate heroes, often blending with the author's self-image; by embedding old prejudices, screwed in with steel nails as if they were plaques, deep in their meretricious prose. Historiography can memorialise in quasi-perpetuity those who stand and celebrate what has been made to fall. Carr knew that much, but when he attacked Trevor-Roper's injunction that the historian must 'love the past' they describe, he omitted to deal with the problem of artefacts that are propaganda, misrepresentations of the past built in stone, glorifications of inequality and brutality wrought in alloyed copper.

Let's be clear. Once a statue is erected, it is much harder to remove than it is to change the reading list. A discipline can more easily critique an outdated or wrongheaded view of the past and move on than a society can remove a statue. Robes of rock, porphyry faces, granite hair, marble feet, brass hands polished by human touch; from childhood encounters onward the statues we come to know become benchmarks for the duration of time. But when the materials of divinity, of royalty or of the commemoration of sacrifice have been used to present racism, slavery or British colonial violence as immovable and inalienable things, somehow eternal and sovereign, stone figures dethroning humanity, then we must be willing to measure them against our present time, to remove these ongoing violent distortions of the past. To overthrow a false memory is always a generative act. To overthrow amnesia enacted through memorialisation could never be iconoclasm.

Most of these are not new observations. In his book *Les damnés de la terre*, published in 1961, the very same year as Carr's *What is History?*, Frantz Fanon evoked the world of European colonialism as 'a world of statues':

> A compartmentalised, machinist, immobile world, a world of statues: the statue of the general who led the conquest, the statue of the engineer who built the bridge; a self-confident world, crushing spines flayed by whips with its stones: this is the colonial world . . . The colonial regime owes its legitimacy to force and at no time tries to hide this aspect of things. Each statue, that of Faidherbe or Lyautey, of Bugeaud or Sergeant Blandan – all these conquistadors perched on colonial soil never stop representing the exact same message: 'We are here by the force of our bayonets.'

Fast-forward to the footage of Colston falling, blindfolded, the rope slung around his shoulders and feet, dragged and drowned in the harbour, shared across the world. Like any image, and like the statue itself, this is not a frozen moment in time; it is a duration. Colston was already falling back in the nineties. Colston is still falling.

Let's infuse our history-writing with this knowledge. Let's correct Carr's vision of the archaeologist and their 'basic facts'. Anti-racist history is not a metaphor but a physical process of dismantling position and privilege, re-purposing the historian's resources, and reimagining our shared past. In the 2020s history is co-production. In the 2020s history takes place in the streets as well as in the libraries and the seminar rooms. In the 2020s history-writing must allow for the possibility of fallism. The remembrance of absence, of loss that endures, a void from which we can still learn. Today all history is rewriting history. Some statues are more weapon than memorial, but a history book can be handled like the archaeologist's trowel, as if each word were excavated, sherd after sherd. Sometimes it's necessary to dig through the fabric of memory and human endurance. Glorious memory. Sometimes you have to write history like you're pulling down a statue.

Selected Further Reading

Ana Lucia Araujo, *Slavery in the Age of Memory: Engaging the Past* (London: Bloomsbury, 2021)

Marc Bloch, *The Historian's Craft* (trans. P. Putnam) (Manchester: Manchester University Press, 1954)

R.G. Collingwood, *The Idea of History* (Oxford: Clarendon Press, 1946)

Dan Hicks, *The Brutish Museums: the Benin Bronzes, Colonial Violence and Cultural Restitution* (London: Pluto Press, 2020)

Dan Hicks, 'Why Colston Had to Fall' *Art Review* (9 June 2020) https://artreview.com/why-colston-had-to-fall/

Dan Hicks, 'The UK government is trying to draw museums

into a fake culture war', *Guardian* 15 October 2020.
https://www.theguardian.com/commentisfree/2020/oct/15/
the-uk-government-is-trying-to-draw-museums-into-a-fake-
culture-war

Dan Hicks, 'Necrography: death-writing in the colonial
museum', *British Art Studies* issue 19 (2021), https://doi.
org/10.17658/issn.2058–5462/issue-19/conversation

Achille Mbembe, *Out of the Dark Night: Essays on
Decolonization* (New York: Columbia University Press,
2021)

Rhodes Must Fall Movement, Oxford, *Rhodes Must Fall: The
Struggle to Decolonise the Racist Heart of Empire* (London:
Zed Books, 2018)

Ann Laura Stoler, *Duress: Imperial Durabilities in Our Times*
(Durham, NC: Duke University Press, 2016)

Erin Thompson, *Smashing Statues: The Rise and Fall of
American Monuments* (New York: W.W. Norton and
Company, 2021)

Michel-Rolph Trouillot, *Silencing the Past: Power and the
Production of History* (Boston: Beacon Press, 1995)

Chapter 7

How can we write the history of disability?

Jaipreet Virdi

I really think that this lie that we've been sold about disability is
the greatest injustice.

Stella Young

He is the real Batman.

Gliding his white staff in front of him as he approaches the
stage to deliver his TED Talk, Daniel Kish teases the audience
with the first sense of his superpower. 'It is people's perceptions
of blindness,' he says, 'that are far more threatening to blind
people than blindness itself.' Blindness is often perceived as a lim-
itation, one that traps a person in a dark unknown. Yet the fate
of blind people, Kish explains, is not always one of misery, terror
or dependence. As with any other disability, blindness requires
a person to adjust to their environment and figure out the best
means for navigating through barriers and challenges to achieve
a sense of freedom. Blind since he was thirteen months old, for
Kish freedom comes from the 'clicking' noises he makes – sonar
perception, or echolocation. These flashes of sound bounce off

objects and back to him, enabling him to mentally perceive the space around him and move through it with comfort and ease. With sonar perception, Kish gains a 360-degree worldview, an adaptation that not only forces us to rethink the experiences of blindness, but also encourages us to shift away from our exclusivity of vision.

Kish's story is not an inspirational one, though he certainly might be inspiring to some people. The tools he uses to manage and live with blindness are not part of an 'overcoming story' but an experience that exists outside of a medical agenda, beyond cultural constructions of dependency and debility. It is an experience that is Kish's own, shaped by his perspective of the world, a perspective, perhaps, that is simultaneously ordinary and extraordinary. This story forces us to change our expectations of what people can be capable of – if we witnessed more blind people riding bicycles and ceased to marvel at the scene, then our understanding of seeing would transform. And as Kish tells it, once this transformation occurs, then more blind people could essentially, quite capably, 'see'.

Our expectations of disabled people are incredibly powerful because they can form standards of 'success' that might not always be achievable. Echolocation is a physiological process used by some mammals (e.g. bats, dolphins) to emit sounds into their environment to determine how far objects are in the vicinity. It is a marvellous skill that is rarely deployed by humans. Kish isn't the only blind person to harness it – Ben Underwood, the 'Boy Who Sees Without Eyes', was another – but there's this implication that if this skill is the ultimate achievement for blind people, then those who are unable to master it have 'failed' or are 'less than'. In other words, when we talk about disabled people and the tools that they use to navigate the world – whether it be echolocation, white canes, wheelchairs, hearing aids, computerised technology – we must accept that disability is not, nor can it ever be, a 'one-size-fits-all' model.

We have been told that disability is suffering, that when it comes to broken and deformed bodies and minds, it is kindness to cure, if not eliminate the differences. But this is a lie. As Australian activist Stella Young tells us, we are sold this lie countless times, that disability is 'a Bad Thing', and that those who somehow manage to live with their disability are exceptional. Living with disability merits adaptation. Understanding disability requires acknowledging the variability of human experience. Writing disability history necessitates centring disabled people: just as race, gender and sexuality are used as analytical lenses for examining historical events, so too can disability. After all, as historian Douglas Baynton asserts, 'Disability is everywhere, once you begin looking for it, but conspicuously absent in the histories we write.' Examining history through disabled people, rather than the perspectives of able-bodied society, moves us away from the medical gaze and challenges tropes of how disabled people are represented in these histories.

Monstrous bodies and blessed peoples

Disability has always been part-and-parcel of human experience. Evidence from archaeology, ancient papyrus, pottery, art, legal documents, scriptures and mythology demonstrates that kings, noblewomen, tradesmen and gods alike were blighted by physical or mental deviance.

In Mesopotamian mythology, Nihmah's creation of a blind

man was turned into a musician by Enki, who declared all imperfect beings would be fitted with a suitable task useful for human society. Hod, son of Odin and Frigg, was also blind, as was the Bengali goddess Manasa, the Māori ancestress Matakerepō, Lumukanda the rebel slave of Zulu oral tradition, and the prophet Tiersias whose sight was taken by the Greek goddess Hera in punishment. Fertility deities also appear as disabled: Bes, the Egyptian god of childbirth is depicted as a bow-legged dwarf; in some Native American cultures, Kokopelli is depicted as a humpbacked flute player; and the Japanese deity Sukunahikona who assisted Ōkuninushi in building the world is also a dwarf. The Rigveda, the oldest of the Vedic Sanskrit texts, chronicles how Vinata's impatience for the hatching of her eggs resulted in Aruna, the god of dawn, being born with no legs or genitals, while the Mahabharata describes how the cunning Dhritarashtra's crown was objected to by Vidura, who claimed no blind man could properly rule a kingdom. Chinese mythology tells us of T'ien-lung ('Heaven-Deaf') and Ti-ya ('Earth-Dumb'), the two attendants to Wên Ch'ang, the god of literature. The mirthful Japanese deity Ebisu is lame and deaf, while the smithing Greek god Hephaestus remained with a shrivelled foot after being thrown from Mount Olympus.

These stories tell us the extent to which blighted bodies are associated with trickery, culpability or punishment, just as much as with chance and variety; they also reveal that ancient societies had no strict category for 'disabled' since no defined standards of normalcy existed – all beings, disabled or otherwise, could have a place and task to fulfil within their societies. The ancient Greeks may have prized the virtue of beauty as justification for abandoning deformed babies, but the Athenian state also provided pensions for disabled workers; moreover, contrary to the romantic athleticism of ascending the winding and uneven path to the summit of the Acropolis, recent evidence indicates that a ramp was built, and that ramps were available at other healing sanctuaries and sacred sites. The imperial households of wealthy Romans contained enslaved hunchbacks, dwarfs and deaf-mutes purchased at the 'monsters' market' – sometimes at exorbitant prices – for entertainment or as pets with talismanic qualities. Meanwhile, disabled children born into wealthy families were nurtured and educated, as was Emperor Claudius, who likely had cerebral palsy and/or Tourette's. Even the *dilsiz* (the mutes and deaf-mutes), who worked for centuries in the *Enderûn* (Interior Service) at the Ottoman courts in Istanbul, obtained privileged status and their system of sign language was adopted by hearing courtiers.

One thing that remains constant across the centuries is that disabled people continuously encountered negative stereotypes. Aristotle's claim that 'there are errors in nature as well as art' positioned people with congenital deformities as aberrations for addressing whether 'accidental births' were harbingers of doom or souls blessed by divinity. The medieval monsters – the strange beauties, wondrous anomalies and frightful, fantastical beings – were framed as a metaphor of religious morality employed in marginal illuminations and as proof of marvellous races living in the periphery of the known world. In *The City of God*, St Augustine expresses that the world is variegated and that monsters are evidence of divine will; so influential was his framing of monstrosity that it even shaped how Catholics and Protestants justified their religious insistence during the Reformation. Such thinking even wove in deep sexism: outspoken, radical women who abhorred their natural place could be divinely punished by their birthing of a stillborn monster.

Within the symphony of creation, of tales of the wondrous and blessed, was a synthesis of stigma and altruism that shaped how disabled people were perceived – as innocents, criminals, beggars or monsters. Within these perspectives, as Henri-Jacques Stiker writes in *Corps infirmes et sociétés* (translated in English as *A History of Disability*), also 'lies the silhouette of the disabled . . . sharply contoured, taking us down the depths of as yet unthought social ideas'. What histories of disability, then, do we write if we extract monstrosity as part of disabled living? What new perspectives do we uncover when we re-examine legends and fables from a disability perspective? Is the madness of Margery Kempe evidence of disability disguised as mysticism and ecstasies, or merely a representation of how disabled people hoped to be positively perceived within their society? Applying new research methodologies can also encourage new disability histories, as with the retrospective diagnosis of Richard III's scoliosis replacing his Shakespearean portrayal as a 'poisonous bunch-back'd toad'. Or it allows us to revisit the extent to which disability shaped a person's experiences: Alexander Pope, the hunchbacked poet, rarely referred to his disability in his writing, but his suffering through Pott's disease likely shaped his literary poetics.

Rethinking the monstrous further enables us to trace how markers of disability can be infused with meanings. Disabled bodies are often positioned against normates, such as how Saartijie Baartman's – the so-called Hottentot Venus – displayed body represented imperial exploitation, with the freakery used to prove the inferiority of non-white people, or how literary depictions of scarred faces are used to signify bitterness and evil. Disability can be used as a metaphor, but it's crucial to remember that disabled people are not metaphors. They are extraordinary bodies, Rosemarie Garland Thomson tells us, whose enfreakment and imperatives of agency can enrich our understanding of un/remarkable lived experiences of disability. Positioning them historically requires acknowledging the limitations of metaphorical and mythological discourse. After all, stories of freaks and monsters – of Millie-Christine, Tiny Tim, lion-faced Jo-Jo, Joseph Merrick the Elephant Man, Schlitzie the 'Pinhead', and many more – are chronicles of *real* lives, of how disabled people have been treated and the kinds of identities they created for themselves.

Beyond the margins

In 1939, faced with the threat of Nazi persecution, educator Karl König and his colleagues fled Austria to Scotland. There, they founded Camphill Village, a curative school based on Rudolf Steiner's anthroposophy, with the aim of creating a new social order: a community of developmentally and intellectually disabled and abled people living and working together in an ecovillage to honour the dignity and spiritual integrity of all. Through this 'life-sharing' approach, they demonstrated how disabled people could thrive within a community created for inclusion – a stark contrast to institutionalised solutions and medical 'fixes' for disabled people as implemented across much of the global north.

Our modern concept of disability emerged within the seventeenth-century colonial plantation economy and chattel slavery, and the eighteenth-century rise of industrialisation. Increasing demands for labour in booming industries strained workers' bodies, producing injury, illness and disablement that risked their capacity to work; moreover, some industries – such as coal mining – were marked with their own occupational hazards, eventually shaping mutual aid societies and workplace health and safety regulations. Industrial capitalism not only integrated disabled people into the workforce, but injuries and impairments on the job were common enough occurrences that workers regularly continued labouring despite their debilities to avoid being marginalised or losing their employment, while enslaved people were forcibly required to prove their value. Self-sufficiency and *ability* to work became valued. Those unable to work or without community support were thus labelled as 'unproductive citizens' and relegated to impoverished second-class social citizenship, dependent on charitable altruism or else sent to pauper asylums and workhouses – including children, the elderly and the chronically ill.

Industrial capitalism's reliance on workers' bodies created new approaches for thinking about how disabled people lived and the pressures they faced to 'correct' their bodies and demonstrate their productivity. By the mid-nineteenth century, the emergence of industrial medicine, statistics and improved surgical techniques became inextricably intertwined with the Victorian values of hard work and self-improvement, values that would reverberate throughout the new century and across colonial lands. Medical science became a knight in shining armour weaponised to eradicate disability. Disabled people turned to prostheses, patent medicines and a host of surgical promises to fix themselves at the same time as public health measures and vaccination campaigns were striving to eradicate disabling contagious diseases. The emergence of alienists and moral treatments guided by eugenic thinking further propelled therapeutic optimism for chronic – though not necessarily curable – cases, requiring an expansion of charitable institutions. So, too, came standards of normalcy, of measuring and defining the disabled body against the norm, such as Galton's composite portrait, an imaginary figure possessing average features that bore no resemblance to real life. As displays of begging heightened and greater numbers of scarred ex-soldiers returned home, some nations even passed 'ugly laws' to limit their presence within public spaces. Disability became seen as a medical condition to be cured, rather than an ordinary aspect of human life. Erasing disability through segregation, assimilation or murder became justified as a step in eliminating incurable difference.

Much of this history has traditionally placed disabled people in the margins, 'viewed as bodies and lives gone wrong, as failure of medicine and technology', as scholar Rod Michalko asserts. There's a rich history here worth uncovering, in how disabled people navigated amongst a multitude of medical options levelled against them, and how they liberated themselves from cultural stigmas associating disablement with dependency. How did disabled people push back against the cure rhetoric? Deaf people, for example, flourished in their own signing communities and thrived with their own cultural identity, even despite the forcible implementation of oralism that attempted to tear their communities apart. In England, disabled children in the Guild of the Brave Poor Things created a collective identity that meaningfully addressed the ways people living with dissimilar disabilities tended to face the same social barriers and medical pressures, even if the guild's construction of disability as a tragedy was damaging for their members.

Crucial, too, is the importance of asserting – if not reclaiming – the experiences of prominent historical figures whose disability has been overlooked or erased, sometimes literally. At the Bodleian Library, for instance, art restorers uncovered that an eighteenth-century painting by Pompeo Batoni of physician George Oakley Aldrich depicted the sitter with his facial disfigurements – extremely rare in portraiture – but was later overpainted to conceal them. Unless self-asserted, the disability experiences of many others have been glossed over in the history books. To name a few: geologist James Hutton, actress Sarah Bernhardt, suffragette Adelaide Knight, abolitionist Harriet Tubman, activist Mary Church Terrell, painter Dorothy Brett, entrepreneur Otto Weidt, explorer John Wesley Powell, politicians Winston Churchill and Franklin Delano Roosevelt, artist Frieda Kahlo, musician Mzee Morris, revolutionary Apolinario Mabini y Maranan, poet Jhamak Ghimire, teenager Emmett Till, Cherokee chief Wilma Mankiller, and writers Audre Lorde and Maya Angelou – and countless others, both known and unknown in the annals of history.

Nor should we forget the unhealthy disabled, or that (traumatic) medical experiences can be tangled with one's disabled identity. 'I am a construction,' artist Riva Lehrer writes in her memoir. 'I've had 47 surgeries . . . I've always thought of the scars of my creators and that my body has been . . . changed and reconstructed and shifted.' She is a Golem, a 'medical monster' made by doctors who scrawled diagnoses on medical files and forced her, and others like her, to identify themselves by their medical names. These are people who exist on the borderland of medical and disability histories, a place where congenital and contagious diseases can dramatically reshape bodies and communities. What stories can we uncover upon re-examining disease histories through disability, especially once interwoven with socioeconomic inequalities and racial and ethnic health disparities, such as with tuberculosis, smallpox, polio, syphilis, HIV/AIDS, or imagined diseases such as hysteria and Drapetomania? And let's not ignore those with invisible disabilities, or considered to be not 'disabled enough', or even those who refuse to be labelled as disabled – all people whose stories are necessary if we are to write more inclusive histories.

Innovators, inventors, tinkerers

The archaeological discovery of a tomb near the city of Thebes in 1997 unearthed an exciting new avenue for disability history. Found attached to the mummified body of an Egyptian noble-woman – likely a priest's daughter, the evidence suggests – was an engraved wooden toe affixed to leather binding and tied around the right foot. Dating as far back as 1069 BC, this makes the toe the oldest prosthesis ever discovered. The 'Cairo Toe', as it became known, reframes our conception of disabled bodies, as researchers have learned that the prosthetic was refitted several times to the shape of the woman's foot to account for the stresses caused by her gait. It also demonstrates how disablement was not always stigmatised or concealed. The toe, after all, was designed to be worn with open-toe sandals.

From simple wooden blocks to computerised exoskeletons, prostheses have always been a part of disability experience. Prostheses are 'the range of detachable, wearable, implanted or integrated body parts', as historian Katherine Ott defines, a broad category of devices that provide people with support to do the things they want to do. Disability is not a discrete identity category, however, and thus, neither are the prostheses nor the identities of prosthesis users. Furthermore, most 'disability things', as Ott describes them, are framed within a restorative narrative of cure or as a performance that reveals assumptions about the grotesque and freakish, even more so when bodies are adorned with artefacts. Prostheses are social objects with a complex set of meanings that affect the daily lives of disabled people. They are material evidence for viewing how individual agency can contribute to, and shape, assumptions about medical interventions and the social boundaries of normality, or become ambivalent tools for freedom. Injection needles, for instance, can provide a diabetic with medical autonomy, while at a psychiatric hospital they serve as vehicles of therapeutic care and overt medical control.

Forging bonds between objects and bodies can be highly visible performances of citizenship, one in which the disabled body is reshaped, strapped or assisted with technologies. Specific objects – Walt Whitman's cane, Harriet Martineau's ear trumpet, Charles Darwin's walking stick, Andrew Gawley's steel hands, Dorothy Brett's hearing aids or Ed Roberts' motorised wheelchair – also become crucial indicators of how disabled people accommodated themselves to 'worlds not designed for them'. Oftentimes, adaptation necessitates innovation. In the seventeenth century, German paraplegic clockmaker Stephan Farfler built the first self-propelled wheelchair. One of the first amputees of the American Civil War, James Hanger, designed a hinged artificial leg to replace peg legs. Robin Cavendish and Teddy Hall developed a motorised wheelchair with a built-in respirator to free the latter from confinement to his bed. Shut out of 'talkies', deaf silent actor Emerson Romero created closed captioning for deaf people to enjoy films. Betsy Farber designed new kitchen tools that were easier on her arthritic hands. Exclusion from technology or technological systems can also spur sources of innovation for accommodating disability, such as the way that talking books and text-to-speech scanning machines created new reading formats. Imported devices claiming to 'cure' deafness in nineteenth-century British India, for example, were mainly colonial designs that did not necessarily translate to everyday experiences of deafness; thus, Indian designers made use of more affordable materials to construct their own prosthesis designs. The Jaipur foot and the standing wheelchair that retails for approximately US$200 are part of that legacy.

No assistive technology, however, can be fully useful if they are limited by social and economic constraints. From activists breaking kerbs to demands for sign-language interpreters at all public events, in the twentieth and twenty-first centuries, access became connected to the idea that design should benefit *all* people. This idea is inherently political as well, for access requires the removal of barriers – architectural, political, social, environmental, medical – that prevent disabled people from achieving full civic participation. As technologies are integrated into social life through computers, smartphones and video conferencing, creating an 'accessible environment' becomes essential for addressing how prostheses are accompanied with the need to restructure social relations and political activism. What good is a world in a pandemic connected by Zoom, if there is no closed captioning? Or heavily visual social media platforms with no alt-text descriptions?

Alongside the political roots for designing accessible environments, disability design is rich with DIY history connected to a legacy of consumers, innovators and tinkerers. To assert agency within the material–human divide, nearly all prosthetic users maintain their devices to better align them to their bodies, though not all: some disabled people, of course, perceive their prostheses as a 'fix' and some outwardly reject them. As scholar Meryl Alper points out, assistive technologies have 'historically been difficult for consumers to obtain and learn about because such knowledge tends to belong to specialized professional groups'. Nevertheless, polio survivors created grasping tools cobbled together from household objects to reach things placed out of reach; deafened users became actively involved in improving amplified telephony when companies fell short of meeting their needs; athletes took apart wheelchair components to make them speedier and lightweight for competitive sports.

While all technology is assistive and disability design is essential, not all 'disability things' are useful or necessary. Sign-language gloves, stair-climbing wheelchairs and portable GPS for blind people are examples of what design activist Liz Jackson terms a 'disability dongle': 'a well-intended, elegant, yet useless solution to a problem' that disabled people never knew they had. Rather than serving as substitutes for access, these technological fixes further propagate barriers to inclusion and full equity by forcing disabled people to shoulder the burden of accessibility. They also ignore the lived experiences of disability, much as how cyborgification, techno-futurism and transhumanism have transformed disabled people into metaphors and fantastical subjects rather than acknowledge them as cyborgs as some prefer – bionic people with real lives who create and use assistive technology.

Instead, 'they want us shiny and metallic and in their image', the cyborg Jillian Weise tells us, and when they cannot be, they become tryborgs, fake cyborgs who are 'terribly clumsy in their understanding of cyborgs because they lack experimental knowledge'.

Intersections

There are scratch marks on the wood and traces of dried blood. The narrow box could not have been more than six feet long, three feet wide and maybe a foot-and-a-half high, with a hinged lid that could be latched shut. Certainly not enough space for an adult human to move around or sit up. The slats alongside the sides barely invited enough light. This is an 'Utica Crib', a shallow wooden cage developed in 1846 by Amariah Brigham, director of the New York State Lunatic Asylum at Utica, after a similar device used at the Marseilles Lunatic Asylum. Considered an improvement on restraint shackles and straitjackets, these innovative devices were used to curtail disruptive and unruly patients, protect them from self-harm, or deployed as macabre punishment. By the end of the nineteenth century, Utica Cribs could be found in most mental institutions. I've examined – somewhat horrified – two versions in museum warehouses. They are more than boxes of terror, however: they are material evidence of disability history, perhaps amongst the darkest chapters, but nevertheless a reminder of how different society could be if we accepted difference as an aspect of human variation and not as justification for conforming to the norm.

Disability history no longer needs to be passive and inert. Centring disabled people within their own histories shifts the discourse towards pride, power, invention, independence, inclusion and community. But we must not ignore the intersections here either, of how racism and classism operate on the lives of disabled people of colour, or that systemic racism means disability tends to be more prevalent in communities of colour and low/impoverished ones. The histories we write about disability, then, cannot be complete without these intersections.

Disability has always been central to our lives. From debates about qualifications for democratic citizenship, to the ravages of war-scarred bodies, improvements in medical technologies, and controversies about access and accommodation, people have grappled with issues of disability in both their personal lives and in the public arena. Disability includes the richness of individual experience and creativity; it is deeply rooted within a long history of activism and struggle for equality. If history is a process that requires a constant reinterpretation of facts, it must also be a practice that requires inclusion – the people whose histories have long been glossed over, trapped in medical files or valued only for inspiration need *their* stories to be told. Representation matters.

Acknowledgements

I am grateful to the generous community of scholars and disability activists on Twitter who provided global historical examples of disability and thus enriched the breadth of this essay.

Selected Further Reading

Meryl Alper, *Giving Voice: Mobile Communication, Disability and Inequality* (Cambridge, MA: The MIT Press, 2017)

Douglas Baynton, *Defectives in the Land: Disability and Immigration in the Age of Eugenics* (Chicago: University of Chicago Press, 2016)

Dea H. Boster, *African American Slavery and Disability: Bodies, Property, and Power in the Antebellum South, 1800–1860* (New York: Routledge, 2012)

Susan Burch and Hannah Joyner, *Unspeakable: The Story of Junius Wilson* (Durham, NC: University of North Carolina Press, 2007)

Susan Burch and Michael Rembis (eds.), *Disability Histories* (Urbana: University of Illinois Press, 2014)

Rosemarie Garland Thomson, *Extraordinary Bodies: Figuring Physical Disability in American Culture and Literature* (New York: Columbia University Press, 1997)

Aimi Hamraie, *Building Access: Universal Design and the Politics of Disability* (Minneapolis: University of Minnesota Press, 2017)

Sara Hendren, *What Can a Body Do? How We Meet the Built World* (New York: Penguin Random House, 2020)

Stefanie Hunt-Kennedy, *Between Fitness and Death: Disability and Slavery in the Caribbean* (Urbana: University of Illinois Press, 2020)

Riva Lehrer, *Golem Girl: A Memoir* (New York: One World, 2020)

Paul A. Lombardo, *Three Generations, No Imbeciles: Eugenics, The Supreme Court, and Buck v. Bell* (Baltimore: Johns Hopkins Press, 2008)

Rod Michalko, *The Difference that Disability Makes* (Philadelphia: Temple University Press, 2002)

Kim E. Nielsen, *The Radical Lives of Helen Keller* (New York:

New York University Press, 2004)

Kim E. Nielsen, *A Disability History of the United States* (Boston: Beacon Press, 2012)

Fred Pelka, *What We Have Done: An Oral History of the Disability Rights Movement* (Cambridge, MA: University of Massachusetts Press, 2012)

Sarah F. Rose, *No Right to be Idle: The Invention of Disability, 1840s–1930s* (Durham, NC: University of North Carolina Press, 2017)

Sara Scalenghe, *Disability in the Ottoman Arab World, 1500–1800* (New York: Cambridge University Press, 2014)

Susan Schweik, *The Ugly Laws: Disability in Public* (New York: New York University Press, 2010)

H.J. Striker. *A History of Disability* (Ann Arbor: University of Michigan Press, 1999)

Bess Williamson, *Accessible America: A History of Disability and Design* (New York: New York University Press, 2019)

Bess Williamson and Elizabeth Guffey (eds.), *Making Disability Modern: Design Histories* (New York: Bloomsbury, 2020)

Alice Wong, *Disability Visibility: First-Person Stories from the Twenty-First Century* (New York: Vintage Books, 2020)

Chapter 8

Can our emotions have a history?

Helen Carr

'*L'histoire des sentiments: cette grande muette.*'
('The history of emotions: that great silence.')

Lucien Febvre, *Annales* (1956)

'How peaceful life would be without love, Adso.' In the 1986 movie *The Name of the Rose*, Sean Connery plays Franciscan monk William of Baskerville, and in a moment of emotional fraternal confession, Baskerville schools his junior apprentice Adso, played by Christian Slater, on the difference between love and faith: 'Are you not confusing love with lust?' Based on the eponymous novel by the medievalist Umberto Eco, the movie is set in the early fourteenth century in a Benedictine Abbey where Baskerville has travelled to solve a series of murders. The investigation triggers a variety of responses from its characters – fear, suspicion, joy, shame, love and lust – all emotions felt by a handful of medieval monks that appear to be those very same emotions we are familiar with today. William Baskerville's pithy line, 'how peaceful life would be without love', from the (imagined) perspective of a medieval monk, begs the question: how did our ancestors experience love? Indeed, how did our ancestors experience the numerous distinguishable and indistinguishable emotions we feel every day?

Trying to verbalise or even understand our own feelings, let alone the feelings of others, sometimes feels like an impossible task. How can you put into words the feeling of your child smiling for the first time, or the agony of a romantic rejection, the feeling of someone walking *really* slowly in front of you when you're rushing to catch a train, or . . . the loss of a loved one, or fear of our own mortality? These feelings are often intimate, but they can also be physical and fervent. They can be both fleeting and consuming – sometimes in tandem.

Intangible and evanescent in the present, past emotions and their meanings have also evolved or completely changed. For example, stress is an emotion we try to avoid today. It is an emotional reaction to our high-octane, high-speed, achievement-driven society. Avoiding stress has prompted the rise of entire industries built on stress management and the practice of relaxation. Our ancestors in the eighteenth century, however, considered stress very differently. Stress was a positive emotion which counteracted an epidemic in the wealthier classes of over-relaxation and indolence, said to be induced by a lifestyle of luxury and leisure, sex and tea. This principle applies elsewhere in history, and past societies and cultures experienced emotions differently to how we experience emotions in the present. If we cannot project our understanding of feelings onto those who lived before us, and if there is no way of truly knowing, why should we study past generations of feelings as well as facts?

As emotions inform our actions today, they did so in the past –

emotions informed the facts the historian 'collects', 'cooks' and 'serves' in whatever style appeals to her. To neglect a history of emotions is to neglect an understanding of the past. To feel emotion is an inherently human experience, and by exploring the felt emotions of the past we can begin to investigate and interpret a realm of feelings that influenced the way the past took place, by bridging the gap between the then and the now. It is by exploring the emotions of the past, the felt experiences: anger, love, fear, happiness, grief, that we can begin to sympathise with the past as much more than a corpus of ascertained and accepted facts about people who lived, loved and left traces of their existence. But where do we begin?

Theories and ideologies about emotions and feelings have been postulated since the third century BC, when the Greek Stoic philosopher Chrysippus of Soli wrote his most famous philosophical treatise *On Passions* – four books discussing the Stoic philosophy behind the passions, or as we would call them, emotions. These passions, or emotions, have since been interrogated by the naturalist Charles Darwin in the nineteenth century, by scientists, neuroscientists and psychologists of the twentieth century, and more recently by historians searching for evidence of feeling.

A way into such an oblique investigation is firstly by interrogating the very meaning and origins of the word 'emotion', which emerged from the French *émotion*, a term used to explain an agitation, or physical movement – like a flock of birds disturbed by a noise. Thomas Dixon, a founder of the Centre of the History of Emotions at Queen Mary University of London, has demonstrated that the term 'emotion' to describe a state of mind is a relatively new one.

In December 1819, the Scottish moral philosopher Thomas Brown was delivering a lecture in Edinburgh when he collapsed before the audience. Only four months later, Brown died but his lecture series was posthumously published as *Lectures on the Philosophy of the Human Mind*. It is in this book that he introduced a new term into psychosocial language; a new category to boldly unite the fluctuations of the human mind: 'emotion'. Two centuries later, emotion is a common term. However, its meaning is a point of contention; even Brown, the father of 'emotions', acknowledged that the exact meaning of emotions is 'difficult to state in any form of words'. To unpack the complex history of emotions, we cannot then search for the term 'emotion' as we understand it before the eighteenth, or even the nineteenth century. This is a difficult task when 'emotion' or 'emotional' is ingrained in our daily lexicon. Our ancestors did not have emotions, they had feelings. Terms that can be applied to pre-modern sources are 'passions' (troubling feelings that were uncontrollable and powerful, like anger) and 'affections' (gentler feelings, like satisfaction). Both words are arguably more understandable and easier to define than 'emotional'.

Despite this, psychologists have favoured Brown's term and adopted 'emotions' in the attempt to define human feelings and categorise them into a series of 'basic emotions'. In the 1970s, the psychologist Paul Ekman argued these basic emotions were fear, anger, disgust, happiness, sadness and surprise. Though psychologists such as Lisa Feldman Barrett would contend that emotions are subject to environment or social condition, Ekman argued otherwise: that basic emotions were universally experienced by all people and all cultures, thereby forming the basis for modern understanding of emotion. As part of Ekman's thesis, he also provided a visual aid for these basic emotions: a series of faces he suggested as 'universal' expressions – a grimace, a creased-eyed smile, a wide stare. These sorts of expression are akin to the 'emojis' popularised in text conversation to illuminate our emotional state. Happy face, sad face, really angry face, embarrassed face, curious face, in-love face. Paul Ekman promoted his understanding that emotions are universally shared, and since then evolutionary psychologists Lena Cosmides and John Tooby have gone as far as to suggest that the human mind has not evolved since the Stone Age. They would argue that we experience the same basic emotions as early humankind.

By contrast, in 1939 sociologist Norbert Elias published *The Civilising Process*, in which he argues that our emotional development has advanced and civilised since the Middle Ages. He suggests that we have become more emotionally rational due to an increasing awareness of personal and societal shame, as opposed to the shameless, socially unaware people of the medieval past. His theory perpetuated the characteristic trope of medieval peoples as axe-wielding, hysterical, weeping troglodytes: emotionally unrefined in comparison to our socially and morally aware selves. The subject of Adso's affections in *The Name of the Rose* is a peasant girl, depicted as more creature than woman as she ferally crawls from the gutter covered in dirt with straw in her hair and violently seduces Adso. The girl is the type of 'shameless' medieval caricature Elias had in mind.

In order to determine or challenge these theories about emotions, historians call up the surviving fragments of the past that remain available – the sources. In the nineteenth century a wave of historians established the modern understanding of history: they blew away the dust, unearthed and transcribed a variety of historical documents in order to ascertain a series of accepted facts about the past. But in doing so they favoured unambiguous facts – dates, names, battles and so on – and neglected the ambiguous, intangible emotional past. It was not until 1941 that this 'great silence' was addressed by historian Lucien Febvre, co-founder of the Annales (a school of thought that looked to social sciences to help study history), which provided the manifesto for the study of the history of emotions. In his book *A New Kind of History,* Febvre extrapolated the necessity of 'the emotional life of man and all its manifestations'. He called for a new examination of what remains of the past, to examine textual records, paintings, sculpture, literature and music: 'I am asking for a vast collective investigation to be opened . . . on the fundamental sentiments of man and the forms they take. What surprises we may look forward to!' Since Febvre's call to arms, historians have addressed the evidence available offering various interpretations of the emotional past, in the attempt to form an understanding of the world our ancestors walked in and how they might – just might – have felt about it.

In the search for these 'fundamental sentiments of man', historians face the troubling task of abandoning their understanding of the present in order to try to understand the past. This problem is endemic to studying history. Our own biases regularly influence the evidence we seek. E.H. Carr describes this stumbling-block using fish as his analogy:

> facts . . . are like fish swimming about in a vast and sometimes inaccessible ocean; and what the historian catches will depend, partly on chance, but mainly on what part of the ocean he chooses to fish in and what tackle he chooses to use – these

two factors being, of course, determined by the kind of fish he wants to catch. By and large, the historian will get the kind of facts he wants. History means interpretation.

In searching for evidence of emotion let's alter Carr's analogy: '*words* are like fish swimming about in a vast and sometimes inaccessible ocean . . .'. Historians of emotion are driven to certain words or sources that are representative of their personal choice, their own understanding, experiences and context. We cannot always know, however, exactly which words described what feelings for the generations before us.

One example is 'nostalgia'. Today, we might use the word nostalgia in recollection of a positive experience: nostalgic for a childhood memory, foodstuffs or a landscape. However, the word 'nostalgia', created in 1688 by the Swiss medical student Johannes Hofer, identified something quite different. A combination of the Greek *nostos*, homecoming, and *algos,* pain, nostalgia was used to describe severe homesickness: trauma that was physically painful or in extreme cases even fatal. Nostalgia in its original form was then only applicable in its time; to look for the word beyond this would be misinterpreting the emotion described.

This same principle applies to emotion words used in twenty-first-century vocabulary. Two regularly used acronyms, LOL and FOMO – 'laugh out loud' and 'fear of missing out' – would be inappropriate in any interpretation of the past. Equally, words such as *apatheia,* meaning to be without passions or extreme troubling feelings; or – most applicable to our collective experience of a pandemic – *acedia,* an ancient Greek word for feeling destitute within one's own surroundings and company. The fifth-century monk and theologian John Cassian described this feeling as a 'listlessness', a type of stillness and lethargy induced by lack of stimulation and change of environment. However, following a year working from the confines of our own homes, absent from friends and family with one day dripping into another, this fifth-century emotion feels more appropriate and expansive than FOMO.

Although language is generally applicable to its time, the historian of emotions William Reddy argues that language is crucial in the search for historical feeling. Yet, in practice there is a difference between modern history and pre-modern history. Due to the Reformation, war, destruction and time, sources before and for the Middle Ages are sparse. Medievalists have searched for evidence of emotion in artistic representations such as tapestries, paintings and sepulchral art, but they have also turned to larger bodies of written evidence – administrative or political documents. As emotions are unpredictable, mercurial, and difficult to pin down, language used in documents such as court records can help evidence feeling. There are examples of defamation in communities and cases of rape – *raptus* – which must be examined closely, as they can sometimes evidence an elopement or forbidden relationship, as well as non-consensual sex.

In the search for personal emotions in the Middle Ages, historians have turned to evidence surrounding preparations for death. Verbal directions for the construction of a tomb (often a meticulously considered and expensive exercise) might include emotion words in engraved epitaphs as a means of memorialising. Instruction for burial beside one's spouse or family might evidence love. For example, John of Gaunt and Blanche of

Lancaster were buried together at St Paul's Cathedral, their effigies clasping hands: a popular gesture of love in the second half of the fourteenth century. Hand-clasping demonstrates medieval married love as an emotional experience that was literally carved into stone as a symbol of endurance. This touching portrayal of 'stone fidelity' is most famously celebrated in Philip Larkin's poem 'An Arundel Tomb' based on the tomb of Richard FitzAlan, 10th Earl of Arundel (d. 1376), and his second wife Eleanor of Lancaster (d. 1372): 'what will survive of us is love'.

One of the most potent examples of the emotional gravity of impending death, and one of the most abundant sources of language regarding such emotional preparation, is wills. Wills in the Middle Ages were composed by scribes, beginning with religious and legal formulae. They are also much like wills are today: a practice of leaving one's worldly possessions to loved ones, or institutions meaningful to the bequeather, and – on occasion – evidence of the reasoning for those choices. By studying the items that are written into wills, and to whom they are bequeathed, we are studying language with material objects. This can in turn reveal a repertoire of emotional life practices. Wedding rings, or rings of troth plight, were usually bequeathed to family – a tangible representation of commitment and love. Wills can also evidence the emotional process of childbirth. Bed linen used by a mother who died in childbed could be bequeathed by a father to his surviving daughter as a reminder of her mother's suffering and the fear, elation and sorrow that came with childbirth. The relationship between a person and their household, friends or servants can be made clear in wills. In 1459, Joan Cotyngham from York bequeathed her intricately embroidered tabards (a type of tunic) to two of her friends, going into great detail about their value. Often, the more personal the item – clothing, jew-ellery, bedding or a bed opposed to plate or kitchenware – the more precious the relationship. There are examples of wealthy men and women bequeathing valued possessions to household servants, indicating feelings of affection, gratitude or even love.

Although much of our understanding of emotions is through the verbalisation of a feeling, whether that is the spoken or writ-ten word, an equally powerful and illuminating expression of emotion is performance: emotion in itself can be a performative action. One of the most exceptional examples of emotional per-formance in medieval history is in *The Book of Margery Kempe*. Margery Kempe was a fourteenth-century bourgeois woman from Lynn in East Anglia, who turned mystic following the birth of her first child, and is known to posterity for her multifarious expressive revelations of Jesus Christ. Margery travelled various pilgrim routes, from Canterbury to Jerusalem, dressed in white, expounding her visions and constantly, loudly weeping – infuri-ating those who shared her passage to shrines across Europe and beyond. Unpopular Margery was scorned by her critics as a heretic, and nearing the end of her life she dictated her ex-periences to a scribe (possibly her son), thus composing *The Book of Margery Kempe*. Although it was not discovered until 1934, it became a crucial source for looking at social, gender and emotional history in the Middle Ages. The *Book* provides evidence of emotional words like *schame* (shame), joy, *dispeyr* (despair), which all occur frequently. These words provide evi-dence for Margery's understanding of her own emotions, but her performance of them can also help to illuminate the emotions of her contemporaries. Her experiences are her own, but they can also act as a mirror for a wider network of individuals and communities: those who encountered her and responded with emotion. As a historian of emotions Barbara Rosenwein points out, there were two 'emotional communities' who responded to Margery's expressions: those who supported her and those who loathed her. From within the *Book*, we are given the most insight regarding the latter. As Margery recounted, on pilgrimage to Canterbury she was 'greatly despised and reproved because she wept so hard, both by the monks and the priests and by secular men nearly all day, both morning and afternoon'. The *Book* records some of the horrified reactions to Margery's emotional performance; her enemies went as far to proclaim, 'You shall be burnt, false Lollard.' Despite the *Book* being largely focused on the polemical attacks on Margery, she also found some support and empathy for her personal emotional crusade. In Rome she met a priest who wept with her and elsewhere she was encouraged by others to persevere in her plight, including by her jilted husband. He had 'compassion' for her cause, but according to the *Book*, Margery never regarded him with much affection.

Margery Kempe is a rare surviving example of emotional performance and she viewed the world through the lens of faith. In this, Margery is not alone. Religion and faith were imbued with morality and daily sensations were experienced in the context of a deeply religious environment. Religious beliefs about emotions dictated the experience of the emotions themselves: for example, guilt or lust was concomitant with sin, and sin required repentance.

When in 1348 that biomedical disaster, the Black Death, tore through western Europe, belief informed reason and emotion. Although we confidently name the emotions that people experienced during this period, we can only look at performance and practice and what they might suggest. As communities across Europe were consumed by bubonic plague, thousands of flagellants roamed England and the rest of Europe, processing in their hundreds as they whipped the beaten, bloody flesh of their own backs. Men and women literally flagellated themselves to experience the same agony as Christ, as He was whipped and tormented on his journey to Calvary. The pain these people inflicted upon themselves was a result of a system of beliefs around humanity and its inherent wretchedness.

These religious sensations of the Middle Ages are palpable; scenes of the Last Judgement innumerably decorated walls of churches prior to the Reformation. One of my favourite churches – to which I drag any willing companion – is the Church of St Peter and St Paul in Pickering, Yorkshire. It illuminates the medieval experience. Beneath the chipped, crumbling plaster that dusts the floor (and one's shoes) are remarkable surviving medieval wall paintings, following the liturgical calendar. One can only imagine the emotional impact on people who gazed at the 'Descent into Hell' scene as men are engulfed by red flames morphed from the head of a fanged demon. These scenes are ominous and terrifying. Similarly, at the Victoria and Albert Museum in London, there is an altarpiece of c.1400 with forty-five scenes of the Apocalypse from Master Bertram's workshop in Hamburg. One of these forty-five scenes shows angels prepared for carnage as the seventh seal is opened and destruction is unleashed. The piece is tarnished, chipped and stained with missing panels, but it is still evocative and furious.

In a similar tone, Dante's *Inferno* narrates the experience of the dead through the punishing vestibules of Hell, marking the clarity of consequence between a life of virtue and a life of sin.

The 1277 text, *On the Gift of Fear,* prompted sermons about demonic torture of the damned. God was great and merciless; 'serve the Lord with fear, and rejoice with trembling' (Psalm 2:11). Fear, guilt, love and relief were shared emotional experiences at the heart of the medieval community: they were social and religious bonds.

Emotions were not only felt by individuals, but by communities en masse. In 1360, in a small town in Lausitz in Central Europe, an infectious hysteria broke out. Citizens danced manically through the streets without rest, food or water, until their feet and flailing limbs were bloodied, bruised and numb. Some were said to writhe and contort on their bellies, dragging themselves along with the crowd – likely the result of extreme exhaustion – and many were branded as heretics, their squirming bodies pinned down as holy water was forced down their throats. The case in 1360 was the earliest recorded example of 'Saint John's Dance' or the 'Dancing Plague', later dubbed 'Choreomania' – an uncontrollable, convulsive urge to dance. The historian John Waller has suggested that St John's Dance was induced by mass psychogenic illness. According to Robert Bartholomew, senior lecturer in Psychological Medicine, 'Mass psychogenic illness arises from long-term anxiety and features motor agitation . . . includ[ing] twitching, shaking, trouble walking, uncontrollable laughing and weeping, communication difficulties and trance states.' The main clue to this diagnosis is the fact that the dancers appeared to be completely disassociated from their bodies: physically exhausted and starved, they nevertheless kept on dancing. Plague, environmental devastation and socioeconomic destruction were harsh realities in late fourteenth-century Europe, and although we cannot ascertain exactly what emotion this collective performance represented we can understand it as a consequence of the condition of the community.

It is not only through contemporary accounts that we can understand emotional performance but through the stuff of the past, in particular the arts. Well beyond the Middle Ages, creative movements were galvanised by emotional expression, becoming synonymous with human feeling, often when the appreciation of humanity was jeopardised by politics, industry, progressivism or science.

Imperial heroics and military accolades became a popular genre in England during the Seven Years War (1756–63), a global conflict between imperial superpowers, England and France, across five continents. In this period, paintings would shape British understanding of the events on the battlefield and served as propaganda for the war by evoking sentiment amongst viewers. These paintings attracted swathes of Englishmen and women, moved to tears or anger at the tragedies that befell their countrymen. The most socially, emotionally impactful painting of this period, prompting an enormous queue to view it in situ on opening day at the Royal Academy, is Benjamin West's epic *Death of General Wolfe* (1770). West portrays a scene of both heroism and tragedy. The smoke of gunfire swallows the sky in an ominous grey cloud and the faint outline of the mud and chaos of battle decorates the background. In the foreground, the thirty-two-year-old General Wolfe swoons in the arms of his fellow soldiers and officers rush towards him, in the final moments of the decisive Battle of Quebec. His eyes roll back as a doting officer dabs his ribs with a bloodstained handkerchief and an allied Mohawk kneels (typifying the eighteenth-century stereotype of the 'noble savage') with his chin in his hand, observing the last moments of England's great hero. General Wolfe did not truly die in such a dramatic performance, but West chose to portray this moment of pathos as a lamentation: Wolfe, the national hero, as a martyr for empire and Britishness. *The Death of General Wolfe* allows some insight into the emotional context of the late eighteenth century, promoting nationalism, heroism and celebrity. But it also demonstrates the power of performance: to represent emotion and to emote. West's portrait of the expiring war hero is as much a piece of emotional theatre as it is a history painting.

If our emotions are performative, they also have the capacity to be powerful. They can evoke, emote and empower for good and ill – to inspire or to incite. In the first week of 2021, Donald Trump arguably incited his supporters to attack the Capitol building, and thereby US democracy, in the most dramatic political performance in recent history. The words 'anger', 'trauma' and 'fear' dominated the headlines and the world watched in horror as the walls of the Capitol were scaled by furious rioters. The global response to the event was defined by emotion, prompting the *New York Times* to ask: 'What are your reactions to the storming of the Capitol?' What had certainly become clear is the power of emotion to influence, to corrupt, and to compel a people into insurrection and destruction.

But emotion can also be inspirational. Emotional language and performance are intrinsic to positive activism. The suffrage movement in the early twentieth century saw women passionately rise up against systematic and stifling sexism. These women often physically expressed their emotions through violence and anger: an emotion at the time that was considered deeply masculine. Female rage has historically, and arguably continues to be, considered unsettling and inappropriate. In 1981, the feminist writer and civil rights activist Audre Lorde delivered a keynote speech at the National Women's Studies Association annual conference. Her speech lauded anger as a powerful weapon, beseeching women to 'tap [that] anger as an important source of empowerment' and stating, 'every woman has a well-stocked arsenal of anger potentially useful against those oppressions . . . focused with precision it can become a powerful source of energy serving progress and change'. Almost thirty years after Lorde's empowering oration, the greatest outburst of female rage since the Suffragettes broke out in 2017, the #MeToo movement. It also empowered women through empathy and collective anger, to speak their trauma around sexual abuse.

In the twenty-first century we consider ourselves more emotionally self-aware than the 'stiff upper lip' of generations past. Today talking therapies are an accepted norm, wellness is an industry, and mental health is a social and political buzzword. We clearly accept emotions are important, yet they were as much a lifeblood and mental rhythm to our ancestors as they are to us.

Considering the history of emotions forces us to embrace the evanescent intangible stuff of which we are made: the uncontrollable, indistinguishable emotional rhythms that make us human. In order to forge a vision of the emotional past, we can and must empathise with the past by looking over our shoulder at the emotional experiences and vision of our ancestors. By doing so we can and should make space for our emotional present and increase our collective, societal sensitivity to the emotional practices and experiences of others.

Selected Further Reading

Books

Katie Barclay, *The History of Emotions: A Student Guide to Methods and Sources* (London: Macmillan, 2020)

Rob Boddice, *The History of Emotions* (Manchester: Manchester University Press, 2018)

Damien Boquet and Piroska Nagy, *Medieval Sensibilities: A History of Emotions in the Middle Ages* (Cambridge: Polity Press, 2018)

Michael Champion and Andrew Lynch (eds.) *Understanding Emotions in Early Europe* (Turhnout: Brepols, 2015)

Thomas Dixon, *From Passions to Emotions: The Creation of a Secular Psychological Category* (Cambridge: Cambridge University Press, 2003)

Lucien Febvre, *A New Kind of History: From the Writings of Febvre* (Routledge and Kegan Paul, 1973)

Helen Hills and Penelope Gouk, *Representing Emotions: New Connections in the Histories of Art, Music and Medicine* (Abingdon: Routledge, 2005)

Margery Kempe, *The Book of Margery Kempe*, translated with an Introduction and Notes by Anthony Bale (Oxford: Oxford University Press, 2015)

Barbara Rosenwein, *Generations of Feeling: A History of Emotions*, 600–1700 (Cambridge: Cambridge University Press, 2016)

Tiffany Watt Smith, *The Book of Human Emotions* (London: Profile Books, 2015)

Theodore Zeldin, *An Intimate History of Humanity* (London: Vintage, 1998)

Articles, chapters, blogs and podcasts

Thomas Dixon, '"Emotion": the History of a Keyword in Crisis', *Emotion Review*, vol. 4, no. 4 (October 2012) 338–44

Lucien Febvre, 'Pour l'histoire d'un sentiment: le besoin de sécurité', *Annales, Économies, Sociétés, Civilisations*, 11th year, n. 2 (1956) 244–7

Rachel Hewitt, 'From the vapours to sad face: a history of emotion', *Guardian* (13 October 2017)

The History of Emotions Blog, Queen Mary University London: Conversations about the history of feeling. https://emotionsblog.history.qmul.ac.uk/

Audre Lorde, 'Keynote Address: the NWSA Convention', *Women's Studies Quarterly*, vol. 9, no. 3 (1981): 7

Susan Matt, 'Recovering the Invisible: Methods for the Historical Study of the Emotions', Peter Stearns and Susan Matt (eds.), *Doing Emotions History* (Chicago: University of Illinois Press, 2013), pp. 41–54

Queen Mary History of Emotions podcast (2016–2020)

Chapter 9

What can prehistory and ancient history tell us about being wise?

Bettany Hughes

As an ancient historian, suggesting that history cannot be fully understood unless we return to its earliest detectable roots – to the world of the ancients – is, perhaps, predictable. But this steer is not simply chronological, it is etymological. Our word history derives from the Ancient Greek – *historiā*. From the sixth century BC onwards *historiā* was coined in Greek-speaking communities to mean above all rational inquiry. *Historiā* was not originally confined by time. And crucially, the past in Ancient Greek was *protuxō*, 'that which happened before' (and could happen again), arguably a more helpful nomination of 'previous' than the c. AD 1300, Middle English incursion *passen* – 'to have gone by'. So although the tendency has been to see history as a means of imposing order onto the complex chaos of previous times, and to generate both reasons and reasonable explanations for the vagaries of individual and collective past lives, we need to look back to the ancients to understand that history is itself an approach, not a thing; history is a driving motivation to understand the facts of the world, and to comprehend the forces and purpose of human behaviour. History is a robust, rational framework in which to explore events – but also to uncover our irrational, unreasonable or seemingly inexplicable motivations for action; our sentient understanding of, and engagement with, the world.

If human behaviour is driven by instinct as well as by instruction, by stories as well as systems, then a temporal catalogue of human action and its impact has to deal as much with inquiry into the ineffable and internally personal, into the felt, as into the evidenced and what we choose to classify as 'reason', or indeed reasonable. And with that emphasis on understanding, history – I would argue – is increasingly at the business-end of human operations.

This volume asks, What is history, now? Living as we do, not in an age of information but an age of influence, our historical approach needs to adapt and evolve. The practice of history can usefully employ a painter's rubric; an appreciation that the truest and most telling representations of a factual subject are those which focus not just on the visible object, but also on that which connects them – the spaces around. History, at its most vigorous, is the study of gaps and fault-lines. It can employ immersion in 'the spaces in between' as a dynamic form of historiography. As historians we should, naturally, in terms of research and interpretation, strive to fill what has been neglected, censored, suppressed, denied, forgotten or ignored. And there's more . . .

History can productively seek out methods which help to access feelings – the elusive psychology of past behaviour. To best chart that path it is helpful to trace history's own physiological genesis, to find its neurological origins, to 'find the beginning' – exactly as is challenged in the opening lines of one of the oldest works of European literature (a work, at times, of history by accident), *The Odyssey*:

> Launch out on Odysseus's story, Muse, daughter of Zeus,
>   Start from where you will, sing of his time . . . and for our time
>   too!
> Tell the old story for our modern times . . . Find the beginning . . .

Physically, where is history born? What is its origin – not in the field, or on the page, or in time, but within us?

The story of history – history as in the study and understanding of 'that which happened before' – begins with mind-gaps, because history is a byproduct of memory. Memory sits, neuroscientists now explain, not in the equivalent of a contained, cerebral chest of drawers, but in a series of electrical connections right across our brain. Memory is the synaptic spaces in between; it is junction. It is also imagination. We cannot have a future thought unless we access a past experience – physical or psychological. We only think thoughts about the future by thinking back. Memory allows our minds to travel both forwards and backwards in time. We use the same brain mechanisms to imagine a meeting in the future as we do to remember an encounter in the past. Physiologically therefore we are creatures of memory; if we deny the past, we do not simply etiolate our present, at a molecular level we cauterise our future, and our potential as humans.

As is so often the case – the ancients understood this, 2600 years or so before it was proved by science. The creative purpose of memory helps to explain why in the Greek tradition, Memory – the goddess Memnosyme – was considered one of the firstborn and most powerful of all deities. Memnosyme's union with

154

Zeus – the God of Success and the Skies – birthed the Muses, divine forces responsible for all science, arts, literature – and all knowledge. Memory had a serious job of work to do – the known world was the product of Memory mating with Power. This exalted appreciation of remembering also explains why the keepers of memory were held in such great esteem by early civilisations. The proponents of the first work of epic poetry – the Epic of Gilgamesh in Sumerian and Babylonian culture, dating to c.2600 BC and featuring characters and experiences evidenced in the archaeological record – were high-status palace officials.* From the walls of 'Nestor's' Palace at Pylos in southern Greece, painted fragments dating to c.1400 BC have been found of a bard singing tales of heroes of old to the inhabitants of the throne-room – the regional court and gathering-place for invited foreign dignitaries and traders – to the accompaniment of his tortoiseshell lyre or kithara. These rhythmic, verbal, broadcast histories were a foundation of Greek epics such as Homer's *Iliad*

---

* Versions of epic Assyrian poems – trumpeting the success of their excessive warrior-king Tukulti-Ninurta I, who ruled for thirty years from the 1240/30s BC, and was said to have taken 28,000 prisoners in a single campaign – were carefully gouged into inscriptions – on rocks, stele (ornamental slabs of stone or wood) and walls across the Middle East:

> Glorious is his might, it sco[rches] the [ir]reverent in front and
>   behind;
> Blazing is his impetuosity, it burns the unsubmissive left and right;
> Fearful is his splendour, it overwhelms all his enemies.
> He who . . . the extremities of the four winds, all kings without
>   exception live in dread of him.

This is oral memorialising, history replicated and transmitted internationally.

and *Odyssey*, which have now been shown to contain lines that scan in the proto-Greek language of the Bronze Age Mycenaean culture. Given that Homer's Trojan War epic history-story-poems alone run to 15,693 and 12,110 lines, all memorised, the Epic of Gilgamesh to at least 32,000 words (with twenty new lines discovered on a tablet from southern Iraq in 2015), and the Mahabharata to 280,000 verse lines or 1.8 million words, the feat of the remembrancers is phenomenal. Epics were the curators of an oral tradition – delivered in a performative style, in public, and they clearly mattered.

An *epos* was originally defined as a story with meaning. Epics were shared missives of fact, feeling and, critically, of weaponised understanding. The first lines of the Epic of Gilgamesh were identified only in 1998 – they put a premium on both physical dominance and, crucially, wisdom: 'He who saw all, who was the foundation of the land, who knew [everything], was wise in all matters: Gilgamesh.'

So, before history as we know it was born, who were the curators of memory, and memory's almighty child, knowledge? Well, interestingly, not just men – women held roles as wisdom-merchants in a number of Bronze and Iron Age societies. The notion of female sagacity and agency leaves its trace in the respect given to divine female intellect – the Babylonian goddess Nisaba was the keeper of stores of grain and of wisdom, the Hindu Saraswati was 'she who has speech' or 'she who purifies with her words', Seshat was the Ancient Egyptian goddess of writing and wisdom and books, Japan's Benzaiten the personification of wisdom; the figure of Woman Wisdom in Hebrew scripture was Hokhma (responsible for practical, emotional, intellectual, moral wisdom and law-keeping) who championed a language that was intellectual and emotional, stating that both are true. Living, breathing women too were wisdom-keepers; Mycenaean aristocrats were allowed at council; the biblical judges Esther and Deborah understood law and customs – witness the Song of Deborah, which celebrates the wisdom of a woman, and the Song of Miriam that asks 'Does only Moses have a voice?'

So female thinkers are there in the DNA of human society – they have a platform, but the stem cell of the urban-based cultures of the Middle East, Indian subcontinent, North Africa and the eastern Mediterranean can appear rather different. The storage of memory and access to memory changed with the widespread advent of writing, coinciding with a militarisation of society and a diminishing of the female role. The pen (or rather the cuneiform wedge, the stylus and the reed-brush) and the sword grew mightier with fascinating synchronicity loosely 4000–3000 years ago. And in the archaeological record – where female figures (and figurines) had been conspicuous by their presence – at the very moment writing appeared as an elite mode of communication, female power visibly withered. Even when present, it was typically neglected – the discovery and identification of the first named female author in human history, the prolific priestess-poet Enheduanna, operational in 2200 BC in Babylon, merited only one small paragraph in the excavation notes of 1925/7. With their voices stifled, it is little surprise that women have been consistently written out of history. Written history begins in fact when women have lost their voices.*

---

* And we still have quite some catching up to do. It should be noted that at the time of writing this essay, the Wikipedia entry on global History checks by name, or references, 190 male historians and three female, with nine other women mentioned, all listed under the category of Feminist History.

So, if we are to attempt to access the testimonies of those individuals or experiences beyond or barred from the written record, we have to leave the libraries and archives and study-rooms, to find history elsewhere – in the spaces, intervals and lacunae.

A physical absorption in the past of material remains, or in the rhapsody of time-related travel, can be one way to break out of the carapace of dominant cultural identities and dominant forms of historical record. When we remember a moment in ours, or in another's life, we reconstruct it, we have the sense of re-experiencing the experience. So by reverse logic, when we follow and recreate a sparse trail left by the more elusive inhabitants of the past, there can be the chance, through the lived experience recorded or alluded to, of appreciating a truth which has escaped the formal, historical record. The chance to be in a place or situation that allows what *historiā* originally encouraged: for us to be in two times at once.

This kind of immersion is a more holistic, and journalistic, approach to history – a method which has, traditionally, created some anxiety in the Academy. And yet Herodotus – the Father of History no less (as nominated by the acute Roman lawyer and politician, Cicero) – was in every sense an embedded journalist. The good journalist's duty is to generate a space where experiences can be shared, memories and ideas heard, facts and opinions, especially those suppressed or neglected, revealed. Herodotus's testimony (some, frankly, fanciful and gullible) is thrillingly capacious. The Hellenistic historian Polybius, too, vigorously asserted that historians should be 'men of action' and that an opinion on history was best derived from first-hand testimony and the physical experience of the historical locus. These eyewitness, immersive, immediate approaches are arguably sympathetic with the original meaning of history. Because a hundred years or so before *historiā* was coined to describe rational inquiry in the sixth century AD, in his epics detailing the story of the Trojan war and its fallout, Homer describes an *istwr* as a witness, sometimes as a judge, a participant who experiences a phenomenon so as to better analyse it.

This is a lived, immersive approach to understanding that still has heft. Witnessing first-hand twentieth- and twenty-first-century volcanic eruption and tsunami damage – generating floating piles of pumice ten feet deep – can help to explain the reference to 'floating shoals of mud' during the destruction of Plato's proud Atlantis (I would argue a mythical and allegorical interpretation of the real eruption of Thera in 1615 BC which devastated cultures around the Mediterranean and beyond).

To be juddered by earthquakes in Ithaka, Athens and along the Turkish coast forces an appreciation of the craven honouring of the sea, sky and earthquake gods who dominated this region from 5000 BC to AD 500. Witnessing the fifty-four ancient shipwrecks in a stretch of water between Fourni Island and Asia Minor, where the wind whips water into 200-metre-high whirling sprays against a sheer rock face known locally as 'the Cape of Death', is one explanation of details of the whirlpool and rock-smashing horror of Scylla and Charybdis in the adventures of Odysseus. Caught out by a freak swell on the Ikarian Sea, described in Homer's *Iliad* as a stretch of water 'teeming and raging like a mob roused by a demagogue' while travelling to the likely locations cited in *The Odyssey* – a full seven hours which my crew and I only survived in our sailboat by gripping on to a vertical ridge that should have been horizontal – we landed at the island of Mykonos shaken and salt-drenched.

Just as the Ancient Greek hero Odysseus was storm-washed up on Calypso's isle and ended up luxuriating with oil baths and massages provided by his host, for the next few days sleep, hot baths and terra firma felt like a physical and psychological necessity. My tetchy annoyance at Odysseus's inability to drag himself away from Calypso and back onto his boat to continue homewards to his wife Penelope dissipated a little. Indeed, that entire six-month Odysseian expedition helped our peripatetic crew of historical researchers internalise and understand more deeply *The Odyssey*'s message of resilience and agency – that collaboration is the only means not just to survive, but to thrive, and that life may throw up unexpected challenges, but to live is to take that journey.

The early Greek authors, in particular Homer and Herodotus, are truly flag-bearers for immersive, instructive memorialising. Authoring his vast *Histories* – a lifetime's work – exhilarated by the adrenaline of being part of an underdog culture that had defeated, against the odds, the dominant superpower of the day, the Persians – Herodotus was writing with hope 'that human achievement may be spared the ravages of time' (Book 1.1). And, critically, his method and purpose were *apodexis* – revelation or display. For Herodotus the point of history was that it be a shared experience. And, remarkably, in the *Histories*, thanks to immersion, what could have been a triumphalist display-exercise in lionisation was anything but chauvinistic. Instead, the travelling scholar is remarkably inclusive, asserting that great deeds were achieved by Greeks and non-Greeks alike. He spends much on-page time trying to experience the world from within another's skin: Herodotus is shocked that the Persian Emperor Cambyses mocks the religion of the Egyptians, reasoning: 'Everyone believes his own customs to be far and away the best . . . only a madman would think to jeer at such matters' (Book 3.38). And the Persian King of Kings Xerxes, on whose empire 'the sun never set' (Book 7), and whose forces had brutally attacked Herodotus's home-town Halicarnassus (modern-day Bodrum in Turkey), is allowed attributes of strength, valour and soul.

The understanding may partly stem from the father of history's own rainbow experience. He was either Carian, or of mixed Carian-Greek parentage – a Greek-speaking Anatolian with a Phoenician dialect in a Greek world. Herodotus was also probably a failed revolutionary, who may have tried to oust a pro-Persian Greek dynasty and as a result ended up a refugee in Samos. But his empathy also stemmed from a key principle: *xenia*, guest-host friendship, the acceptance of the need to welcome the unknown across thresholds, to cross borders and boundaries, to embrace strangers as friends and the strange as well as the familiar. For Herodotus, history was all about making a present-day journey to find a connection across time and space.*

There was another ancient, hyper-connected understanding of the world, which has been categorised as anti-rational, but which, once again, science now buttresses and which contemporary historical inquiry should embrace ever more vigorously. We now appreciate chemically that we are part of a bigger matrix, but it is clear from manifold sources that highly successful ancient cultures long-believed that humans were connected at an

---

* Fascinatingly, we now know that reading stories and history empathetically triggers the production of oxytocin, the 'cuddle chemical' that encourages us to care about the lives of others.

atomic level to the rest of the universe. The evidence is there in the Neolithic cultures of Malta and Gozo, where 5000 years ago giant east/west-facing underground temples were carved and whole communities buried together, the half-rotten corpses covered in red ochre, in the anticipation that the flesh would be reborn: an acceptance that matter never disappears, it just takes on another form. For the Old and New Kingdom Egyptians death began the journey to another life. Pharaohs, buried in the time-travelling resurrection machines of the first mastaba tombs, then pyramids, then rock-cut burials, were being prepared for their journey through the skies back to the stars. We now understand that in terms of chemical composition we are both star dust and earth. By sponsoring state-busting projects such as the building of the Great Pyramid on the Giza plateau – as a means of rejoining the 'indestructibles' – Egypt's pharaohs were subscribing to the carbon-block concept of biochemistry.

And just as carbon molecules circulate in our universe's system, so the carbon molecules of culture may move, but they never vanish. The white lead and kohl-rimmed faces we see on the frescoes of women on the Late Bronze Age walls at Akrotiri on Santorini, Tiryns and Mycenae in the Greek mainland, are still applied – exactly – to the last detail of red suns on cheeks, chin and forehead, by some Muslim brides of remote villages in Bulgaria. When we wish *Salaam* or *Shalom* – peace on one another – we are using an ancient Babylonian word – *shul* – which means a whole, a thing that is not broken. We might be familiar with Shylock's 'If you cut me, do I not bleed?' speech in the *Merchant of Venice*, and think it refreshingly progressive – but Shakespeare's endeavour would also have been recognised by the inhabitants of fourth-century AD Smyrna – Izmir as it is now, in Turkey – where one of the city's sons, Quintus, feels his way around sexual inequality by giving the following speech to the Trojan Hippodamia, inspired by a Queen of the Amazons, Penthesilea:

> Not in strength are we inferior to men; the same our eyes, our limbs the same; one common light we see, one air we breathe; nor different is the food we eat. What is denied to us that the gods have bestowed on man?

What indeed!

The list goes on. Female ♀ signs on lavatories around the world commemorate the goddess Venus's astrological symbol. The ♂ on male cubicles is the symbol of the god Mars. The Christian tradition of monasticism was originally inspired by itinerant Buddhist monks travelling the silk routes of the Near and Middle East, and reading *Celestial Bodies* by Johka Alharthi, the first female Omani novelist ever to be translated into English, we find the sustained use of Platonic allegories – as Arabic folk-myth – cited in the oral, poetic culture of 1970s Omani harems. We swim every moment of every day in a cultural ocean that has also lapped the feet of other societies and other times. It is why we can feel connected to the other, and can learn from communities of the deep past, from women and men of all degrees who were learning how to live in the world, as a human-dominated world was working out how to live with itself.

Just as the evolution of the bordered, distinct academic disciplines in the nineteenth century (the taxonomy of archaeology as a science distinct from history; the favouring of Greek, Latin and Hebrew over Sanskrit in many Western universities) evolved in the twentieth century to encourage historians to think thematically about historical inquiry, perhaps the new millennium should support a more organic and borderless approach – an understanding of the connectivity of history that is at once progressive and, with no little irony, at the same time prehistoric.

Because immersion in prehistory can help us with the very definition of the concept of what history is – then and now. The root of the word history in Proto-Indo-European seems to be *wid-tor* – a wise agent. *Wid* meaning to witness, understand or see. *Wid* also gives us our word vision. History, wisdom and vision therefore share a common root – a notion of active clarity and clear-sightedness. The author of historical method, Thucydides, was inadvertently spot on when he opined that history had been invented as a tool 'so mankind could see more clearly'. Well, now feels the time to make good on that tight relationship between sapience, history and perception, to allow history to be an active agent in the service of wisdom.

At almost exactly the same time that *historiā* emerges as a robust method, 2500 years ago, when society is feeling its way towards rationality and when individuals are starting to become economic and intellectual actors, not just dominated by landowning or religious elites; when we start to share lives together in large groups understanding that our minds have agency, then questions start to have real value. Inquiry becomes not seditious but central to what it is to be human. Positing that only the wise admit to the voids in their wisdom, thought-leaders such as Socrates, Confucius and the Buddha challenged us never to stop seeking out the gaps – 'the unexamined life is not worth living', to quote Socrates via Plato; and to be, literally, lovers of wisdom – a philosopher is one who has *philia* (love) for *sophia* (wisdom).

Socrates expanded on this, denouncing the dangers of cataloguing the world without comprehending it. The hemlock-drinking philosopher gets my vote. Psychological inquiry, philosophical quests, emotional intelligence and a haptic immersion can be usefully associated with the acquisition of historical knowledge and understanding.

So the answer to the question What is history, now? should, more accurately, be another: What is wisdom, now? And the search for the answer to that, surely the most fundamental of interrogations, can only be a series of questions and explorations. Because we also now realise that our own memories – and therefore all memories – are narratives, narratives constructed to match our feeling of what our lives should be (and, therefore, were). Memory is more often than not consistent with our identity. It is important to embrace a head-on understanding and recognition of the power we have to imagine into existence our pasts, and therefore our present. We are the stories we tell about ourselves. The process of memory is physical, dynamic, protean, sometimes false, sometimes true. Given that histories (and stories) are frequently used to justify the creation of new futures, the histories and stories that are told, and shared, matter exponentially – which of course forces the value of memory and of history as a collective experience. If the human mind was born from idea-exchange – as a critical mass of the cognitive group at least 70,000 years ago passed ideas between one another that fired and grew – the fact that the online cognitive group has now reached critical levels, exchanging ideas and truths of all kinds, makes it incumbent on every participant, historian or other, to endeavour to bring wisdom to the party.

Technology and history are also linguistic womb-mates. The

Proto-Indo-European root *tek* originally meant to weave together, or to foster the young; would it not be a wonderful thing if the sharing technology of the digital age could inject into the ether of influence, and the economy of attention, the wisdom of 'that which has happened before'? In the deep past we see the acoustic and then the Greek alphabet sponsoring the common reader – new technologies put to the service of history could happily nourish the common thinker.

The response, therefore, to the bracing challenge of this collection is that if we accept that there are as many ways to understand history and to enact historiography as there are ways to be human, history can be an ever-expanding companion to the lived experience. Indeed, it can fulfil its original mission twenty-six centuries ago: to witness, consider, and inquire rationally. If there is one thing my physical journeys through history have taught me, it is that powerful civilisations leave behind great monuments, great civilisations leave behind powerful ideas. Memory and mind (and in fact muse and museum) share the same root – *men* – three letters which also, as it happens, give us our word man. Linguistically, a man is not a male thing but a thinking thing. I think and therefore I am, I remember and therefore I am, part of the brother- and sisterhood of man. It is the sourcing of prehistoric word-ideas such as *men/tek/widtor*, and ancient records of early human experience, that enliven our understanding of now. History gives us all the time in the world to think; history reminds us to remember, to think better. Who knows, perhaps by reaching back through time, and across experience, beyond the textual, we may one day alight upon the Mother of History too – and indeed, on the all-time beauty of wisdom.

So what is history, now? History as a process has returned to its roots and moved beyond the page, its purpose is vision and witness. When history is transparent, whether its subject is the rational or the irrational, it allows us to see clearly: history today is what the ancients originally conceived it to be – the ally of a future that chooses to be clear-thinking, clear-sighted and wise.

Selected Further Reading

D.W. Anthony, *The Horse, the Wheel, and Language: How Bronze-Age Riders from the Eurasian Steppes Shaped the Modern World* (Princeton, Oxford: Princeton University Press, 2007)

P. Cartledge, *Democracy: A Life* (Oxford: Oxford University Press, 2018)

J. Cook, *Ice Age Art: The Arrival of the Modern Mind* (London: British Museum Press, 2013)

K. Cooney, *When Women Ruled the World: Six Queens of Egypt* (Washington, DC: National Geographic, 2020)

K. Cooper, *Band of Angels: The Forgotten World of Early Christian Women* (London: Atlantic Books, 2013)

B.W. Fortson, *Indo-European Language and Culture: An Introduction*, 2nd edn. M.A. Malden (Oxford: Wiley-Blackwell, 2010)

S. Goldhill, *Love, Sex & Tragedy: Why Classics Matters* (London: John Murray, 2005)

D.W. Graham, *Explaining the Cosmos: the Ionian Tradition of Scientific Philosophy* (Princeton, Oxford: Princeton University Press, 2006)

N. Harrington, *Living with the Dead: Ancestor Worship and*

Mortuary Ritual in Ancient Egypt (Oxford: Oxbow, 2012)

B. Holmes, *Gender: Antiquity and its Legacy* (Oxford: Oxford University Press, 2012)

Homer, *The Odyssey* (trans. E.R. Wilson) (New York: W.W. Norton and Company, 1988)

B. Hughes, *Venus and Aphrodite* (London: Weidenfeld & Nicolson, 2019)

M.H. Munn, *The Mother of the Gods, Athens, and the Tyranny of Asia: A Study of Sovereignty in Ancient Religion* (Berkeley, London: University of California Press, 2006)

C. Phillips, *Socrates in Love: Philosophy for a Passionate Heart* (New York, London: W.W. Norton, 2007)

Chapter 10

Why diversity in Tudor England matters

Onyeka Nubia

Historians have sometimes found it appropriate to envisage English history as a book with white pages and no Black letters in. And historians often write a narrative where Africans and other people of colour are automatically the 'other', 'stranger', 'Johnny-come-lately' or 'the enslaved'. This distortion skews our understanding of English history and makes it difficult to see Africans as active participants in England's story.

Moreover, Tudor history is a popular preoccupation, and often it is here where Africans are assigned tropes that explain away their significance. For example, Kenneth Little in *Negroes in Britain* (1947) wrote that he doubted 'if the Blackman whether of African or East Indian origin was a familiar figure [in England] until well on in the [sixteenth] century, except as a chance visitor or when imported from Portuguese and colonial territories [in Africa and the Caribbean].' These words 'familiar figure' and 'imported' in the quotation above suggests that Little thinks there were very few Africans present in Tudor England, and that those who were there were enslaved and 'property', belonging to

Europeans. Little's statements are simple and reductionist, but his sentiments are echoed by more recent historians such as Kim Hall. The trajectory of her book is insightful, but unfortunately she repeats similar notions that Africans in Tudor England were marginal and inconsequential, 'too accidental and solitary to be given a historical statistic'. Hall implies that their presence was not significant enough to warrant any serious academic analysis or public recognition. But recent research has revealed that African people can be retrieved from English records, and their presence, status and significance disrupt established historical narratives. The existence of these Africans offers a challenge to narratives of Englishness that continue to ignore or marginalise them.

To understand the status and contribution of Africans in Tudor England it is helpful to recognise that racism has not always been institutionalised or systematised. Some of the reasons for this are that Tudor England did not inherit from its medieval past race laws, conventions or customs that determined people's status by their colour. Race laws emerged in England at the end of the seventeenth and into the eighteenth century. They were supported because of the economic profits engendered from colonialism and enslavement. These profits created an economic imperative that made racism institutionally necessary. It is at this time that African people were stigmatised as less than human in many parts of the world. Proponents within anthropology and other sciences, as well as theology, supported this. And intellectuals that included Carl Linnaeus, Immanuel Kant, Erasmus Darwin and Josiah C. Nott helped to institutionalise quasi-scientific and philosophical theories that promulgated inequality. Meanwhile, European lawyers refashioned the slave laws and customs of antiquity, pilfered from Greek and Roman apologists such as Aristotle, Euripides, Plutarch and Cicero. And these lawyers originated monstrous social and legal conventions, which denied humanity to Africans. These conventions became woven into the fabric of seventeenth, eighteenth and nineteenth-century British societies. They made being English exclusive and white.

However, in Tudor England, status was primarily determined by social standing, lineage, birth, gender and, to a lesser extent, wealth. During the Tudor period, Africans seem to have been free to determine their status in the same way as other people. African people's status was not restricted by government legislation or public policy. It was in the private sphere of English society that their status was determined. This meant that, in Tudor England, there were no laws on race that disqualified Africans such as Henrie Anthonie Jetto from holding office, voting, owning property and so on.

Jetto lived in Holt in Worcestershire and was baptised there on 3 March 1596 when he was twenty-six years old. He was described in the records as a 'Blackemore' and his surname 'Jetto' (from 'jet', black) probably also referenced his complexion. He had six children, more than thirty-two grandchildren and over seventy great-grandchildren. Jetto now has hundreds of descendants living in Holt, the surrounding areas and elsewhere. Jetto was a yeoman – which meant he held land worth more than forty shillings – and was an active member of his local community. As an independent man of property, he could vote in local elections. He was also literate and wrote his own will, which he signed on 20 September 1626. This will is one of the oldest written by an African in English records.

There is no evidence that Jetto's ethnicity meant he was legally deprived of his status in Tudor England. The English courts at that time were unwilling to take away liberties acquired by birth or denization without a legal reason to do so. Nevertheless, some historians have suggested that two letters and a draft proclamation, created in the reign of Elizabeth I, attempted to take those rights away. But upon closer inspection, these documents prove the contrary. The letters are dated 11 and 18 July 1596, and the draft proclamation was written in 1601. These documents appear to label Africans as inferior and divide them from other 'liege' subjects. But careful investigation proves that these documents need to be recontextualised as opportunistic ruses that originated outside of the halls of government, and which were never supported by law. They certainly did not result in mass deportations or expulsions.

Africans in Tudor England could still demand *habeas corpus* if they were wrongly arrested and detained. Their rights were *in personam* (personal). The action in defence of these rights was also *in personam*. This meant that some personal rights were defended in public spaces, although the action remained 'private'. The idea of natural rights was known, but not necessarily vocalised as it is today. The English courts, especially at the end of the sixteenth century, were strong advocates of judicial activism and pursued an aggressive policy of limiting the infringement of liberties, especially by powerful members of the state, merchants, and so on. The judiciary, including the Court of the Exchequer, King's Bench, and the Courts of Common Pleas, pursued this idea, meaning that individuals could pursue a claim for loss of rights, even where the claimant had not suffered financial loss. The common law was willing to protect natural rights so long as the victim had *locus standi* or a 'sufficient connection' to bring a cause of action. Leading jurists at the time, including Edward Coke the attorney general, James Dyer and Edmund Anderson, chief justices of the Court of Common Pleas, agreed on that, if little else.

The result was that Tudor jurisprudence was a battleground for conflicting rights. In some ways, men of power could claim their right and power over their households as an absolute and unfettered one. And some used classical and legal reasons to substantiate this. But, equally, people sought to defend their own liberty or that of others by reinterpreting notions of reasonableness as standards of equity. They claimed protection under the law. These cases include, in 1470, an African woman named Maria Moriana. In Southampton, Moriana's employer attempted to have her sold as if she were a slave. It was her local community that sought a legal remedy to protect her rights. The court agreed that she could not be denied her natural rights, even if she had accidentally given them away, because she, the 'said Oratrice' was an 'innocent' and could not 'read or write English or Latin'.

And then there is the 1579 case of a 'said Ethiopian [unnamed] who utterly refused to work for his master', one Hector Noviemies. The court ruled that Noviemies had no remedy against his servant and could not compel him to work. Early modern jurisprudence was capable of ruling against the men of power who arbitrarily assumed absolute authority over their households.

Africans in Tudor England would not have found themselves automatically denied access to their rights on the grounds of tradition, and Africans travelling to England from elsewhere had similar opportunities to become domiciled or an English denizen (a citizen that has rights). After all, the process of becoming domiciled or a denizen was really about being naturalised and adult baptisms were often an important aspect of this process. The fact that most of the visible Africans in English records are baptised indicates that they had probably gone through a naturalisation process. Once these Africans were christened, their legal status would have varied little from their white counterparts. This is especially true as Africans were integrated into their parishes, and for them to be singled out for detrimental treatment would have meant extracting them from families and communities in which white people were also a part.

We should avoid reactionary notions that automatically and perpetually 'other' Africans in English history. And when we say Africans, we use the term generically; it includes African women. African women lived in an English patriarchal society, but they had the capacity to negotiate their own agency. For example, Mary Fillis of Morisco is recorded in the Tudor parish records in more detail than her white female counterparts. Mary was a commoner and her record is the longest for any commoner in the memorandum daybook for St Botolph-without-Aldgate. In the daybook the writer recorded at her baptism that 'now taking some hold of faith in Jesus Christ, [Mary Fillis] is desirous to become a Christian.' The same document refers to the fact that in 1597 she had lived in England for thirteen or fourteen years. This would have meant she was between four and six years old when she arrived on English shores. It is stated that she came 'from Morisco' and that her father's name was 'Fillis of Morisco, a shovel maker and basket maker'. Although some historians have interpreted this to mean that she originated from Morocco, Morisco is more likely to be 'the land of Moriscos', in what is now Spain. Despite the last Moorish stronghold of

Granada being defeated in 1492, Moors continued to live in the Iberian peninsula. In 1568 there was a Moorish revolt that was put down very harshly by the Spanish authorities. Later still more draconian measures were put in place. Moorish people began to leave and travel to parts of North and West Africa and places such as France, the Italian states and England. This would suggest Mary's father was one of those émigrés. The Moors of the Iberian peninsula were internationally famous for their skills and abilities, so it is not surprising that English record-keepers thought it necessary to quote Mary's father's profession and repeat this several times. The background of Mary Fillis is therefore very important in our understanding of why a woman and commoner would be celebrated in her parish. We do not know what happened to Mary — but we should be cautious of imposing an automatic inscription of inferiority on her.

English history includes Moriana, the 'said Aethiopian', Jetto and Mary Fillis, and this 'Island's story' is degraded if there is no space to acknowledge or recognise them. Jeremy Isaacs, the founding chief executive of Channel 4, stated in 1973 that there was a 'National Resource of Memory'. At present that national memory is distorted by nineteenth-century norms, and prescriptions emerging from the developing science of race at the end of the seventeenth century. This means it is very difficult for us to understand Africans in English history except through that lens. Of course, it has always been the case that some areas of history are more popularly studied and researched than others. But this does not fully explain why Imtiaz Habib's book *Black Lives in the English Archives* (2008), was the first book published by a mainstream British press to codify this history. And this indifference towards diversity is illustrated by the fact that *Blackamoores:*

Africans in Tudor England (2013), was the first book on the status and origins of Africans in Tudor England. Some might ask why it has taken so long for detailed research about Africans to be published by a British press, in what is otherwise a popular period of English history. It is also disappointing, but startling that both books emerged outside of mainstream British academia. These books, and others such as Miranda Kaufmann's *Black Tudors: The Untold Story* (2019) and Hakim Adi's *Black British History: New Perspectives* (2019), can aide our understanding of English history.

Diversity is sometimes viewed as a modern idiom imposed arbitrarily on moments in history. But research into English history reveals it as fact. This fact is not shaped by polemics but evidenced by records written by Englishmen. These records in the archives reveal Africans and other people of colour as an integral part of this island's narrative. This history matters, and it should not be political to acknowledge this diversity. Rather, we should be excited to learn about another aspect of England's past which until now has been obscured.

Selected Further Reading

Susan Adams et al., 'The Genetic Legacy of Religious Diversity and Intolerance . . . Christians, Jews, and Muslims in the Iberian Peninsula', *American Journal of Human Genetics*, 83: 6 (2008), pp. 725–36

Hakim Adi (ed.), *Black British History: New Perspectives from Roman Times to the Present Day* (London: Zed Books, 2019)

Lauren Benton, *Law and Colonial Cultures: Legal Regimes*

in World History, 1400–1900 (Cambridge: Cambridge University Press, 2002)

Imtiaz Habib, *Black Lives in the English Archives, 1500–1677: Imprints of the Invisible* (London: Ashgate, 2008)

Miranda Kaufmann, *Black Tudors: The Untold Story* (London: One World, 2019)

Onyeka Nubia, *Blackamoores: Africans in Tudor England, Their Presence, Status and Origins* (London, 2013; new edition, London: 2014)

Onyeka Nubia, *England's Other Countrymen: Black Tudor Society* (London: Zed Books, 2019)

Robert Rees Davies, *The First English Empire: Power and Identities in the British Isles 1093–1343* (Oxford: Oxford University Press, 2000)

Chapter 11

How can we recover the lost lives of women?

Suzannah Lipscomb

They were nobody special. So now they are the invisible, the forgotten, the historically negligible, the 'dead multitudes', the minor figures, the chorus. They were not the Great Men or kings or occasional queen that pepper History's grand narrative. They were ordinary women – the illiterate, the poor, the marginalised and the enslaved – the billions who left barely a hint that they had ever existed. They are the women from and about whom we have only traces – single sheets of paper, or perhaps not even that much; those who left no documents in their own hand; those who appear to us only, fleetingly, through the eyes of others; those whose words, when attended to at all, have been written down by someone else. Yet, their lives were as actual and as meaningful as those who left behind a great wealth of documents, and as actual and meaningful as our own. How can we reclaim them from historical oblivion? Can we restore them to history?

When Sally Alexander, the great historian and feminist activist, was in her twenties and reading for a diploma in History at Ruskin College, Oxford, she helped found a lively academic movement called the History Workshop. At a Workshop in 1969, she proposed a meeting for historians interested in talking about women's history. This was the year that men walked on the Moon. But while mankind was taking a giant leap forward, womankind was assumed to be at a standstill. For Alexander recalls the 'gust of masculine laughter' as she made her suggestion. Three years earlier, writing in the *TLS*, E.P. Thompson had popularised the study of 'history from below' – history that focused on the experiences of ordinary people – and this is what the History Workshop had been set up to do. But for those laughing men ordinary people did not, apparently, include women.

As it turned out, of course, Alexander was on the right side of history. In the 1970s 'Women's History' began by telling the lives of 'women worthies' – notable, high-profile women about whom much was known – but in the 1980s feminist historians started to look for everyday women and the structures that shaped their lives. They sought out female agency and the qualities of women's experience that distinguished it from men's, recuperating women as the subjects of history and considering what history might look like from a woman-centred perspective. The only trouble was: how to find these ordinary women?

History is a discipline that relies largely on documents. Modern historians might have access to archived photos or recordings, and archaeologists may unearth material evidence of the past, but much of what we know is simply what was written down. So how can we access the experiences, thoughts and feelings of those who could seldom write and who scarcely warranted a mention by those who could? E.H. Carr told us that 'History consists of a corpus of ascertained facts. The facts are available to the historian in documents, inscriptions and so on, like fish on the fishmonger's slab. The historian collects them, takes them home and cooks and serves them in whatever style appeals to him.'* Carr's breakthrough was observing that the historian chooses which facts to take and serve up – but what if the facts aren't in the documents? What if those fish were never caught?

Historians have demonstrated that the archive is a site of power. The sources in it may give the illusion of transparency, objectivity and completeness, but the stories they tell about the past are partial and censored. The information we have is shaped by power: it determines whose perspective mattered enough to make it into the documents, who is silent and invisible, what is absent, what cannot be known and what has been erased. Those who were exploited or oppressed or simply peripheral and marginalised could not leave their narratives to posterity in the same way as men of power could. There are questions that the archive refuses to answer, and the narratives that the archive does provide to us are, consciously or unconsciously, shaped in such a way as to justify the dominance of the powerful. The archive is unreliable. This is a particular problem for those of us who study women – especially women who were largely powerless. When ordinary women emerge from obscurity it is only because they had an encounter with the powerful. As the philosopher Michel Foucault put it, that power 'marked them with its claw was what gave rise to the few words about them that remain for us'.

If we have very few sources about such women and those are far from neutral, how can historians possibly represent forgotten lives? The answer is to treat the source like an enemy – attack

* His choice of pronoun says much about the study of history in 1961.

it and force it to give up the secrets it is trying to hide. Back in the 1940s, Walter Benjamin said we should 'brush history against the grain'. Ann Laura Stoler called it 'upside-down reading'. Historians now commonly talk of 'reading against the grain'. To read documents against the grain means to scrutinise them with a different purpose in mind to the one the authors intended. It means constantly veering away from their priorities, preoccupations and pronouncements. It means reading between the lines in search of subtexts, listening for silences, and, says Saidiya Hartman, 'breaking open the stories they told in order to narrate' our own.

One type of source that has often been read against the grain to explore women's lives is inquisition and court records. These are records of interrogations, hastily written by (male) scribes, who shifted first- and second-person testimonies to third-person narratives, relied on often-used formulae, and did not always indicate where an inquisitor's leading questions ended and the answers began. Even at their most 'authentic', therefore, they cannot be assumed to be faithful transcripts of female speech. But they can be a place to look for the lives of ordinary women.

So, what does reading against the grain mean in practice? I tried to do this when writing my book, *The Voices of Nîmes*. I drew on the records of the Protestant Church of Languedoc in France. Each local church set up a consistory, which served as governing body and moral tribunal. It was a patriarchal insti-tution, designed to reinforce the rule of husbands and fathers and to ensure moral probity, especially regarding sexual sin. As women were believed to be morally weaker and sexually insatia-ble, this endeavour meant attempting to control women. Reading these records, I constantly had to resist the temptation to focus on what the consistory thought mattered. This sense of being drawn towards the consistory's obsessions and motivations probably explains why the handful of people who had read these manuscripts before me had ended up writing books of ecclesiastical history. But it is possible to read the documents against the grain because, unlike criminal and civil courts in the same period, the consistory's scribes carefully recorded the words of all the women who appeared before the tribunal. As a result, the registers I examined contain over a thousand testimonies by and about women – and not just the rich. There was no fee to initiate a case, which meant the Church had inadvertently created a mechanism that women – even the very poor, servants, widows and others without social status – could use for their own purposes. In these pages, therefore, I found, for example, maidservants accusing their masters of sexual assault.

One case in particular shows how this might work. In December 1600, Marguerite Brueysse claimed to be pregnant by her employer Anthoine Bonnet, whom she accused of rape. We don't know how old Brueysse was, or anything about her background, but it was typical for girls and women to act as servants in their teens and early twenties. It was not a case she could have taken to law, even had she been able to afford to, because a raped woman had to prove her active physical resistance. Most people at the time believed women were naturally lustful and would yield voluntarily, and medically it was thought that women had to climax in order to conceive, so a pregnant woman claiming rape was doubly disadvantaged. Nevertheless, at the consistory, Brueysse was able to record her side of the story, albeit in the context of a discomfiting cross-examination by the man she accused of assaulting her. Bonnet was an influential man, probably in his fifties or sixties, and, as such, quizzing Brueysse directly was his prerogative. He asked her when the supposed rape had happened. Her reply, restored from the consistory's script to a first-person account, is illuminating:

> It was in the month of April after your return from Castres. One day, when I was clearing dung into the ditch in the garden, you ordered me to go into the stable and there you threw me on a pile of rye and knew me [carnally] by force. You stuffed a handkerchief in my mouth to stop me shouting out. And, afterwards, you gave me money and made me great promises.

As his questioning continued, Bonnet tried to discredit and undermine Brueysse, portraying her as promiscuous, blaming the pregnancy on someone else, and even disputing whether the stable would have been a practicable place as rye was slippery. But despite his efforts, the consistory came to the conclusion that it was she who was telling the truth. Shocked and angry, Bonnet burst out, 'You do me a great wrong to believe a whore rather than a good man.' He vowed to appeal their decision. We hear nothing more of the case; we do not know what became of Marguerite Brueysse and her child. She flickers before us briefly – but her case shows us that if we look for women's perspectives in unlikely places like the consistory registers, we can glean details of their everyday lives, see how they operated in moments of crisis, and how they could even occasionally persuade men of power to back them – even in the records of a system designed to keep women in check.

More punitive systems than the consistory compound the problem of whether we can find women's 'authentic' voices.

This is especially true in the records of judicatures that relied on torture to exact confessions. Drawing on the trial records of accused witches in sixteenth- and seventeenth-century Germany, where torture played a key part in securing admissions of guilt, Lyndal Roper found that scribes only noted the precise relationship between how it was applied and the testimony produced in unusual cases. An instructive example is that of widowed peasant Gertrauta Conrad from the village of Ober Wittighausen, who was accused of witchcraft in 1595. At first, she robustly denied being a witch, but after being suspended by her wrists for five hours, she confessed that she had learned to fly. Later she added that she had first met the Devil in a meadow; he had come to her for sex in her chamber and kitchen, and she had hidden the money he gave her away from the servants in an old butter churn.

Mostly the witchcraft records disguise how confessions emerged. Interrogations took place over weeks or months, and sometimes the 'clean' copies of trial documents summarised the final confession, with a victim's contradictions, retractions and denials erased from the record. In addition, to stop the pain and in a state of disorientation, many accused witches adopted the scenarios posed to them, so confessions reveal as much of the fantasies of the interrogator as of the interrogated. Witches' testimonies, nevertheless, contain extensive life histories and, reading against the grain, it is possible to pay heed to the small inconsistencies, slips, emotions, and vivid details that shed light on women's experience of everyday life – like hiding money from the servants in a butter churn.

But what can we make of those women whose existence in the sources is even more ephemeral? Some merit only momentary mentions. They appear solely in fragments – what Verne Harries calls 'archival slivers'.

Certain subjects naturally beget an anecdotal, fragmentary record. In researching her book, *Mother: An Unconventional History*, Sarah Knott found one historical constant: it has always taken two hands to hold a baby. The traces we do have about motherhood testify to the way an infant interrupts narrative. Letters break off: 'Baby is stirring so I must stop,' writes Rebecca Wylie to a relative in Indiana in 1875. Or the stuff of the cradle was thought too mundane to warrant a mention. Historic mothering only comes to us piecemeal in stray remarks, passing anecdotes, or nuggets of recorded conversation.

Where gender intersects with differences of race, ethnicity, sexuality or class, we see especially scant sources. We can count on one hand the extant autobiographical narratives from the millions of enslaved women who endured the Middle Passage.

There are, however, methods by which we can attend to these archival fragments. One is a sort of Lectio Divina: we read the text closely and contemplatively. We contextualise, gently unpack each phrase, and acknowledge what we do not know; we treat it to what anthropologist Clifford Geertz called 'thick description'.

In 2016 historian Diana Paton was handed a bundle of letters found in a Scottish attic. They included a single sheet written by a formerly enslaved woman, Mary Williamson of Jamaica, to her London-based master Haughton James in October 1809. Paton knew how extraordinarily rare it was. So she pondered each phrase, investigated every lead, and located every other source she could find relating to James (about whom she found much) and Williamson (about whom she found little). In her article about it, Paton discusses Williamson's self-description as a 'Brown woman' – meaning she had European as well as African ancestry – and her account of her manumission as the result of a sexual encounter with a white man, James Tumming, who 'fancied her'. 'Williamson', writes Paton, 'presents herself as, literally, a commodity: he fancied her, bought her . . . took her with him.' Paton explores how, on Tumming's death, Williamson chose to move back to the estate where she had been enslaved to be close to her sisters – 'every relation I have in the world are there' – and support them materially as much as she could. Her letter to James was a rhetorically sophisticated plea for help after a new overseer, responding vindictively to the passing of the British Act for the Abolition of the Slave Trade in 1807, had threatened to 'make your people sup sorrow by spoonfuls', destroying Williamson's house and the one she had built for her sisters. From Paton's close reading of this one letter, we get a rare female perspective on sexual encounters between white men and brown women, and the normally hidden importance of family relationships in slavery.

There are challenges in working from scraps. Camilla Townsend has written about the Indigenous woman variously known as Marina, Malinche or Malintzin, who was both translator for and (possibly unwilling) mistress to Spanish conquistador Hernan Cortés during his conquest of Mexico, and who left not a single page of testimony. She stresses the utter importance of not 'projecting motivations and feelings onto the woman that she in fact never harbored'. As much as possible, we must refrain from imposing our own biases, romanticising, or speaking for our subjects.

We must also resist our desire to force stories to an outcome. Fatima, an enslaved Muslim Berber woman from North Africa, was found by Mary Elizabeth Perry in a single document in an Inquisition case in 1584 in Malaga, Spain. According to a cleric, when Fatima was hospitalised with plague, she had chosen to convert to Christianity and had been baptised. Later she professed that she was and always had been a Muslim, and that the baptism had been performed when she 'was crazy and without sanity and without judgement'. The Inquisition condemned her as an apostate. For having maliciously denied her baptism, she was confined to a convent for religious instruction and subjected to two hundred lashes – a punishment that might have proved fatal. We know neither anything about Fatima's life prior to this case nor whether she survived. We must live with the discomfort of not having an ending.

There is also a far greater problem. Not only must we contend with the absences and erasures of the archive, we also must reckon with a kind of 'epistemic violence' – violence is encoded in the way we know about many women's lives. Enslaved women, for example, appear in archival documents almost exclusively when being beaten, mutilated, violated and executed. Marisa J. Fuentes cites the testimony of Captain Cook, from the House of Commons Sessional Papers of 7 March 1791, in which he spoke of something that happened about ten years earlier:

> One instance in particular happened during my stay in Bridge Town, in Barbados, that appeared to us truly shocking – Returning home one evening with Major Fitch, of the 90th regiment, later than usual, we heard for a considerable distance the most dreadful cries that could come from a human being; and as we approached the square in Bridge Town, we found that those cries came from the house of a man that sold liquor,

> and we heard repeated application of the whip to a creature
> whom we apprehended to be dying . . . a Negro girl of about
> nineteen, chained to the floor, and nearly expiring with agony
> and the loss of blood.

Our only knowledge of the life of this unnamed woman is of her torture – and that only because it happened to be overheard. All that we know of her is all these passing white men knew of her: her suffering. How can we avoid writing histories that endlessly rehearse the violence against these dead women and render them forever the object of titillation and pity? How can we do more, asks Hartman, 'than recount the violence that deposited these traces in the archive'?

Is it possible to press against archival limits? In the late twentieth century, anecdotes and fragments were regarded as pretty worthless evidence. Historians in training were advised to amass a vast empirical base of quantifiable evidence from which to generalise, and to distrust sources that could not be corroborated. This is fine if they exist – but if we only tell the stories of those about whom we have copious sources, we will keep on telling the same stories of the people in power. Like the archive, we will be complicit in keeping the marginalised marginal. What might it mean, asks Hartman, 'to think historically . . . about life eradicated by the protocols of intellectual disciplines?'

One protocol we might usefully forsake is maintaining the voice of a distanced, omniscient narrator. Writing about historic motherhood, Knott trammelled her wide-ranging anecdotes by following the narrative of her own experience of becoming a mother – the quickening, birthing, nursing, holding and crying. Shifting from the third-person pronoun to writing in the first person is what Maggie Nelson has called 'presencing' – being present in one's own text. Knott describes it as a 'radical form of empathy' between past and present, historian and reader. It provides a narrative thread (and therefore a way of consuming history) where evidence tends to the fragmentary. It also foregrounds the lack of objectivity of which Carr warned us.

There is another pronoun shift that can reorient our thinking. Fuentes, who frequently encounters in her research harrowing testimonies like that above of those who witnessed the violent assault of enslaved women, suggests a technique borrowed from narrative history. Rather than repeating each scene from the point of view of the white male punisher or observer, instead reorient the narrative to see and feel it from the point of view of the woman in pain:

> In 1780 or 1781 a young unnamed enslaved woman 'about nineteen years old', chained to the floor inside her owner's tippling house near the 'square' . . . cried out so loudly she could be heard from 'a considerable distance'. Exhausted, bleeding, and near death, she struggled with consciousness after three separate beatings, each thirty-nine lashes, with the cowskin whip wielded by her owner. It was the sound of her straining voice . . . and the sharp noise of the whip hitting her body that brought Captain Cook and Major Fitch of the 90th Regiment inside the tavern to witness and attempt to stop her punishment. She heard them demand entrance . . .

It gives us, Fuentes says, 'an alternative way of witnessing these scenes'. The pivot isn't merely a storytelling technique; it is an ethical and empathetic approach that attempts to represent the agency of the silenced woman.

189

Shifting pronouns can take us closer to certain truths, but it isn't straightforward. I practised a version of it earlier when giving Brueysse's testimony against her rapist. I said Brueysse starts, 'It was in the month of April after your return from Castres . . .' – but because my source was in the third person, I don't actually know if she did say that. Word for word the record (in French) states: 'Said it was the month of April after his return from Castres.' Did Brueysse direct her answer to Bonnet? Given she was speaking French, and later Occitan, did she use the respectful *vous* or *vos* of a servant to a master, or the familiar and disrespectful *tu* of a woman to her rapist? Or might she, refusing to meet his eye, have defiantly directed her responses to the consistory, referring to Bonnet in the third person? 'It was in the month of April after *his* return from Castres.'

In asking those questions, I've employed another technique that scholars have suggested for these lost histories: to use the subjunctive to ask empathetic questions about 'what might have happened or might have been said or might have been done'. For example, of a disturbing early twentieth-century photograph of a nude prepubescent child reclining on a sofa, Saidiya Hartman writes,

> Anticipating the pressure of his hands, did she tremble? Did the painter hover above the sofa and arrange her limbs? Were his hands big and moist? Did they leave a viscous residue on the surface of her skin? Could she smell the odor of sweat, linseed oil, formaldehyde, and clothes worn for too many days? Did she notice the slippers, tattered shirt, and grubby pants, and then become frightened?

These questions could be called 'speculative' (a word historians use to insult each other), but by embracing speculation, Hartman makes us heed the silences of the archive. The archive offers nothing of the experience and feelings of this little Black girl, and the thousands of other obscured lives she represents, but these leading questions create imaginative possibilities – even if the ideas they contain cannot be verified.

Such questions are just one way in which Hartman tries to compose counter-histories that are written critically, creatively and speculatively. She dubs this 'critical fabulation' and says it is written 'at the intersection of the fictive and the historical'. She introduces techniques borrowed from novels to 'fashion a narrative, which is based upon archival research'. This means recreating scenes, transcribing indirect and reported speech into dialogue, stretching the narrative beyond the chronology of the archive, and posing counterfactuals. Elsewhere she gives the name 'close narration' to a technique by which her voice, direct quotations from the sources and speculative elements are interwoven. In *Wayward Lives, Beautiful Experiments* (2019), she uses these approaches to explore the lives of young Black women in the US in the early twentieth century. She argues that the archive produced by the state to legitimise the confinement and punishment of these women was itself full of fictions, fabrications and fabulations that rendered them criminal, deviant and pathological. This was a world in which, between 1882 and 1925, teenage girls could be arrested and imprisoned if they were judged 'in danger of becoming morally depraved' – a conclusion that could be reached if they had casual sexual encounters or serial relationships, went drinking and dancing, were out after dark or were found without 'just cause' outside their homes.

Hartman's work rests heavily on the official archive – the journals of rent collectors, sociological surveys, transcripts of trials, photographs of slums, reports by social workers and parole officers, criminal investigations, psychological interviews and prison case files – but it

> elaborates, augments, transposes, and breaks open archival documents . . . I have pressed at the limits of the case file and the document, speculated about what might have been, imagined the things whispered in dark bedrooms, and amplified moments of withholding, escape and possibility, moments when the vision and dreams of the wayward seemed possible.

A careful study of her text and notes shows how closely tethered she remains to the archive, even as she tries to consider the plausible but unprovable, and wrestles with what that archive will allow her to know or wants her to conclude. In so doing, Hartman builds on the work of scholars such as Natalie Zemon Davis, who noted in *The Return of Martin Guerre* that when confronted by inconclusive accounts, she did her 'best through other sources from the period and place to discover the world they would have seen and the reactions they might have had'. Davis described the result as 'in part my invention, but held tightly in check by the voices of the past'.

Yet, take away the words 'in part' and you have a description of Hilary Mantel's *Wolf Hall*. The techniques of reorienting scenes, critical fabulation, the subjunctive mood and close narration are fictive, not fictional – but at times it can be hard to see the difference. So what is the line between critical fabulation and historical fiction?

The honest answer is that it is Rizla-paper thin. Much of it depends on the integrity of the historian (often manifested in her footnotes). But I think it also depends on recognising that the archive itself isn't telling the whole truth and nothing but the truth. The silences, fabrications and violence in the archive mean that these are people about whom we are unlikely to ever have more sources. To demand more be found before their stories can be told is a way of choosing not to tell the stories of women – especially Black women. Reading against the grain, thick description and critical fabulation are methodologies that are appropriate when there is no other way to enter a story – because there is no other way. And, ultimately, we need them because the stories we tell about the past determine the nature of the present we live in and the future we're building.

In the end we cannot fully recover the lives of women dispossessed by history. Ours is a project premised on impossibility; there are many stories we will never know. 'Having been nothing in history . . . having left no identifiable trace around them, they don't have and never will have any existence outside the precarious domicile of these words,' wrote Foucault. They don't have and they never will have – but they did have. They did exist beyond these words. Ultimately, it is this that drives us – it is an act of love to do this recuperative work, even while we know we cannot fully retrieve them. And we can, at least, partially reclaim these women from oblivion. We can choose not to collude in the erasures and fictions of the archive or in promoting the narratives of the powerful, and we do so by reassessing our methodologies and the limits of our practice as historians. We can reject a blanket insistence on quantifiable data, large sample sizes, corroborative sources, and modes of thought and narration that rule out any reconsideration of lost female lives. We can imagine new ways of writing history. Why does it matter that we do? If we can write these new histories of women – and point out unflinchingly why we can only write them in these ways – then maybe men will no longer laugh at the idea that women might be important enough to talk about.

Selected Further Reading

Books

Robin Briggs, *The Witches of Lorraine* (Oxford: Oxford University Press, 2007)

Natalie Zemon Davis, *The Return of Martin Guerre* (Cambridge, MA: Harvard University Press, 1983)

Natalie Zemon Davis, *Women on the Margins: Three Seventeenth-Century Lives* (Cambridge, MA: Harvard University Press, 1997)

Marisa J. Fuentes, *Dispossessed Lives: Enslaved Women, Violence and the Archive* (Philadelphia: Pennsylvania Press, 2016)

Saidiya Hartman, *Wayward Lives, Beautiful Experiments: Intimate Histories of Social Upheaval* (New York: W.W. Norton, 2019)

Olwen Hufton, *The Prospect Before Her: A History of Women in Western Europe, 1500–1800* (London: HarperCollins, 1995), 2 vols

Sarah Knott, *Mother: An Unconventional History* (London: Penguin, 2019)

Suzannah Lipscomb, *The Voices of Nîmes: Women, Sex, and*

Marriage in Reformation Languedoc (Oxford: Oxford University Press, 2019)

Lyndal Roper, *Witch Craze: Terror and Fantasy in Baroque Germany* (New Haven and London: Yale University Press, 2004)

Camilla Townsend, *Malintzin's Choices: An Indian Woman in the Conquest of Mexico* (Albuquerque: University of New Mexico Press, 2006)

Michel-Rolph Trouillot, *Silencing the Past: Power and the Production of History* (Boston: Beacon Press, 1995)

Articles and chapters

Michel Foucault, 'Lives of Infamous Men', in *Power*, ed. James D. Faubion, trans. Robert Hurley et al. (New York, 1967), vol. 3, pp. 157–75

Catherine Gallagher and Stephen Greenblatt, 'Counterhistory and the Anecdote', in *Practicing New Historicism* (Chicago: University of Chicago Press, 2000), pp. 49–74

Saidiya Hartman, 'Venus in Two Acts', *Small Axe* 26 vol. 12, no. 2 (2008), 1–14

Seth Moglen, 'Enslaved in the City on a Hill: The Archive of Moravian Slavery and the Practical Past', *History of the Present* 6.2 (2016), 155–83

Diana Paton, 'Mary Williamson's letter, or Seeing Women and Sisters in the Archives of Atlantic Slavery', *Transactions of the Royal Historical Society* 29 (2019), 153–79

Mary Elizabeth Perry, 'Finding Fatima: A Slave Woman of Early Modern Spain', *Journal of Women's History* 20.1 (2008), 151–67

Stephanie E. Smallwood, 'The Politics of the Archive and

History's Accountability to the Enslaved', *History of the Present* 6.2 (2016), 117–32

Wendy Anne Warren, '"The Cause of Her Grief": The Rape of a Slave in Early New England', *Journal of American History* 93.4 (2007), 1031–49

Chapter 12

How do we write the history of religion?

Miri Rubin

The historical study of religion is probably one of the areas that E.H. Carr described as posing 'fundamental challenges . . . to the current way of doing things'. In recent years, the study of systems of belief has changed as a result of the introduction of research and approaches by historians whose inquiries were not mainly anchored in their own religious beliefs and commitments. The new histories of religion more broadly have been informed by other concerns, and reflect the radical diversification of the study of history and its aims. We should study religion in the past by considering how we have come to do so in recent years. In the second half of the twentieth century new approaches developed which still inform our practice and which continue to be revised and refined. As one who studies Europe over half a millennium or so following c.1000, I share with you the developments in the study of that long period. These have often been pioneering and have inspired historians of other times and places.

The new history of religion is practised by a wide range of scholars and informed by a whole range of new questions and methods. While religion had been treated as a thing apart, pertaining to a spiritual realm and operating within a providential order, it is now treated as a human phenomenon of great significance, rich and dynamic, yet amenable to all the methods of inquiry that the humanities employ: religious texts are subject to literary analysis, religious rituals can be interpreted with the help of anthropology, religious institutions can be seen as political operations, and theologies can be understood through the operation of gender.

The study of religion had for centuries been the practice of clerics and a form of religious work. It was usually associated with particular institutions – monasteries, the papacy – and fitted recent events into established schemes of Christian history, often beginning with Creation. The Reformations introduced a strong polemical element into writing the history of religion, and a purposive 'rewriting' of history by Catholics and Protestants, each still within a providential framework which supported the truth claims of their respective faiths. As Christianity became increasingly diverse, and extended its global reach, attempts at sacred history encompassed new regions, achievements and failures. These prevailed into and beyond the eighteenth century, when another orientation in the history of religion developed – a critique not of any strand of Christianity but of religion in general. The most powerful example is Edward Gibbon's *The History of the Decline and Fall of the Roman Empire* (1766–1788), a rewriting of the history of Rome through a critique of Christian institutions and devotional styles, such as monasticism.

The history of religion took another turn in the nineteenth century as history writing became a profession often supported by states and practised in universities. Be it the Republican orientation of French education, or the blend of Anglicanism and nationhood which characterised English scholarship, writers of the history of religion aligned it with a path to nationhood, and to the essential characteristics of that nation. And practitioners of religious history usually dealt with the 'confession' or denomination to which they were born; when Catholics treated Protestants it was often to attack. Much history of religion was written by priests or ministers and, in the Catholic tradition, by monks and some nuns. They brought to their writings a certain immersive expertise, of course, but in many cases also a preordained sense of historical explanation and purpose.

All this means that religion is no longer studied as a thing apart; indeed, the opening up of the study of religion to historians and their whole array of methods has resulted in its being one of the most fertile areas of history. Pioneers who have inspired generations of historians have honed their efforts in studies of religious faith and practice: Caroline Walker Bynum has innovated by exploring the importance of the body in religious practice and experience in the Middle Ages; Natalie Zemon Davis has demonstrated the underlying ritual patterns of religious violence in sixteenth-century France; Eamon Duffy has studied parish-based religion embedded in local materials and artefacts and recorded in churchwardens' accounts; Carlo Ginzburg sought personal religious beliefs in the most impersonal records of the Inquisition; Lyndal Roper has shown the operation of gender in Protestant households; and R.W. Scribner noted deep continuities in devotional habits even across the period marked by the Lutheran Reformation. This opening up of the sphere of religion to new modes of inquiry was conducted in two interlocking manners: bringing new approaches to bear upon religion, and identifying new types of sources, textual and later visual and material, which bear witness to past experiences of religion.

Religion as a cultural system

The early twentieth century saw a number of influential efforts to systematise the study of religion just as its influence in the (Western) world seemed to be waning. Max Weber (1864–1920) associated modernity with Protestantism as a religion of personal responsibility which also oriented people towards flourishing in worldly affairs. Emile Durkheim (1858–1917) developed a universal model for religion's role in social life, delivered through the rhythms of ritual. At the same time anthropologists, whose work arose from ethnographic engagement, explored the interconnectedness of all aspects of life – including treating the supernatural – within belief systems they were able to observe, notably Bronisław Malinowski (1884–1942) and E. E. Evans-Pritchard (1902–1973) in their ethnography of magic and cosmology. Religion had a logic and delivered ends – it had a function – in support of hierarchy, binding kinship, explaining the cosmos and offering remedies to illness and loss – what we may call magic. Their works, and those of post-war anthropologists, especially Mary Douglas (1921–2007) and Clifford Geertz (1926–2006), offered those historians in search of approaches to religion useful concepts and tools. Geertz taught historians to see religion 'as a cultural system' and explore its power to underpin all social and political relations; and Douglas encouraged historians to understand the preoccupation with purity and danger at the heart of so many religious rituals.

What does this mean for historians? To see religion as a cultural system is to understand it as a language with its internal logic, its registers, styles and complex meanings. Language is a system, it has rules, and historians profited from understanding those rules and their manifestations in practice. Social historians sought relations between classes and the making of hierarchy through religion, and feminists emphasised the rules of gender incorporated into religious life. The move was also one from institutions to communities, from the history of doctrines and the structures which supported them to the uses of religion in lives, in place, and in practice. Religion became as diverse as the people who lived it, in the sense that all religion was the religion of people in communities, but religious institutions also had the power to inform, persuade and coerce. Some parts of the array of religious behaviours were deemed heretical, and invited the attention of courts and inquisitors. Hence both the wide range of beliefs and the responses to them that now form the subject matter of the history of religion.

This historical approach removed the privilege of official religion and placed alongside it other types of authority and influence in religious life. Historians turned to mystics and hermits, to charismatic preachers, to those deemed overzealous or odd, and treated as witches or heretics. Above all, the exploration of women in religion has extended the realisation of how religion manifested itself in people's lives.

Women and gender

History so often reflects the mood of civil society and as more women attended universities, became academics and conducted research in the second half of the twentieth century, some of them pursued the feminist questions raised in their lifetimes by second-wave feminism. The study of religion benefited from this energy too, and especially for those periods when religion was hegemonic and central to the understanding of all aspects of life. Historians of medieval and early modern Europe responded creatively, and they did so by discovering hitherto little-known voices of religion: the twelfth-century abbess Hildegard of Bingen of the Rhineland, who was a prolific mystic, composer and scientific writer; the mystic and religious polemicist Marguerite Porete from northern France who was burnt at the stake in 1310; the wife, mother, then traveller and mystic Margery Kempe from a patrician family in Lynn in Norfolk; and many more. What began as an expectation that a 'female voice' might be found soon gave way; there were conservative voices, and radically alternative ones; women who welcomed the consolation of male priesthood, and those who challenged it. Caroline Bynum made an important intervention in 1987 that has inspired a great deal of research and understanding since: that women seem to have identified most particularly with the suffering body of Christ and with the humility of his sacrifice.

Alongside these early studies of women who left religious texts or had merited admiring biographies – hagiographies – more modest lives in religion were revealed through engagement with other types of sources. The Church sponsored inquisition and inquiry into suspect religious belief and practice, and these have left us with records of investigations, including the testimonies of individuals. From southern France and northern Italy in the thirteenth century, in parts of the Holy Roman Empire in the fourteenth, and from fifteenth-century eastern England the voices of women and men, explaining their religious beliefs, emerge: often highly critical of the Church, often expressive of private religious understandings: they readily expressed the view that contact with God did not depend on the priest and his work at the altar. These were often sceptical of clerical authority, and expressed an unmediated and highly emotional interest in the suffering of Jesus and his mother the Virgin Mary. Feminist historians also inquired into the gendered nature of the language of religion: in hagiography, devotional writings, and visual representations of saints. Women have been shown to have been active in religious voluntary organisations – known as confraternities – which spread from the thirteenth century, where a more intense devotional experience was promoted than that in the parish. These were hubs for the enactment of religious drama, penitential processions, collective recitation and chant, and the commemoration of dead members.

Studying the religion of those women who devoted their lives to religion outside institutional settings was often a turn to non-Latin texts by or about them, and this in itself is a step towards making the field of religious experience more diverse, moving it beyond the clergy, theology, doctrine and church administration. Indeed, from those who have studied religious texts for and by women has emerged the term 'vernacular theology'. It aims to acknowledge the existence of a realm of reflection on theological questions outside of universities, within women's communities and even by lone women in their solitudes. Such was Angela da Foligno (1248–1309), who turned her room in her parental home into a 'cell', and there received visions but also reflected on the nature of Christ. Or the religious woman from Brabant, Juliana of Mount Cornillion, who reflected on the absence of a

Eucharistic feast in the Christian calendar and so lobbied with her bishop, and ultimately the pope, for the creation of Corpus Christi, one of the most substantial Christian feasts.

As historians refined their understanding of women's religion they noted that while it was always a sphere which caused anxiety, and so oppressive action, on the part of many ecclesiastical leaders this was not a universal response. Some religious men found inspiration in the devotions and religious leadership offered by abbesses; others saw in exemplary women useful models for lay religion more broadly, and hence wrote hagiographic accounts of the exemplary religious women who had impressed them. Prominent religious women frequently caused dispute between those men who wielded authority over their lives. Such men could disagree as to whether inspired women were a good thing or bad, though they all agreed women could not teach or preach.

Some of the questions arising from this better acquaintance with the religious lives of women have helped historians think about lay religion in general. Women's religion was vernacular, with some access to Latin in liturgy, and so was that of most lay (that is, non-clerical) people. Lay people all depended on the sacramental authority of priests, but also sought to enhance their own involvement. Women contributed to the upkeep of parish churches with the crafts they used in their homes; lay people participated in processions, and were invited to respond to religious drama by responding to Latin cues with vernacular ones.

At its outset the new history of religion sought to identify a realm of 'popular religion' apart from and in some opposition to official scripts taught and legislated by church authorities. As research became more diverse, and its results ample, what has emerged is a picture – varied by region – of a quite active and creative involvement of lay people in religious life. They did so by reading and writing vernacular religion, by creating voluntary religious organisations, and in efforts to personalise religion for themselves and their families, in their professional organisations, cities and communities. In doing so, they engaged professional religious people, used – and shared – skills of reading and writing, and embraced many of the opportunities to feel, hear, touch and smell religion. For religion was material in its conception and was delivered through the senses.

Material religion, emotions and the senses

Christianity introduced a God made Flesh in a clear break from its Jewish origins, and so it became a religion preoccupied with the body and with the material traces of the divine. God was made flesh: his body left its marks on the landscape, sanctified places in the Holy Land, and appeared even after death to his followers before ascending to heaven. By the twelfth century Europeans were taught that at the altar each priest consecrated bread and wine into Christ's own body. The places and body parts of saints offered the hope of intimate contact with virtue and the power to heal. Europe was criss-crossed with pilgrimage routes superimposed on the routes of trade and communication. Materiality was at the heart of the Christian experience, in its liturgy, in the spaces created and adorned for worship, and in the belief in a God whose human body could be consumed – in the form of bread – by every believer. This sacrament, and all others, were operations of 'invisible grace' through the visible sign of matter: holy water in baptism or blessed chrism for the anointing of those on their deathbed.

Holy remnants and the sites that contained them, and Christ's body itself, were joined by holy books. The word made flesh was also the word written down in the gospels, and the book became a central emblem of Christianity. Books represented Christian truth even to those who could not read; books were displayed at processions, made luxuriously beautiful, and crafting books occupied the waking hours of many monks. Historians of religion and historians of the book now work together in their efforts to trace the many uses of books – as objects, as containers of knowledge, as symbols of authority – in religion. Books contained more than words – they were filled with figurative images and diagrams, devotional emblems and musical notation. Access to them was determined by vocation, education and wealth: in the first millennium monasteries contained most books; from around 1400 so many books of prayer owned by lay people in England and France have survived that historians are able to study quite intimate habits of prayer and devotion.

People handled their prayer books, read from them, heard the sound of leaves turned over, and they chanted from them. But even without these aids to devotion, Christian life involved a great deal of sense experience at its core. Bells marked the passing of the hours and called Christians to prayer; lights marked out holy spaces, especially at the altar and in processions; incense reminded believers of the operations of the Holy Spirit, and marked the entry into churches and chapels, where distinctive sound of voices in song and prayer were to be heard. All life is a sense experience, but religious life had its own array of prompts and appeals to the senses. Historians have now recognised this, and work to incorporate sound, image, smell and texture into their research.

Work with images started early and it is hard now to think how religion was ever understood without them. Even modest parish churches were decorated with imagery in support of basic tenets, depicting habitually the Crucifixion, Heaven and Hell, the Virgin Mary and Child, as well as biblical tales. Images also informed more private meditations, as they interacted with prayers within prayer books. By the fourteenth century, the demand for images was so great that craftsmen experimented with methods of mechanical reproduction of engravings to meet the demand, efforts that were precursors to the development of print in the following century. Similarly, mass-produced books, pilgrimage badges and devotional figurines were being produced and traded in the thousands across Europe, reminding us of the intersection of craft, religious interests and economic capability in the making of the material culture of religion in Europe. Consumption in the religious sphere went hand in hand with new technologies and the development of specialist markets in Europe over the later medieval period.

Creative ingenuity responded to religious ideas and enriched the life of Europeans through a material culture available for personal use or collective appreciation. Think of the exciting idea of the Shrine Madonna: a sculpture of the Virgin hollowed out as a container that can be opened. Here is a material realisation of the idea that Mary's body contained the divine and gave birth to a saviour. Or think of the rosary: a simple chain of beads, each associated with the invocation of the Virgin or memories of the Passion, a devotional aid developed in the very late fifteenth century and which has since become the mainstay of Catholic personal religion. These could range from simple wooden beads on a string to carefully engraved silver beads on a gold chain.

Matter afforded cues for devotional action and tactile support for personal prayer. Objects such as these are ideas shaped into matter and activated into practice. They now also attract the attention of historians of religion.

Religious diversity, influence and exchange

Everything we have seen so far shows that the study of religion has sought to include a broader set of historical actors, to identify practices alongside norms and prescriptions, and to appreciate the materiality of religious life. No doubt prompted by the valuing of diversity in our own societies, there is a greater recognition of coexistence and intertwining, sometimes hybridity, in the life of Jews, Christians and Muslims – and in some regions with Armenians, Greeks and Cumans. Relations between these religions carried different qualities. The attitude to Jews was a fundamental feature of Christianity, and it was expressed through ideas of Supersession – that Christianity replaced the claims of Judaism – and with an array of narratives, many born in the Middle Ages, which imputed to Jews evil intent towards Christians. Jews were present in most European cities, often in long-standing settled communities, yet also set apart by the practice of their religion and some limitations on their civic rights.

Thinking about the Jewish presence in Christianity concentrates historical attention on the cultural processes by which religion is formed and experienced. Polemic is one such mode: religious identity fortified by definition and opposition to another. This process of identification of Christianity's 'others' – the process of invention, of definition, and sometimes of persecution too – was highlighted influentially in R.I. Moore's book of 1987,

The Formation of a Persecuting Society. His argument sees the establishment of the authority of the Church in the twelfth century through the development of knowledge and institutions – in religious education, theology, education, law, liturgy – but also through the definition of what was un-Christian: heretic, Jews, prostitute. This meant that Christian intellectuals developed ways of portraying Jews as mirrors for reflection on Christian identity, even as Christian monarchs sought to regulate and secure Jews' presence in their states as vehicles for economic and commercial growth. Historians and art historians have identified the intensification of preoccupation with Jews' presence in Christian history. Jews with evil intent were painted into scenes of the Crucifixion by 1200, as they had not been in earlier centuries, and in devotional poetry they were depicted as the special enemies of the Virgin Mary. In the tense and violent decades after the Black Death, Jews and others – witches, Muslims, Hussites, usurers – were all painted as dangers to Christian well-being. The rhetoric of 'othering' was carried over in the sixteenth century to describe Protestants, as the preoccupation with religious difference now encompassed other Christians alongside non-Christians. On all sides, rulers became more involved in securing orthodoxy and regulating religious life.

Global religion – religion and politics

Our discussion of the historical study of religion began with the move towards a broad array of actors and phenomena: to women, to active lay people, to the vernacular languages, to religion in practice. This was a move away from elites and institutions in Church and society. Yet the global turn of European history and of historians' interest in it has meant that attention is redrawn to the convergence of states and religion, and the action of missionaries and religious orders. Yet all the themes we have discussed above are used by historians as they explore global Christianity, since European Christian ideas and practices travelled with conquerors and settlers; these eventually and inevitably influenced each other. Fernando Cervantes has explored ideas about the devil as these interacted with the beliefs of Native Americans; Romain Bertrand has explored the operation of ideas about witchcraft when applied in the tense setting of the Philippines a decade after the Spanish conquest; and David Irving has studied how Indigenous music was blended by missionaries with Christian chants to create a hybrid form of experience for the many new Christians they were making in the Philippines. Yet the global turn requires attention to structures of power and violence differently sustained and deployed than they were in Europe. And these in turn require an understanding of the religious and political ideas that underpinned the Protestant and Catholic global extension.

The historical study of religion is now clearly marked by a variety of approaches. Historians do not so much expect conformity to an ideal type in religious life, but expect religion to appear in their sources as a subject of contention, as a field for creativity, and one to be used for the establishment of authority. With its powerful narratives and engaging rituals religion lives even among those who proclaim no religious faith; it sets standards in aesthetics and ethics. And since around the world religion is still proclaimed as the highest authority by many individuals and polities, we must work to understand its operations. Here history is our surest guide.

Selected Further Reading

Annabel S. Brett, *Changes of State: Nature and the Limits of the City in Early Modern Natural Law* (Princeton: Princeton University Press, 2011)

Caroline Walker Bynum, *Holy Feast and Holy Fast: The Religious Significance of Food to Medieval Women* (Berkeley: University of California Press, 1987)

Caroline Walker Bynum, *Christian Materiality: An Essay on Religion in Late Medieval Europe* (Princeton: Princeton University Press, 2011)

Madeline H. Caviness, *Visualizing Women in the Middle Ages: Sight, Spectacle, and Scopic Economy* (Philadelphia: Pennsylvania University Press, 2001)

Fernando Cervantes, *The Devil in the New World. The Impact of Diabolism in New Spain* (New Haven: Yale University Press, 1997)

Fiona J. Griffiths, *Nuns' Priests' Tales: Men and Salvation in Medieval Women's Monastic Life* (Philadelphia: Pennsylvania University Press, 2018)

D.R.M. Irving, *Colonial Counterpoint: Music in Early Modern Manila* (Oxford: Oxford University Press, 2010)

R.I. Moore, *The Formation of a Persecuting Society: Authority and Deviance in Western Europe, 950–1250* (Oxford: Blackwell, 1987, second edn. 2006)

Miri Rubin, *Corpus Christi: the Eucharist in Late Medieval Culture* (Cambridge: Cambridge University Press, 1991)

Ulinka Rublack (ed.), *Protestant Empires: Globalizing the Reformations*, (Cambridge: Cambridge University Press, 2020)

Reima Valimaki, *Heresy in Late Medieval Germany.*
The Inquisitor Petrus Zwicker and the Waldensians
(Woodbridge: Boydell Press, 2019)

Chapter 13

Why family history matters

Emily Brand

Like that of any self-respecting aristocrat, the life of Vita Sackville-West was drenched in family history. At twelve, to the bemusement of her parents, she formed her 'earliest ambition': to appear at a dinner party 'in a sheet representing a ghost, in order to recite an epic poem composed by myself on the various exploits of my ancestors'. As an adult she styled her hair in imitation of pictures of long-dead relatives, and wove her ancestry into her fiction and non-fiction. The most direct of these, the family biography *Knole and the Sackvilles* (1922), closed with the death of her grandfather in 1908: he 'became a name like the others, and his portrait took its place among the rest, with a label recording the date of his birth and death'. With one final breath he passed seamlessly from 'family' to 'family history'.

Admittedly, it is easy to cultivate this particular vision of the past with ready access to centuries of well-preserved heirlooms, records and traditions – and all the more tempting to do so if it sets *us* on a more advantageous footing. As a result, family history has long been a favourite trove of treasures for the privileged, who have in return unhelpfully bestowed upon it a lingering whiff of conservatism, antiquarianism and self-indulgence. In reality, a century after the publication of Sackville-West's *Knole*, the turning of a collective cold shoulder by those seeking to understand 'proper' history amounts to dismissing a potential historical goldmine.

First, a distinction between two related concepts. The study of *genealogy*, strictly speaking, involves the compilation of names, dates and places to construct the framework for a family 'tree'. (I have always preferred the imagery of 'roots' – in a messy, egalitarian tangle, stretching to goodness knows where – over the neat medieval vision of (often male-focused) branches and less important (often female) leaves. But that is perhaps less aesthetically pleasing.) For colour, character and meaning, we must delve into *family history*, taking into account an endless list of factors – including social context, gender, ethnicity, geography, profession – and creating a narrative to breathe some life back into the dead. In the words of Scottish historian Adam Ferguson in 1798, 'Mere names of Father & Son with dates & Successions always vanish from my recollection . . . I need some adventure or trait of Character to give them Substance and make an impression.'

Though the disciplines of *history* and *family history* have been set on different paths, they are entwined and inseparable, sharing many of the same tools, methods and objectives. (This is perhaps demonstrated most explicitly in the correlative but distinct work on the social history of the family, as pioneered by scholars such as Lawrence Stone and Philippe Ariès.) The best way to counter outdated views about the histories of specific families is simply to bridge this gap by writing them, and writing them *well*, with all the scholarly rigour and resources at our disposal. But can writing – and reading – such focused narratives really tell us anything *new* about our shared past, or shed light on other avenues of historical inquiry? What does the popular hunger for family history tell us about our present, and could it even influence the future?

While it is often valued and articulated in culturally distinct ways, the desire to feel connected to our ancestors is a deeply human impulse that transcends era, culture and class. We find it in ancient Rome, where family memory and emulation of one's forebears were a key tenet of the virtuous citizen. We see it in the oral traditions of the West African *griots,* who commit generations of history to memory; and of the Māori, for whom the concept of a genealogy of all things, or *whakapapa*, functions as an explanatory framework for the world. In other societies it has co-existed as a means of private commemoration and – less creditably – a dubious route to power.

It is unsurprising that a preoccupation with *lineage* in particular should squat at the heart of Western culture. As the nations of Europe were forged, hierarchies of power – from the monarchy itself, to hereditary peerage, to simple ownership of property – centred on a system of dynasty and inheritance. Kinship connections were also instrumental in the birth of America, where politically loaded genealogical questions can still threaten to make or mar a career. The blossoming of popular print in the eighteenth century made the unwieldy British pedigree an easier beast to tame, as comprehensive peerage lists became widely available. Elsewhere, the less privileged meditated on their ancestry in other ways: generations of births and deaths scrawled in bibles; family groups immortalised in embroidery, and decorated with flowers and hearts; names carved into heirloom chests by the successive generations of women who owned them.

During the nineteenth century the professionalisation of history as a discipline took a chisel to the study of genealogy: first dislodging it to form its own subsidiary line of inquiry, and then relegating it to the domain of the hobbyist. In 1897, John Franklin Jameson – a professional historian and key figure in the establishment of the American Historical Association – lambasted the pointless 'addiction of historical societies to genealogies'. 'Volumes upon volumes of it have been printed', he complained. 'Search through the whole tiresome mass, and do you get a handful of historical wheat out of all this chaff, this pitiful accumulation of names and dates?' This reluctance to take something so popular seriously has not quite been shaken off, and conflation of 'genealogy' with 'family history' has seen both swept up in similar criticism.

Nonetheless, both have since flourished on either side of the Atlantic. Since the 1970s especially, hundreds of institutions have sprung up to professionalise, promote, and codify standards of practice. This reflected and facilitated an explosion of popular interest often attributed in part to the success of the 1976 novel *Roots*, in which the author, Alex Haley, 'traces' an African American ancestry and claims to be reunited with a lost heritage. In recent decades this reciprocal, supply-and-demand relationship has been mirrored by the advent of the internet and the accessibility of historical records databases, plus the popularity of television shows hooked on family history. Both tap into the attraction of narrative-driven family histories, but also provide audiences with the impetus and the tools they need to begin their own.

At the dawn of the 2020s, answers around the legitimacy and value of family history as a discipline are yet to be settled. The combination of scholarly disinterest and the (admittedly growing) issue of crowd-sourced databases being flooded with the errors of inexperienced contributors does little to rescue the field from those old accusations of unreliability and irrelevance. And yet, we are presented time and again with powerful examples of how ancestry is inextricably bound up in our understanding of not just the past, but ourselves and the societies in which we live. Perhaps more than anything else, the continued uses – and misuses – of our shared pasts offer enlightening testament to why the narratives we choose to tell about family history matter.

The writing of family history can take many forms, from century-sweeping non-fiction to intimate group biographies, or a focus on a particular historical moment through the eyes of one family. In some cultures it is more meaningfully expressed in verse or song. It forms the basis of documentaries, dramas and museum interpretation. The benefits range from the purely practical to the deeply personal. The uses of genetic testing in predicting and treating inherited illnesses are a vital medical development but – being tied more closely to DNA than to family history – lie beyond the scope of this essay. But the written word also wields influence, as we can see in the ways ancestral narratives can be employed to promote not just individual reflection but also popular understanding of, and engagement with, wider histories.

First is the question of individual identity. Both the living and the dead provide endless testimonies to the deeply personal power of ancestry as a means of forming a sense of identity, or a feeling of 'belonging'. Modern surveys of those conducting family history research tend to elicit a common motivation: they want to investigate 'who they are', where they 'came from', and how they fit into the vast swell of history. This introspective impulse is often criticised as egotistical and trivial, but it can lead us in many positive directions.

The pull to locate our own beginnings is inevitably particularly strong for those who have been somehow disconnected from their ancestry, whether by adoption, migration, a family history of enslavement, or the systematic destruction of cultures. In these circumstances, filling in and understanding those blanks can be life-alteringly formative and emotionally cathartic. Investigations can also create a new site for family bonding as an untapped network of kinship opens up. More generally, narratives about the past can offer an (admittedly sometimes dubious) device for explaining aspects of ourselves. Most traditionally the concept of exalted lineage – whether distinguished by wealth or some heroic deed – can be used to shed a sort of lustre on its descendants (merited or otherwise). The Romantic poet and ancestry devotee Lord Byron found solace in a supposed 'inheritance of storms', which he felt not only explained his streaks of misfortune but also justified his unruly behaviour. 'It is ridiculous to say', he insisted, 'that we do not inherit our passions, as well as the gout, or any other disorder.'

It can also stir artistic and professional output. Like Byron, novelist Thomas Hardy continually ruminated on the melancholy idea of fallen pedigree and it infused much of his fiction and poetry. Family narratives can inspire careers, prompting people to emulate admired relatives – in the military, for example – or devote their professional lives to tackling those intriguing unanswered questions. The 2020 documentary *Enslaved* showcased the work of maritime archaeology group Diving with a Purpose, which protects, documents and interprets African slave trade shipwrecks. Many of its members spoke directly of their wish to restore a voice to silenced ancestors, and the emotional gravity of their work was movingly reflected in their responses to both successful expeditions and those memories and experiences that proved impossible to recover.

With our sense of self more comfortably settled, those histories can then communicate our identity to the outside world. In 1711 Jonathan Swift's friend Anne Long requested that he 'make a pedigree' that she could present to her new neighbours: 'the people here want sadly to know what I am'. (In a society built on kinship and patronage, questions were evidently forthcoming.) Vita Sackville-West went further, as writing her family history enabled her to reassert her own place within it. Though her sex barred her from inheriting her beloved Knole Park – which passed instead to her uncle – through her writing she found a way to possess and inhabit it in print.

In an increasingly secular society, perched between these private meditations and public displays is an attempt to wrestle with one of the biggest questions of all. At its most existential, exploring one's family identity – and crucially *passing on that knowledge* – can even provide a means of coping with the concept of mortality, as we create a legacy of stored knowledge for the next generation.

Second, reflecting thoughtfully on our ancestral connections can nudge us towards lasting shifts in *collective* memory and identity. Exploring history through this lens often complicates an established picture, forcing us to question how we view the past. For some – especially those already nursing a particular idea about where they 'come from' – the results can be disarming. In her own sweeping account of her family history, author Alison Light describes how discovering generations of migration across twelve different countries not only unsettled her idea of 'Englishness' but also highlighted the arbitrariness of imposing national boundaries over the vagaries of human life. In an age still fired up by 'patriotic' spirit, this perspective – cultivated en masse – could invite important public discussions about national identity and the popular imagination. An optimist might even hope that by inquiring into and acknowledging its own diversity, an informed society would be more inclined towards toleration and acceptance.

Elsewhere, it can help to foster a sense of affinity among people with shared roots in migrant or diaspora communities. Crucially, elevating and giving texture to these stories (which are often based on less 'traditional' sources) has the effect of inspiring further research elsewhere; it can even act as a clarion call to others with the means to assist in populating the historical blanks, or simply raise awareness of what has been lost. We see it in the institutions established by the families of Holocaust survivors concerned with erasure and remembrance, and in the defiant reactions of some who – after decades of legitimate residence in the UK – faced deportation during the Windrush scandal of 2018. The website of Black Lives Matter Los Angeles overtly states that the organisation 'draws deeply from spirituality and the path forged by our mightiest Ancestors'. Family history can be activism, and a means of reclaiming and reshaping a hereditary story of grief or loss.

On the other side of the coin lie dark collective pasts, steeped in shame or hatred. How are Nazi affiliations or other historic

WHY FAMILY HISTORY MATTERS

crimes to be reckoned with? The answer is not to be found in the response of actor Ben Affleck, who in 2015 requested that details about his slave-owning ancestors be omitted from US documentary *Finding Your Roots* – as controversy erupted he could merely cite 'embarrassment'. Uncomfortable as it may be, it is only in choosing to confront and articulate our response to these painful narratives that we can hope to comprehend what happened – and effectively challenge similar patterns in modern times.

Third, writing family history wields unparalleled potential for stimulating popular engagement with history in general. Genealogical research is often identified as the third most popular online pursuit (after shopping and pornography). The incurably addicted describe it as a 'gateway drug' to an appreciation for the wider past, as experimenters are transported to the heart of the industrial revolution, the Irish famine or the trenches of the First World War. In many cases, centring the narrative of a family in the midst of such Great Events makes them infinitely more manageable – in the words of literature academic Jerome de Groot, it offers a way to 'navigate through the chaos of the past'. Though never providing a definitive account, it teases out the immediacy of lived experience. In light of this, the yawning chasm between the popular pursuit and the academic world is all the more disappointing. In an age when 'history' is increasingly recognised to belong to everyone, surely bridging the gap would be mutually constructive?

Certainly, increased scholarly input would only add to the continuing professionalisation of the discipline, as well as offering vitalising context and theoretical approaches. Less accepted, unfortunately, is the notion that academia itself could benefit from collaboration with family history. The tools, perspectives and skills honed by focused training in genealogy are rarely incorporated into formal academic education, at least not before specialist postgraduate study. And yet, for the biographer and social historian, they are essential to understanding networks of kinship and the formative influence of ancestry. The necessity of revisiting genealogical records rather than relying on nineteenth-century myth or misunderstanding is often totally neglected. It was even the apparatus of family history that enabled one of the most significant historical discoveries in Britain in modern times: the identification of the remains of Richard III – having been unearthed in a Leicester car park – by tracing a living descendant and matching their DNA.

Looking outwards, the demand for genealogy has directly facilitated the accessibility of historical records that are mined by amateurs and academics alike – first in influencing the use of archives, and then in a hunger for online subscription databases. The sheer weight of its commercial appeal has generated astonishing growth, digitisation and preservation in the wider historical field. If part of the impetus behind scholarly research is to seek wider impact by informing and engaging the public, it seems short-sighted that this existing clamour for history has not been harnessed or even recognised as legitimate.

Of course, such a vision could only be accomplished by emphasising and providing a foundation for the proper respect and rigour due to all historical disciplines. Waters can always be muddied by those who don't properly interrogate their evidence or thoughtfully communicate their findings, and the emotional charge of ancestry is its greatest power and its greatest peril. As with any related field, those who write family history have a responsibility not to misuse it. History has shown that such narratives about the past can be manipulated – even weaponised – in dangerous ways.

Just as family history has the power to impact positively on both the personal and the public, it can also lead us in more troubling directions. Though inevitably influenced by biases and wishful thinking, we must approach our own family histories with an open mind; writing the family history of *others* must always be navigated with care and respect. Not everyone is so fastidious, and not everyone finds the validation they may have been seeking.

The flipside of family history's capacity to confer a sense of identity is that it can also pull a comfortable rug out from underneath us. At its most benign, this might mean we have to come to terms with the fact that an idolised 'ancestor' has no connection to us whatsoever. (I once faced the awkward task of breaking such news to someone who had already commissioned a set of ceramic wares emblazoned with the said Civil War hero's face.) At its worst it can undercut our entire sense of self, even prompting an identity crisis that might take years to resolve. Writing for the *Guardian* in 2018, translator Sequoya Yiaueki lamented the unsolicited discovery – via a DNA test taken by his sister – that he was not of Susquehannock heritage as he had been raised to believe. His father's lies, apparently born of little more than a whim, had profound consequences. 'The stories I have told about myself my whole life are based on certain material aspects that my narrative self depended on', Yiaueki explained. 'Now, I am working from a fractured narrative.'

A concern with genealogy lies at the heart of American society, and routinely expresses itself in political discourse. The presidency of Barack Obama stimulated discussion ranging from one genealogical society's claim in 2008 that he was related to a gaggle of former US presidents (plus Winston Churchill and Brad Pitt), to Donald Trump's self-serving and baseless claims that he was not a legitimate US citizen. In 2018 Senator Elizabeth Warren's long-standing claim of Cherokee roots gained the spotlight, culminating in a DNA test and criticism among her opponents and the Native American community. While the former simply accused Warren of asserting Indigenous ancestry to advance her career, representatives of the Cherokee Nation objected on the grounds that tribal citizenship is rooted in centuries of cultural kinship, not in the bloodline. Suggesting otherwise not only imposed an irrelevant 'settler-colonial' definition of Indigenous identity but dishonoured its legitimate citizens. In a nation forged from immigration and colonisation, divergent definitions of kinship and claims about heritage, identity and appropriation are weighted with particular political significance.

Perpetrated on a broader scale, myth-making can have worrying implications for the public imagination, politics, and even race relations. The emotive punch of family history and collective memory – often entirely unburdened by authentic scholarship – can be unscrupulously re-purposed by those with a particular agenda. The twentieth century provides ample evidence for discomfiting relationships between ancestry, nationalism, immigration and eugenics – and the horrors that can follow. Historian Honor Sachs has also pointed out the 'regressive potential' of ancestral inquiry, highlighting how the explosion of interest in genealogy in the 1970s led to a revival of white supremacist sentiment. The trend threatens to revive with the growing accessibility of DNA testing, which opens the door to easily weaponised concepts of racial 'purity' as well as opportunities for appropriation. Whatever science can tell us here, it is the narrative we form around it that matters.

Challenges to entrenched national stories, however gentle, will inevitably spark backlash. In 2020 the National Trust faced outrage for 'tarnishing' and 'rewriting' British history simply for highlighting connections between stately homes and wealth generated by transatlantic slavery. But attempts to deceive, to exploit or to cast an unhelpful, rose-tinted lens onto ancestral narratives can only be undermined by properly informed counter-efforts like this – here the narrative power of family history comes into its own. In an increasingly polarised world, this seems all the more important.

The future of family history promises to continue in its recent trend of rapid expansion and evolution, and to become even more firmly instrumental to how archives operate. Technological advances will inevitably reflect and respond to the popular fascination with tracing our genealogies, accelerating and shifting the nature of historical research itself as it goes. Without intervention, the wildly profitable collaboration between public archives and private corporations – such as the National Archives and FindMyPast – is also likely to further consolidate the focus of this type of research firmly outside of academia, and encourage millions of 'amateur' hobbyists to contribute. It is a species of participatory history that offers an accessible, digestible and meaningful route through daunting and challenging topics – but it also deserves a more reputable place within the wider field.

Like the now pervasive fields of social history, gender history and local history before it, family history still suffers from a dearth of scholarly respect and theoretical study. Thankfully, countless non-academic institutions – including the Society of Genealogists, the Family History Federation and the Institute of Heraldic and Genealogical Studies – have for decades been rising to the challenge of promoting and professionalising the discipline. Finally, the tide seems to be turning: especially in Scotland, with the universities of Glasgow and Strathclyde paving the way for postgraduate qualifications in genealogical studies. It is a hugely promising development, equipping future generations of historians with the skills to interrogate grassroots sources with the microscopic attention of the genealogist. One hopes that this will lead to more universities assembling genealogy modules to encourage this alternative historical perspective, more critical thinking about often idly accepted sources, and to complement related fields of study: future works of history and biography would be immeasurably enriched.

Throughout human history, the impulse to seek out a meaningful dialogue with ancestors has crossed class, culture, nation and ethnicity. Viewed through such a personal lens, this dialogue – and articulating it through writing, or oral tradition – is arguably history at its most powerful. Family history matters because engagement with it can transform our view of ourselves, how we relate to the world around us, and even provide existential solace for an increasingly secular and ageing population. It complicates visions of collective identities, raises questions about established historical narratives, and can restore the humanity to those who have been stripped of it in life or death. Learning about the particular struggles or achievements of our ancestors fosters a deeply personal act of remembrance, and writing rigorous, unflinching family histories – in whatever form that may take – in turn allows for the preservation of a rich cultural legacy. In the recent BBC documentary series *My Family, The Holocaust and Me* (2020), one participant was asked why he wanted to lay to rest the question of exactly how his Jewish relatives had died. 'I can't say it's good to find out', he replied, 'but it's *important* to find out.' The story itself held the potential to heal wounds that had blighted generations of his own family, but *telling* it prompts many more to reflect meaningfully on a historical trauma with which they may have no personal connection at all.

One of the beauties of family history is that each thread remains perpetually unfinished, and the complete tapestry reaches tantalisingly beyond view. In *Common People*, Alison Light highlights that 'the family history we choose to write, the past we believe in, is always a selection of stories from the many at our disposal'. Vita Sackville-West apparently viewed her 'rotten' and 'mad' ancestry as a sort of personal challenge, joking to her cousin that 'You and I have got a jolly sort of heredity to fight against.' Dipping into my own bloodline, I am drawn to the story of an Edwardian couple who met and married in a Lincolnshire lunatic asylum, while my mother hopes to investigate an old family rumour of a connection to the notorious Captain Bligh. My grandfather would wave away both in favour of tales of derring-do among our troop of Victorian railway workers. As well as clearing a path to our ancestors, these explorations offer the opportunity to commune with our descendants – in creating a legacy of family history through writing, we not only pass on our findings but reveal our own interests and values.

In 1850 the American essayist Ralph Waldo Emerson suggested that 'every man is a quotation from all his ancestors'. For the biographer or historian, the family history of a subject provides an often neglected means of understanding their social standing, their motivations, or even their personality. Networks of kinship and influence become more obvious, and the emotional texture of communities can be brought back to some semblance of life. For those exploring their own ancestry, in each 'quotation' lies a potential lesson, a fresh and intimate glimpse at history; or, as philosopher Roman Krznaric expresses in his book *The Good Ancestor,* the encouragement to think and act with an eye to the long-term consequences. In most cases, our family histories are populated not by lords and ladies but by labourers, by factory workers, by those whose names and voices have long been buried by history. Who else is going to look for them? Who else is going to look for you?

Selected Further Reading

Family histories

Jung Chang, *Wild Swans: Three Daughters of China* (New York: Simon & Schuster, 1991)

Hadley Freeman, *House of Glass: The Stories and Secrets of a Twentieth-Century Jewish Family* (London: Fourth Estate, 2020)

Alison Light, *Common People: The History of an English Family* (London: Penguin, 2014)

Stephen McGann, *Flesh and Blood: A History of My Family in Seven Maladies* (London: Simon & Schuster, 2017)

Tiya Miles, *Ties That Bind: The Story of an Afro-Cherokee Family in Slavery and Freedom*, 2nd edn. (Berkeley:

University of California Press, 2016)

Robert Sackville-West, *Inheritance: The Story of Knole and the Sackvilles* (London: Bloomsbury, 2010)

On genealogy

Bruce Durie, 'What is Genealogy? Philosophy, Education, Motivations and Future Prospects', *Genealogy*, vol. 1, no. 1 (2017)

Jerome de Groot, 'On Genealogy', *Public Historian*, vol. 37, no. 3 (2015)

Honor Sachs, 'The Dark Side of Our Genealogy Craze', *Washington Post*, 13 December 2019

François Weil, *Family Trees* (Cambridge, MA: Harvard University Press, 2013)

Karin Wulf, *Lineage: Genealogy and the Politics of Connection in British America, 1680–1820* (Oxford: Oxford University Press, forthcoming)

Eviatar Zerubavel, *Ancestors and Relatives: Genealogy, Identity, and Community* (Oxford: Oxford University Press, 2012)

Chapter 14

How can museums open doors to the past?

Gus Casely-Hayford

I grew up in a very untrendy London suburb long before music conferred those neighbourhoods with any kind of coolness – a place that even in early childhood felt far away from everything. We lived on a street where the buses terminated. I adored it, loved that sleepy neighbourhood that looked out for everyone, but as I reached teen-age, I slowly began to begrudge that suffocating quiet, grew to dislike that quality of suburban tranquillity that is antipathy to the young. At night I would spend long hours listening to the soft rumba of trains sashaying along distant sidings, fantasising about their ultimate destination; I would catch the crooning of lost drunks stumbling from night buses and be left conjecturing about where they might have lost their way; I would track the reflected beams of car headlights across the ceiling until they evaporated into the darkness and wish that I could follow. The moment I could resource independent travel, I travelled: Western Europe before I could afford it, the Soviet Union before I should have, Central America when the Foreign Office felt it was inadvisable, Asia before it felt obligatory, and of course Africa . . . Africa (the birthplace of my parents) became an early obsession.

I bussed up Africa's spine in my early twenties, traversed its deserts and rivers, spent time unpicking histories from the High Atlas to the Kalahari. I fell in love with African perspectives on histories that I thought I knew, was captivated by new narratives pulled intact from ancient sites and was thrilled by sensing stories that might yet be drawn from its untouched archaeology. History was there to be encountered without fuss or preciousness, it was a continent that beguiled with the magnificent ambient materiality of its past. And alongside the stuff of great history, Africa also afforded its visitors the chance to feel close to affecting intangible culture, to experience living histories; from the epic oral history traditions, to glorious performance and masquerades. It would be the pursuit of these histories, in form and content, that would drive the greater part of my career. My itchy feet would carry me abroad to work, and eventually lead to the Smithsonian National Museum of African Art in Washington DC. But it would be extended periods living abroad that would rekindle my love of the city of my birth. And amidst the Covid outbreak, looming recession, divisive culture wars and Brexit, I returned to London in the spring of 2020 to a new role, founding a new kind of museum, a museological proposition that would allow me to answer that lingering longing from my childhood, of how we might nurture, inspire and liberate young minds hungry for the past.

The 2020s present an opportunity, a moment when the Arts have rarely felt more critical, more important, more potentially useful – and more contested. The current political and economic conditions threaten resources but they also offer a powerful platform upon which to demonstrate the value of the Arts. The Victoria & Albert Museum in London has committed to play a role in this moment, to answering it with something that speaks to new and old audiences alike, that feels like a fitting twenty-first century response to what a museum might be, that can create opportunity, that can drive debate, and uplift, inspire and empower a new generation. The aim is to create a new kind of collections centre and museum in East London: one that offers open access to a body of objects – some 260,000 of them – that was traditionally only accessed by a tiny minority of specialists. Planned around an open central court, the building's glass balustrades and glass floors are designed to truly open up the collection, to immerse visitors within one of the finest single collections of art and material culture ever conceived. This will be paired with a new multi-gallery museum showcasing the work of international artists and makers.

The chief challenge is how we might reanimate the stuff of the past to deliver meaningful opportunity and do so for one of the most economically disadvantaged and demographically complex communities in Europe. To answer this challenge means adapting the museological paradigm for these new audiences, to offer new kinds of engagement and opportunity. How do we animate a historical collection for a digital first generation? How do we find ways to contextualise complex, contested and sometimes painful histories in ways that are not divisive? How do we offer the kind of experiential engagement that might sustainably speak to and *for* a younger and more diverse audience than any other national museum has ever achieved, and to do so in ways that might liberate potential, activate agency and creativity? Perhaps, above all, how do we create a sense of welcome and openness, a feeling for our visitors that we care about creating a narrative with them – a sense, in fact, of communion? We need not look further than our own personal experiences of hospitality, inclusivity, human interaction and warmth to answer these questions.

One Ramadan in my twenties, I got stuck on the road to Taouz. It is an area of southern Morocco that sits on the upper lip of the Sahara, a place where you do not want to be stranded at any time of year; but when drivers are tired and hungry, these roads become even more challenging. We had driven until the road had begun to fail, and then we had gone on – and when the track that had taken the place of the road had itself given in to the desert, we forged our own faltering path between rocky crags and the soft sand. Very occasionally we might build up a little speed, but over and over and over again our momentum was frustrated. However many times we stopped, Hassan my driver simply refused to accept that the rest of the journey would be slow, intricately negotiated, going. Again and again he would accelerate on a virgin patch of road only to be beaten by the sand.

There was complete silence in the car. It was a slightly awkward silence. Hassan was frozen in concentration and frustration; his whole being focused on teasing tiny clues out of coming changes in the camber and texture of the road before the sand overcame us once more. His eyes had the familiar glazed distance of someone who had not eaten or drunk since dawn. It had been easy to track how, as the month of Ramadan progressed, the effects of keeping a daytime fast were becoming progressively tough. Whilst the inevitable resulting physical weakness is a formidable thing to deal with, I have always thought that the greater challenge of extended fasts was dealing with the effects on thought and mood. Like many, my driver compensated by redoubling his concentration, by checking everything twice, by being consciously measured in everything he did. But every sand-forced stop, each physical exertion, told upon Hassan's constitution. You could feel the tension crackle around his attentiveness, almost see him reaching inward, and drawing down deep upon his last reserves. I really wanted to help, to suggest a less uncompromising approach, but with no knowledge of the geography or understanding of the skill Saharan roads demand to negotiate, I concluded that the most useful thing I could contribute was my silence. And so, there was silence.

The Qur'an is sensitive to the particular stresses that complete abstention from food and water can induce in a hot climate. The Islamic scriptures show latitude and tolerance; there are even special allowances for people on journeys. The Ramadan fast was not meant to be seen as a brutal test; Allah desired *ease*, not hardship. The holy month was a time to reflect on our relationship to consumption and community. Although many Muslims are prepared to suffer some discomfort as part of the process, the physical strains, the demonstration of inner strength and self-control were secondary to the potential of the fast to draw communities together in reflecting on God and duty. Sharing the endeavour with friends and family, knowing that you are bound with millions of others in daily patterns of prayer, abstention and consumption has the potential to be profoundly comforting.

Over the final kilometres of the journey as we neared our evening stop, visions of delicious Moroccan delicacies breached my mental defences. I gorged myself in fantasies of cooling light onion and tomato salads; I dreamt of smoky grilled lamb or garlic-infused beef kebabs, and imagined plates of honey-based sweets, and to slake my monumental thirst for mint tea. We were heading toward a guesthouse where the drivers of ancient camel-laden pantechnicons come off the road to pray and recharge before taking on the formidable trans-desert roads. I knew that the chances of fulfilling my gastronomic daydreams were some-what remote, but as we drew up outside the hotel and Hassan switched off the engine, I thought about the hearty foods that I have eaten at truck stops all over the world. If there is one con-sistent feature of truck drivers' diets, it is big plates of tasty food.

Almost anywhere else the three-sided corrugated iron shack would not have dared to call itself a hotel, but out here any safe, clean, stationary refuge from the winds seemed palatial. We shared a small washbasin, luxuriating in every drop of salty, soapy, cool water, and then joined the other men reclining on soft woven carpets on the floor of the multi-purpose room. It was impossible not to feel at home: our limbs and bodies touching and intertwined – the softly hypnotic rattle and squeak of the iron roof twisting in the wind, the comforting hum of hot water boiling – and from somewhere at the back of the room, hidden in the darkness, the slow, deep breaths of a child sleeping. After that merciless journey and with the evening approaching, the inescapably soporific atmosphere had immediate effect. On any normal night, I would have given in to it, I would have drifted off to sleep, but my exhaustion was no match for the magnitude of my hunger and thirst. And I, like everyone else in the room, knew that sleep and food would have to wait until after sunset.

As seems common to every Ramadan dusk, the dying few moments doggedly refuse to give way. The sun had slipped low enough to thread its rays beneath the lower edge of the door. Breath by breath, the last shadows crept up over our bodies and chased away the day. I lay my head back on the carpet, closed my eyes briefly and inhaled the warm smell of spent mint tea leaves, warm bodies and couscous. The day was gone.

After prayer we shared stories of our homes and families as our host began to gather the ingredients to make something I had been longing for all day. Even in the limited space of the single room the hotel owner took care to prepare the mint tea in the age-old manner. *As-hay*, as it is known in Berber, is something that is fundamental to hospitality in Morocco. I watched him, as I have watched patriarchs all over North Africa, throwing strong dark tea leaves into a pot and allowing the mixture to brew. As he worked he looked around the room, studying each guest in turn. He seemed one of those men who had a talent for identifying a stranger's discomfort, for sensing isolation in a room of chatter. With his eyes he directed his daughter to fetch one guest a newspaper and to light a kerosene lamp. He took off his wristwatch, a timepiece that had been loved and polished to the edge of destruction, once gilt edges now a dull brass – and he pointed at its face, I think not to suggest the passage of time, but that this particular moment mattered. Hospitality is an art-form in Muslim cultures, and this was a virtuoso at work. And then he began to tell a long story of getting lost on the Sahel, that ended with the Islamic saying, 'Live in this world as though you are a stranger, a traveller.'*

* There are various translations of this commonly used Islamic saying. Ibn Umar reported: 'The Messenger of Allah, peace and blessings be upon him, said, "Be in this world as if you were a stranger or a traveller along a path."' Source: Ṣaḥīḥ al-Bukhārī 6053, Grade: Sahih (authentic) according to Al-Bukhari.

And once the ice had been broken, when he thought no one would notice, the hotel owner carefully moved the lamp, giving the shy young truck driver the choice to withdraw back into the comfort of the shadows. And so began a process that would last all evening as the hotel owner made ongoing barely noticeable interventions to keep each of his guests comfortable, happy, welcome and at home. The little corrugated-iron hotel in the desert rocked with laughter – even Hassan smiled. The liquid was strained, and copious amounts of sugar added. A small man who had arrived late stood in the doorway. A little more sugar was added to the tea, giving the viscous hot mixture a glassy sheen, before it was returned to the fire and held on a rolling boil as fistfuls of fresh mint leaves were bruised and pressed into a pot. It was then that the real magic began to happen; an aromatic alchemy seemed to begin with smells erupting with an incendiary ferocity across the room: the perfume of spearmint and old gunpowder tea first, leaving in their wake the faint tang of burnt toffee.

The room was now silent, the wait barely tolerable; we all watched the golden piping-hot liquid being poured from pot to pot three deliberate times, each time from a greater height than the last, drawing air through the beverage to enhance the flavour and leaving the tea with a deep frothy head. It was served in glasses lacquered with years of sticky brown tea glaze; steaming hot lanterns of gold that were passed from guest to guest around the room.

I had not consumed anything since dawn. I could have quenched my thirst on water, but I wanted to pay respect to the demands of the day by ending it well. I did not stop to further savour the aroma or consider the moment, I was beyond that –

the edge of the glass burned my lip, on the tongue the ingredients revealed themselves as an unexpected cascade of flavours:
the temperature of the water at first disguised the kick of the
mint, but then the mint bit as a fresh peppery flavour that was
strong enough to cut through the caramel-like sweetness of the
sugar, leaving first the earthy flavour of tea, and then a softer
spearmint sensation on the tongue. For bodies craving calories,
the sugar rush hit like a slap, firing nerve endings, drawing pupils
open and electrifying senses. And then the mellowing afterglow
of the mint began its work to steady and recalibrate nerves. It
is a single mouthful of liquid that I hope I will never forget, a
flavour and method of preparation, a form of subtle intangible
heritage that has remained little changed for centuries, and an
insight into a particular kind of hospitality that so often makes
casual encounters in Muslim countries such a pleasure. These
cultural traditions remain an important mechanism for building
social cohesion; this was the quality of experiential encounter
that Kant would have seen as special, as the very apex of societal
development, moments when communities are bound by shared
experience, mutual respect and trust, when it feels like values
coincide. We followed our tea with a simple but good meal of
thick lentil soup that had that unmistakable flavour of Morocco,
that deep range of sweet and savoury flavours that in traditional
European kitchens would be considered awkward accompani-
ments – but here they tasted perfection. And then more stories of
family and friendship, stories of love and loss and communion,
were shared. For that evening, a tiny room on the edge of the
desert, miles from the nearest town, but with a profound sense
of place, felt like the centre of the world.

Decades after that simple meal on the road to Taouz, that

evening continues to preoccupy me. It has remained the emotional yardstick against which I have aspired to measure my own hospitality, to judge the quality of welcome and sense of place, wherever I have lived or worked. And in thinking about a new museum for the twenty-first century, it is that quality of connection between visitor and host, between strangers, that palpable feeling of being part of something meaningful, that I would seek to replicate. How do buildings and their stewards create such a powerful sense of communion, suggest shared narrative, develop such a potent emotional pull? How do we build a welcome that might evoke in our visitors a feeling of being under the stewardship of people who care? If that hotel on the road to Taouz was to be some sort of tonal guide, then generosity, humility and authenticity are critical. Race, cultural diversity, age, class, educational attainment or familiarity cannot be barriers to engagement, should not connote the nature of cultural ease or degree of comfort that our visitors might feel. Though difference and diversity might be celebrated, there should also be the possibility that they might also be transcended. These in my mind are the qualities of great cultural institutions: they are spaces where we might find a welcome, solace, inspiration, points of coalescence and credible praxis. But to do any of this we must, like the hotel on the road to Taouz, also find the shared narrative to complement the shared space; we need our visitors to feel that our museum is a place of communion, where we are elegantly drawn together by shared stories, history.

Stories are important. Museums are rarely, primarily, about objects, seldom just about their collections. Collections tell stories, they symbolise histories, capture communal continuity. The objects are there to illustrate some bigger truth, perhaps to forge collective catharsis, or drive cohesion – rarely just there on their own terms. However glorious the collection, the story is usually the headline, the narrative is the scene-stealer, the thing that, however subtly it is conceived, lingers longest in the memory.

The mid-eighteenth-century founding of the British Museum coincided not just with the conclusive suppression of the Jacobites (and the consolidation of the British Union), but also with the burgeoning of a new set of wider imperial ambitions. The new national museum presented an important set of nascent narratives, it helped define Britain, and the world, in relation to us. Its founder Hans Sloane, student-botanist, a physician who had worked on slave plantations, was a product of the age: his collection, his ambition, his view of the world were all informed by a moment when the grand Enlightenment themes were being shaped. And the narrative that the collection wove spoke powerfully to that time, it helped to reinforce hierarchies of both nature and humanity in ways that made sense of new thinking, new politics, new encounters and new territories of peoples. It naturally placed the British at the centre of its world, and also at the apex of its intellectual (and, by implication, moral) hierarchies. It made it clear that museums were to become important national instruments, that like the armed forces and the civil service they could be deployed as tools to help in the forging of a sense of nationhood. And the British Museum played its part; an intellectual encapsulation of new confidence, a treasury of objects and narrative; it represented an analogue of the world that the nation sought to navigate, understand and control.

A century on, the creation of three South Kensington museums was driven by a renewed set of similar imperatives, a drive to serve a nation at the dawn of profound industrial and imperial change. Focused on science, natural history and art and design, a new suite of national museums sought to look at the world practically, as a toolbox. Henry Cole, the founder of the V&A, was a very different kind of figure to Hans Sloane. Cole saw the world not as a box of curiosities, but was fascinated by people and skills and by the possibility of cultural transformation.

In 1849, Cole visited the eleventh Quinquennial Paris Exhibition, an exhibition considered the encapsulation of French cultural and industrial ambition. Cole was not impressed. He returned home disappointed at what he saw as a critical omission in the lack of international participants. As he saw it, to tell the story of great culture was to tell a global story. In response, he conceived a Great Exhibition that would mark itself out from all of the European expositions that had preceded it by being truly international in its intent. Cole believed in a kind of universal connection between peoples across geography and time, a connection that was most palpable through contact with cultural excellence, with making – and he wanted to celebrate that in the greatest exposition that the world had ever seen. And he was successful, the Great Exhibition drew people from across the globe – as participants and as audiences. Sixty thousand foreign nationals came to London in a moment that would help to redefine Britain and the nature of its imperial relationships.

One of the earliest visitors to the Great Exhibition was Henry Mayhew, a *Punch* journalist and social reformer – who like almost everyone else was affected by what he saw. Mayhew saw the Great Exhibition as an intriguing study of the creative industries. Whilst this was a platform for international practice – it was also a fantastic advert for the very best British creativity. And the journalist in Mayhew wanted to uncover the communities that were the engines of this national transformation. He travelled east to the least fashionable areas of the city. His description of East London, written at the time of the Great Exhibition, is a condemnation of Victorian urban and civic management, but through the crippling poverty and deprivation he also defined it as a proud place of makers: of tailors, shoemakers, sawyers, carpenters, cabinet makers and silk-weavers. Dickens, who walked the same streets in the same era, described it similarly as a place of 'oil boilers, gut spinners, varnish makers, printers, ink makers and the like'. Like other chroniclers of Victorian London, both men were shocked at how, in this period of growth and advance, those who were making some of the biggest sacrifices were enjoying the least benefit. Today as post-Brexit Britain renegotiates its relationship with the world, it is amongst the descendants of those creative East London communities that the V&A is looking to invest a significant part of its institutional energy. And although East London has profoundly changed, there are things about it that do not change: it remains a place of making, of invention and creativity. And it also continues to be home to some of the most economically disadvantaged and culturally diverse communities in Britain.

To make the desired difference we must be bold. When Cole sought to build a permanent museum, he wanted it to be radical, to liberate rather than control creativity, to galvanise rather than institutionalise ingenuity, but also to become a place of meaningful refuge in a time of huge flux. He hoped his V&A might at its best be truly transformative, that it would offer the kinds of tools that would meaningfully change ordinary lives. And so, he was bold. The V&A under Cole pioneered progressive innovations in museum practice: the first museum to have gas lighting and late opening hours to allow working men and women to visit after work; a café to provide rest and social opportunities; studios and a library for practical study. But Cole's methods and values were nevertheless limited by his time and culture, by a certain patrician surety of what was right, beautiful and useful. Whilst there are powerful and timeless things to take from Cole's vision, today we must accept that there is no monopoly on knowledge, truth, goodness or beauty. We must embrace the fact that whilst we have deep institutional expertise, we do not have a monopoly of the truth; indeed, history and interpretation are at their most thrilling when they are part of dynamic exchanges with makers and audiences. And whilst we would like to leave our audiences changed by engaging with our collections, we would also like our institution to have the potential to be changed by its visitors, to perhaps be like the hotel on the Sahel, a crucible of genuine narrative exchange, to be open and flexible enough to be able to reflect the changing needs and moods of these fluid times. And to deliver that we must work in new ways.

Across the Arts we have enjoyed the benefits of the digital revolution, we have witnessed how digital tools and infrastructure have transformed the distribution and consumption of film and television, how digital engagement has changed retail and patterns of customer engagement. As yet, the museum sector has not found the truly transformative digital paradigms to shift the nature of a museum visit. Perhaps through imaginative integration of digital technologies we might deliver a new kind of engagement and transform the user's experience of a collection. For Gen-Z, a demographic that is used to customisation, that is obsessed with authenticity, we want to craft an environment and experience that will allow our visitors to not just *see* beautiful

243

things, but to offer them the opportunity to engage directly with our collections, and then to leave something of themselves behind. Over time museums will need to become not just a repository of beautiful objects, but also of reflection, testimony and memory.

My hope is that V&A East will become many things to its diverse audience: perhaps a future Hans Sloane might value our storehouse as an open centre of curatorial excellence, maybe a future Henry Cole will celebrate our museum as a catalyst of skills enhancement and a crucible of inspiration and opportunity. But I also hope that future fellow travellers on the road to Taouz will find something comforting in its quality of welcome, and that it possesses the confidence to flex and change to the needs and desires of its visitors. The new cultural landscape requires new kinds of institutions, museums that can re-energise collections for new audiences and recalibrate themselves to the concerns, rhythms and modes of production of our new age, but also tell the essential human stories of the past. We have an extraordinary once-in-a-lifetime opportunity to build an experiential storehouse of art and design, to pair it with an experimental partnership-based gallery and exhibition platform, to create a campus for the imagination, to craft a space for account and reconciliation, a space where we might acknowledge the complex and difficult histories that our collections represent, negotiating relationships of equity, empathy and openness with audiences, communities, artists and makers of the world.

Selected Further Reading

On ambient and transient traditions of African history – oral, performance and masquerade, ephemeral objects

Toyin Falola and Christian Jennings (eds.) *Sources and Methods in African History: Spoken, Written, Unearthed* (Rochester, NY: Rochester University Press, 2005)

On the future of museums and debates around digital cultural heritage

Jane Anderson, *The Routledge Companion to Cultural Property* (London: Routledge, 2021)

Fiona Cameron and Sarah Kenderdine (eds.), *Theorizing Digital Cultural Heritage: A Critical Discourse* (Cambridge, MA and London: MIT Press, 2007)

Contextualising colonial histories within the museum

John McAleer, 'Objects of Empire: Museums, Material Culture and Histories of Empire' in Anne Gerritson and Giorgio Riello (eds.), *Writing Material Culture History* (London: Bloomsbury, 2015)

Dominic Thomas (ed.), *Museums in Postcolonial Europe* (London: Routledge, 2010)

New forms of material engagement

Arjun Appadurai, *The Social Life of Things* (Cambridge: Cambridge University Press, 1986)

Lambros Malafouris, *How Things Shape the Mind: A Theory of Material Engagement* (Cambridge, MA: MIT Press, 2013)

Cultural traditions and rituals, communities, mechanisms for building social cohesion

Charlton Payne and Lucas Thorpe (eds.) *Kant and the Concept of Community* (Rochester, NY: Rochester University Press, 2011)

Building a welcoming environment, how to remove institutional barriers regarding race, cultural diversity and more

Nicole Ivy, 'The Labor of Diversity', *Museum*, January 2016, 36–9

Richard Sandell and Eithne Nightingale (eds.) *Museums, Equality and Social Justice* (2013). Twenty-one essays by academics and practitioners. With a foreword by Mark O'Neill and Lois Silverman

Chapter 15

How making space for Indigenous peoples changes history

Leila K. Blackbird and Caroline Dodds Pennock

The first step in liquidating a people is to erase its memory, destroy its books, its culture, its history. Then have somebody write new books, manufacture a new culture, invent a new history. Before long, the nation will begin to forget what it is and what it was. The world around it will forget even faster.

Milan Kundera, *The Book of Laughter and Forgetting*

LKB: For many, if not all, Indigenous peoples, there is no separation between the past and the present. It is held within traditional ways of knowing and belief that all time and all history are interconnected and co-existing, crucial to culture and well-being. We hold these connections to be sacred. The rupturing of those threads which weave together the present and the past, and living generations to the ancestors, has been a violence beyond the initial acts of colonisation, enslavement, massacre, land theft, displacement, genocide and treaty violations. Mythologised accounts of colonisation are still normal in the classroom, but even they fill far too few pages of our history books. Approaches to studying and teaching the history of the so-called New World have often been inadequate, if not outright destructive. Yet, by making space for Indigenous peoples and perspectives in the present, we can change history into something more honest and dynamic, which also holds great promise for repair.

History is forged into a weapon in the crucible of politics. Carefully crafted versions of the past have far too often been deployed by policy makers and educators to reinforce the perspective of the coloniser and to create national myths. Unfortunately, this has also come to define the relationship between Indigenous peoples and Europeans. For Native Americans, this history is inescapable; it forms the legal frameworks of nation-states, defines borders and citizenship, limits our political sovereignty, and even quantifies our blood. Colonial policies have been used for generations to forcibly reshape and supplant our traditional ways of knowing and being, to break our kinship bonds, and to control our very identities in order to maintain control over the land and its resources. Natives must learn from an early age to carry history on our shoulders, while simultaneously not allowing the weight of it to crush us. We must know, deeply, that we are not victims. We are survivors, culture-bearers and thriving communities. We are still here. This is our land. And we belong to it, not it to us.

It is a creation of historical memory and literature, rather than one of fact, that Indigenous peoples are somehow gone or forever left behind in the past. To think we are unchanging relics creates no path for us to the future. But colonial rule was justified by this logic – that we were 'primitives', incapable of 'civility', modernity or self-governance. That is the foundation of sand on

248

which empires have been built and on which they have collapsed. Likewise, imperial histories are a version of the past that have been hollowed out and rendered incomplete. They are missing the faces, voices and stories of the millions of Indigenous peoples who also lived and loved, who travelled and created, and who were warriors, poets, prophets, healers, diplomats and intellectuals. Erasure is a form of violence that sustains a settler-colonial present.

To view Indigenous peoples as real, living and modern challenges that ongoing colonial reality. As scholars and students, simply shifting this perspective makes it possible to restore agency to Native actors in the past. But it also leads us to making space for living Native people who seek to repair connections across time and place and to mend the threads that tie our ancestors to us and to our future generations. Only when Indigenous peoples are considered capable of having a future are we able to hope and dream it into being. Only by first recognising and honouring the gravity of the past can we then begin to make space for the possibility of reconciliation in the present. That is why we must invest in a history that is capable of centring the many vibrant Indigenous cultures, polities and languages that continue today. It is a vital and necessary project, perhaps now more than ever, and it presents us with an opportunity for strategic collaboration. This piece is an exercise in doing precisely that. By retaining our unique voices and perspectives before joining in conclusion, we seek to provide example. Stories often live in many dimensions.

CDP: In 1961, E.H. Carr called on historians to recognise the ways in which they stood between the past and the present: neither neutral custodians of a dry collection of facts, nor propagandists who used snippets of evidence to embroider their historical fictions. For Carr, history could and should reflect the concerns of one's age, but it must never be overwhelmed by them. As scholars entering the academy, we are taught to walk along this careful precipice: to recognise our biases in order to acknowledge them; to understand how the evidence we choose shapes our story. Yet even six decades after Carr's clarion cry against absolute objectivity, the model of a historian as impartial observer unfortunately lingers. That model also abruptly evokes an uncomfortable relationship of power and curiosity. As Linda Tuhiwai Smith (Māori) wrote, 'research is probably one of the dirtiest words in the Indigenous world's vocabulary . . . it conjures up bad memories'. Scholars of Indigenous histories have to remember that Indigenous peoples' bodies, lives and histories have been the subject of scrutiny for centuries. The idea that a non-Native observer can somehow 'recover' these pasts for 'neutral' scrutiny reproduces a deeply problematic dynamic that has been at the heart of the relationship between the West and 'the rest' for centuries.

For a non-Native scholar working on Indigenous histories, this history is also inescapable, and it must inform my practice. History, Carr wrote, 'is a continuous process of interaction between the historian and his facts, an unending dialogue between the present and the past'. This dialogue is critical, but I see it as a less abstract one than Carr, as a conversation that is not only between the historian and her 'texts' (be they alphabetic, visual, material or oral), but which places between them an awareness that the evidence we study reflects a violent rupture for Indigenous peoples, who still flourish across the world today. As a historian of the Aztec (more properly the Mexica) world, I am used to working with sources that were created almost exclusively after the invasion of Mexico, using texts written by, with, or under the aegis of conquistadors, missionaries, enslavers and settlers. Few Mesoamerican texts survived the Spanish conflagration of the great pictographic archives, which were destroyed by missionary fervour in the first years after the conquest. Even later documents written by the Nahua – Nahuatl-speaking descendants of the Aztecs and their neighbours – are inevitably shaped, in part, by the colonial encounter: by violence, disjuncture and destruction, as well as by adaptation, resistance and syncretism.

As scholars, we learn to read 'against the grain', to look behind the obvious and excavate for evidence beyond the façade, but we are not always able to 'read' Indigenous histories clearly through the cracks of preconception and assumption. Although it is now fairly mainstream to claim that one works in an interdisciplinary way we now call 'ethnohistory' – an inclusive approach which brings together different disciplines and sources, such as art history, archaeology, ecology, landscape, linguistics and anthropology, to illuminate Native histories – the place of contemporary Indigenous communities has remained tenuous. Oral histories are often dismissed as 'anecdote' and Indigenous elders as 'storytellers', as if this were different from being historians. Rather, we must recognise alternative ways of doing, telling and understanding the past, which may explicitly reject Western 'facts' in favour of traditional 'stories', simply because they matter more or contain different ways of knowing. As Susan Gillespie – who rejected relentless archival empiricism in favour of reading Aztec 'mythical histories' on their own terms – wrote: 'there are other "truths" to be found' there. Indigenous epistemologies are valid in their own right.

The study of Indigenous histories should be a work of collaboration and conversation, not just between the historian and her texts, but also with the people she finds there, and those who have come after. In attempting to recover the world of Tenochtitlan, for example, my work in many ways embraces the traditional methods of the cultural historian, but I do this always in the awareness that, although the age of the 'Aztecs' has passed, millions of people still speak Nahuatl, and more than a hundred other Indigenous languages, in Mexico today. Descendants of the Mexica, Zapotec, Mixtec, Tepanec, Olmec, Maya and countless others live in every corner of the country. And although I cannot 'speak' to their ancestors in the way that one may still speak with a living Lakota, Apache or Cree elder about their history, I can help to write a history which centres Indigenous voices and is written in the awareness that it matters to their descendants. When we stereotype Indigenous peoples of the past as vicious, bloodthirsty and brutal, we implicitly excuse the invasion of their lands, the enslavement of their children, and the ongoing racism and oppression experienced by them across the Americas today. I cannot speak for them, but by carefully unpacking the texts, I can try to help them speak for themselves.

LKB: As the old axiom states, history is written by the victor. To most Americans, then, history begins with colonisation. To them, it is not contact and connection but, rather, conquest that defines the modern nation. In the United States, the national origin story is steeped in 'Manifest Destiny', a philosophy by which Anglo-Protestant expansion from the Atlantic to the Pacific and beyond is seen as having been justified, inevitable and a God-given right.

In Canada, competing British and French imperial interests and violence have equally shaped contemporary national realities. But historiography – most often tied to its nation of origin and, therefore, to its nationalism – cannot be entirely devoid of culturally constructed preconceptions or prejudices. This is at the heart of the lesson that Carr taught us. Nevertheless, some of the academy's most prized thinkers have upheld profound biases, even if they have believed their perspectives to be wholly objective. Empiricism is often naivety.

European settlers and their descendants have learned to see themselves as the proud inheritors of the Western Enlightenment tradition, and it is upon this framework that the historical profession has been built. At the turn of the twentieth century, the American Historical Association (AHA)'s Committee of Seven determined that national history education must be a political project, and future AHA president James Harvey Robinson began developing a 'New History' to shape the 'scope and intent of historical study'. In 1916, Robinson and his colleagues established the importance of the subject in the emerging public-school curriculum, offering the US Bureau of Education the promise of being able to create a proper citizenry through education. The profession then began espousing a lasting version of history that exalted 'Western Civilisation' in hopes of defending the world from the darkness of the 'barbarism' of the world war era. Ever since, secondary-school curricula have centred the 'progressive evolution' of the 'Caucasian race' and the Christian faith to global domination, from the ancient Greeks and Romans through 'our shared European beginnings' to the pilgrims and the pioneers who 'discovered' and 'built' America.

As an Indigenous historian in the American academy, I must constantly grapple with these deeply embedded prejudices. Being raised in the Deep South, my childhood history textbooks told tales of 'vanishing Indians' and courageous frontiersmen, of 'happy slaves' and kind fatherly enslavers. In their pages, I could not find my truth or that of most of the people I knew and loved. This is exactly what inspired me to become a historian. However, it has also meant I have had to learn how to walk in two different worlds. Education itself has fractured Indigenous cultures, languages and knowledge production, and institutions have long been part of the European 'civilising' project. For Native Americans, this is deeply bound with trauma. When my mother first learned of my intention to pursue higher education, she warned me not to forget that this system was not built for me; rather, it was expressly built to destroy people like me.

From the 1870s, while white children were being inculcated with the 'civilising myth', Native children were being forcibly removed from their homes, cultures and communities and placed in 'Indian boarding schools'. The first of hundreds operated by either the US Bureau of Indian Affairs (BIA) or private religious groups, the Carlisle Indian Industrial School was established by Brigadier General Richard Henry Pratt under the philosophy of 'Kill the Indian, and Save the Man'. Pratt and those like him believed in what the Canadian Superintendent of Indian Affairs, Duncan Campbell Scott, called the 'final solution' to 'the Indian problem': forcible assimilation to whiteness, or utter annihilation. Likewise, his government developed a policy of 'aggressive assimilation', claiming Aboriginal cultures were unable to adapt to modernity.

The parallel history of 'residential schools' in Canada, the last of which closed in 1996, has lately been at the centre of a national human-rights investigation. Through this investigation, the Truth and Reconciliation Commission (TRC) uncovered thousands of accounts of First Nations, Métis and Inuit children forbidden their languages and cultures, of rampant physical and sexual abuse, and of cruelty, starvation and death. The findings are clear: the legacy of these schools is one of genocide. The consequences of this are still tangibly felt through poverty, disease and despair; Indigenous peoples across the US and Canada have the highest rates of suicide, incarceration, sexual assault and death by homicide per capita than any other racial or ethnic group. Across the Americas, Indigenous people remain disadvantaged by every socioeconomic measure, such as employment, education, health and wealth. But as Tanya Talaga (Anishinaabe) reminds us, 'You are conditioned not to care, you are conditioned to indifference, and there is a violence to that indifference.'

Unfortunately, the United States currently has no vision for truth or for reconciliation, and many of the horrors of the past remain hidden from our history books. Only now in our living generations have Native Americans been able to begin to break this cycle of intergenerational trauma. Unlike the historians who have recently penned think-pieces denying the horrors of slavery and genocide in support of a more 'traditional' or 'patriotic' version of the past, to which they hope we return, I believe we should never locate our national identities within histories that glorify domination. Instead, we should take the time to carefully consider the 'dialogue between the present and the past' and then reflect upon the colonial roots of our shared consciousness. We must be willing and courageous enough to look into the proverbial abyss, to truly know ourselves. This is how we make space to honour those who remain. The truth is, neither coloniser nor colonised can heal through denial.

CDP: As a British historian trained two decades ago at Oxford, I learned that sources matter, that how you choose them and use them shapes the histories you tell. I learned that those histories matter, and that they could be used and abused for political ends. The post-modernists had taught the academy there was no such thing as what Hayden White called a 'value-free history', that narratives were powerful and multiple, and that our interpretations were deeply embedded in our own context, as well as in those of our authors. Post-colonial historians and the work of the Subaltern Studies Group challenged the nostalgic fantasies of Britain's imperial past and, in the US, the New Philology transformed our understanding of Mesoamerica by focusing on the study of Indigenous languages. But, although we were taught to try and recover unheard voices in our work, it was rarely suggested that those unheard voices might be those of our contemporaries. Or, crucially, that the stories we were telling might be part of an ongoing narrative of oppression.

Indigenous history was seen as the past, rather than the present. It was only when I looked outwards, beyond the academy, that I saw the people who were still living with this history. My work is rooted in the scholarship of people like the doyen of Nahuatl studies, Miguel León-Portilla, and his teacher Angél Garibay K. These men did remarkable work identifying and translating millions of words of historic Nahuatl. They believed that Aztec literature and philosophy should take their place in the canon of world civilisations – and they were right:

translation and interpretation are vital tools in understanding the Indigenous past. But they remain part of a tradition of ethnology which focused on observation and translation, rather than on collaboration. León-Portilla's enthusiasm for Indigenous Mexican history was encouraged by his uncle, Manuel Gamio, a distinguished archaeologist and one of the key architects of *indigenismo*, the twentieth-century attempt to create a unified national identity based on the pre-Hispanic histories of Mexico. His work, and that of ethnologists and linguists like Garibay, was vital in reconstructing the history of the Indigenous peoples of Mexico, showing their complexity and significance. But, while Gamio revered the art and culture of their ancient past, he saw contemporary Indigenous communities as potential citizens in need of modernisation and integration in the efforts of the national state.

Indigenismo promoted the Indigenous past and offered some limited benefits to living Native communities, but it was fundamentally an assimilationist project designed to take the 'good parts' of Indigenous heritage and subsume the rest into a homogeneous *mestizo* Mexican identity. Indigeneity – a glorious fossil, disconnected from descendant communities – was appropriated to create a nationalist narrative, while Indigenous people themselves were stereotyped, acculturated and erased, creating what the Mexican ethnologist Guillermo Bonfil Battalla called an 'imaginary Mexico' designed 'to incorporate the Indian, to de-Indianise him'. For him, this invented *indigenismo* stood in opposition to '*México profundo*' (deep Mexico). Battalla saw Indigenous peoples as embodying the 'real' Mesoamerica and as the 'bearers of ways of understanding the world and of organizing human life that have their origins in Mesoamerican civilization', as distinctive communities, individuals, families and regions who maintained parts of their cultures and traditions.

As a museum director, Battalla was one of the first to work directly with Indigenous communities, empowering them as co-creators of their own histories. This model of *indigenismo participativo* (participatory indigenism) sees Indigenous activists partnered with scholars and institutions to empower local communities and revitalise linguistic and cultural traditions. In 2003, Nahuatl and sixty-two other Indigenous languages were officially recognised, but many of Mexico's Indigenous languages remain endangered, putting at risk the history and cultural identity of those communities. At institutions like IDIEZ (Zacatecas Institute for Teaching and Research in Ethnology), Indigenous students and teachers work in partnership with academics to revitalise their language and create scholarship for other contemporary speakers, rather than merely translating for external audiences. There, Indigenous people are not just informants or bystanders, as they are so often made to be. Instead, they are active participants in research and teaching in a place that sees their cultures as 'characterized by continuity, not rupture'.

Such partnerships offer a model that provides the possibility to see Indigenous history as a cooperative effort, rather than as an ivory-tower exploit. Historians too can find collaborative and ethical methods which recognise the value of working in partnership with Indigenous peoples. As an academic historian, I cannot disavow the traditions of scholarship and seizure that form part of the foundations of my discipline. By studying, categorising and labelling the Indigenous past, we have colonised it. To push back against this possession through strategic collaboration is to reimagine history; this is what it means to 'decolonise' this past.

Both: Since the earliest encounters between Indigenous peoples and European invaders, the practice of history has been entangled with colonisation. Texts were burned and cultures recreated in the image of their colonisers. Material objects were seized, scrutinised, and displayed without deference to the communities tied to them, and without understanding their significance or power. Since the sixteenth century, Indigenous peoples' sacred objects and human remains, imbued with spirit, have formed parts of prestigious institutions' prized collections. Tens of thousands have yet to be repatriated. But for Indigenous communities that have been forcibly acculturated and who seek to repair the connections between living generations and ancestors, the ability to reclaim heritage is vital. As Governor Tarita Alarcón Rapu (Rapa Nui) told the British Museum when pleading for the return of *Hoa Hakananai'a*, the giant *moai* statue stolen by the navy from Easter Island in 1868, 'We are just a body. You, the British people, have taken our soul.'

Scholars have now (mostly) accepted the importance of including Indigenous peoples in the histories we tell. 'Frontiers' and 'discovery' have given way to 'middle grounds' and 'entangled histories'. Making space for Native stories has already changed history by transforming our understanding of the dynamics of empire, showing that Indigenous peoples had limited agency within colonialism, and undermining enduring assumptions of European racial and cultural superiority. Likewise, museums are slowly finding ways to engage in what Margaret M. Bruchac (Abenaki) has called 'restorative research', returning looted items to descendant communities and working with Native people to better understand and represent their own past. In 2017, for example, hundreds of cultural objects were repatriated from the Yale Peabody Museum of Natural History, completing what Chief Many Hearts Lynn Malerba (Mohegan) has called 'a sacred circle'. Yale and the tribe also have cooperated on the Native Northeast Research Collaborative, which supports scholarly efforts alongside empowering tribal communities to research their own heritage and affirm their sovereignty. Yet, this is the exception and not the rule.

The stereotype of Indigenous cultures as 'people without history' barely changed between the sixteenth century – when Juan Ginés de Sepulveda justified Spanish colonisation of 'these halfmen (*homunculi*) . . . [who] are not even literate or in possession of any monument to their history except for some obscure and vague reminiscences of several things put down in various paintings' – and 1965, when Hugh Trevor-Roper decried 'the study of pre-European, pre-Columbian America' as 'largely darkness . . . And darkness is not a subject for history.' The denial of Indigenous histories is a continuing colonisation, a device that makes the past unintelligible by erasing lived realities and severing connections across time and space. Only by embracing Indigenous histories, informed by oral and sacred traditions, archaeology and alphabetic sources, as well as deep understandings of landscape and language, can we pierce the supposed 'darkness' which veils the Indigenous past.

We must make space for Indigenous peoples themselves, as partners in our professional practice able to speak their truths. Native American and Indigenous Studies (NAIS) offers a template for collaborative, interdisciplinary practice which recognises that Indigenous communities have linguistic, archival and culturally specific expertise. And Indigenous peoples are confronted every day with the consequences of their histories, often knowing their pasts more intimately than those who once sought to forever erase them. Recent prize-winning works by NAIS scholars like Lisa Brooks (Abenaki) and Christine K. DeLucia have been ground-breaking and transformative, unsettling dominant narratives and compelling readers to take seriously Indigenous perspectives. In tracing the 'memoryscapes' of colonial North America, both rewrite our understandings of the British Atlantic world, making elusive pasts visible through archival rigour layered with living Indigenous knowledge and methods. For DeLucia, 'Memory bridges the "proof" chasm, while history dwells on the vacuum.' Unfortunately, such reorientations have not been unanimously embraced. NAIS has been stereotyped by its detractors as too presentist, 'politically correct', or lacking in objectivity. But as Carr recognised, objectivity is fantasy. History has long been produced to serve nationalist and imperialist agendas and used as a weapon to silence the truths of colonised peoples.

It has always been a privilege of those who get to write history to determine what it is. By protecting the status quo of archival methodologies as the only arbiter of 'truth', historians perpetuate the epistemic violence the archive embodies. By dismissing Native knowledge as inherently 'biased' or untrustworthy, detractors hold white supremacy as the implicit standard. Philip J. Deloria (Standing Rock Sioux) asks, 'Do Native peoples want absolute authority over academic history (framing the questions, conducting the research, generating conclusions)? Perhaps. Perhaps they simply want the recognition of some measure of authority over *themselves*.' Because the lack of self-determination has profound material and political consequences. If the inclusion of Indigenous perspectives and ways of knowing challenges European ways of understanding and telling history, then history will only be richer for it. It will empower us all to deepen our understanding of the past and confront preconceptions of 'truth' mired in generations of bias. In our unending dialogue between the present and the past, Indigenous peoples must be able to speak and to be heard.

Selected Further Reading

Philip J. Deloria, *Playing Indian* (New Haven: Yale University Press, 1998)

Thomas King, *The Inconvenient Indian: A Curious Account of Native People in North America* (Minneapolis: University of Minnesota Press, 2012)

K. Tsianina Lomawaima, *They Called It Prairie Light: The Story of Chilocco Indian School* (Lincoln and London: University of Nebraska Press, 1994)

Andrés Reséndez, *The Other Slavery: The Uncovered Story of Indian Enslavement in America* (Boston and New York: Houghton Mifflin Harcourt, 2016)

Audra Simpson, *Mohawk Interruptus: Political Life Across the Borders of Settler States* (Durham: Duke University Press, 2014)

Linda Tuhiwai Smith, *Decolonizing Methodologies: Research and Indigenous Peoples* (London: Zed Books, 1999)

Tanya Talaga, *All Our Relations: Indigenous Trauma in the Shadow of Colonialism* (London: Scribe, 2020)

Gerald Vizenor, *Manifest Manners: Narratives on Postindian Survivance* (Lincoln: University of Nebraska Press, 1999)

Stephanie Wood, *Transcending Conquest: Nahua Views of Spanish Colonial Mexico* (Norman: University of Oklahoma Press, 2003)

Chapter 16

How East Asia's past is shaping the present and future (or why we ignore China and Japan at our peril)

Rana Mitter

Perhaps the biggest power shift in today's world is the move of political and economic power from West to East, and the rise of China in particular. Yet it is a shift that has been accompanied by only a limited understanding of the history of the societies that sit on Asia's Pacific Rim. In summer 2020, the ITV network showed a dramatisation of J.G. Farrell's fine novel of anti-colonialism *The Singapore Grip*, based on the events of the fall of Britain's Eastern redoubt to the Japanese in 1942. It was a rare appearance of this region's history in British popular culture.

For decades, Western schools in general and British schools in particular had little time for any aspect of East Asian history. South Asia is different – just. Twenty years ago, there was a tiny trickle of Indian history taught in schools, all of it tied to the story of empire, and almost all seen from the point of view of the British. But the great societies of East Asia were almost entirely absent from that syllabus, apart from a late cameo appearance by Japan as the 'other' Axis enemy during the Second World War. By the 1980s, this was beginning to look a little anomalous. Japan was the second biggest economy in the world, and was saving the bacon of the fast-declining British car industry by investing in the north of England. By the early twenty-first century, this emphasis was even more out of kilter. Japan was now 'only' the third largest economy in the world, but that was because it had ceded its place to another East Asian giant: China. When I went to study Chinese in the late 1980s at university, my choice was seen by some as eccentric (my school tried briefly to put me off). Thirty years on, people assumed I had a level of insight aged eighteen about the future shape of the world. I didn't. I just thought that China (and Japan) were interesting places to find out about, particularly in a part of the world that doesn't think about them very much. I still do.

Today, there is a little more awareness of China's modern history in schools, in particular at GCSE level. Yet contemporary politics may be forcing a greater interest in history. Today, as the West scrambles to work out how to deal with the rise of China's economic, military and geopolitical power, there is a rising interest, and even urgency, around the historical origins of this new superpower. And on a wider scale, the Asia–Pacific region has become increasingly important to a Britain unanchored from Europe but unsure where to go next. In spring 2021, the British government issued an Integrated Review on Defence and Security which talked about a 'tilt to the Indo-Pacific', a policy orientation that could include new trade agreements with South East Asian nations, or sending an aircraft carrier to the South China Sea. Yet projections of an imagined future for Britain in today's East Asia rarely show much understanding of the complex historical relationship between Britain and the region.

In this essay, I will discuss two aspects of East Asian history that, better understood, would enhance Western understanding of major global trends: the impact of war and the importance of global history. If there is an overarching theme in the history of modern East Asia, it is the way that the region modernised and became central to the fate of the world without becoming a clone of the West, and without democracy being a necessary or inevitable part of the economic story. In the turbulent 2010s, a further perspective from East Asian history that might have been useful was about the fragility of democracy. The story of post-war Europe, as told in most histories, has become one of inevitable democratisation. In some ways this was a story read backward; the long debate about whether Germany's *Sonderweg* ('special path') was responsible for its descent into dictatorship was fuelled in part by the idea that Germany's lack of democratic commitment before 1945 was in some way anomalous in the European context. The story of Eastern Europe after 1989 also fitted neatly into this model, along with the intellectual framing of Francis Fukuyama and others who argued that liberal democracy was the ultimate norm in politics.

India's history became relatively more familiar to Britons than that of other Asian countries, in part because so much of that story took place in English, and was easily accessible. However, this concentration on India concealed an anomaly in understanding Asia as a whole: in the post-war era, India has been the only consistent democracy in the region apart from Japan (and for two years in 1975–7, even that democracy was suspended under Emergency legislation). This made the Indian experience seem in some way familiar, a democratic offshoot of the favourable parts of the European legacy (liberalism), while politely ignoring the less palatable parts (colonial domination).

The breakdown of liberal democratic norms in the United States under the Trump presidency and in European countries such as Poland and Hungary, or even (on a smaller scale) the willingness of British politicians to use sharp practice to prorogue parliament during the Brexit debates of 2019, might have seemed less surprising if Britons had been familiar with societies that had modernised successfully without liberalising. The case of Nazi Germany, the European descent into dictatorship most studied in British schools, is in some ways so egregious, ending with racial genocide, that it serves to illustrate little beyond its own case (even the most abstruse arguments about European fascism do not equate the Italian or Austrian Dollfuss versions with Hitlerism).

Japan's pre-1945 path, somewhat like that of Germany, involved imperialism and dictatorship that created a form of modernisation, but at a terrible price. Like Germany, Japan's post-war reconstruction was in stark contrast to what had gone before, as the country became a global citizen contributing to a peaceful and democratic world. China's traumas on the path to modernisation were greater even than Japan's. Up to the mid-twentieth century, China was a country as much a victim of global forces as it was a shaper of them. Yet in the early twentieth century, its republican, pre-communist governments still sought to create a modern state. After a world war and a civil war, in the mid-twentieth century, China modernised further, not under a pluralist democracy like Japan, but under a radical experiment in communism that challenged the Soviet Union as much as it did the United States. That modernisation has been underpinned by a range of themes that speak to wider themes in modern history: the impact of war, the power of globalisation, and the legacy of colonialism.

War and the shaping of Japan

The Second World War, three-quarters of a century after it ended, still remains central to the way that Britain defines itself. This is also true for many other societies; Russia recently made it illegal to insult the memory of the 'Great Patriotic War'. The dominant narratives about the 'meaning' of the war in Europe share certain characteristics: what I call a 'circuit of memory', meaning a shared set of ideas and assumptions that define the perceived meaning of a historical event. For most of Western Europe and North America, there has been a circuit of memory since 1945 that projects the war as a conflict against fascism, concentrated in Europe and with the Nazis at the centre, which ultimately led to the defeat of evil and the establishment of stable democracy in the West. Historical detail differs, but in Washington, Paris, London or Berlin, few would deny the key elements of that framework; the defeated Germans shared it just as much as the victorious Americans.

Yet Western understanding of the Second World War, perhaps the historical framework most widely understood and engaged with in Britain today (at least judging by television documentaries, popular histories and school curricula), needs to incorporate the very different frameworks and assumptions surrounding that same conflict in East Asia, not least because those historical assumptions continue to shape the two most powerful Asian states, China and Japan.

For, unlike in Europe, a shared circuit of memory around

the Second World War in Asia, with mutually understood assumptions and narratives, never developed in East Asia, largely because of the Cold War and the Chinese Civil War. In the short years after the end of the war with Japan in 1945, the Nationalist (Kuomintang) government of Chiang Kai-shek made tentative moves to create a new friendship with post-war Japan, on the basis that China would be a key shaper of a new order in Asia. In this scenario, post-war China and Japan would have both been oriented toward the US. As in France and Germany in the same era, this context might have provided the opportunity for two former enemies to form a shared understanding of their past trauma. Also as in Europe, wider support from the US could have meant that both Asian powers were able to create a favourable atmosphere for a shared circuit of memory.

Instead, the Chinese Civil War of 1946–9 took China decisively out of the fledgling pro-American order forming in East Asia. Because of the Chinese Communist Party's (CCP) victory, China allied instead with the USSR. The Korean War followed shortly afterwards and caused a further rift that meant that the People's Republic of China (PRC) and the US remained isolated from each other diplomatically until 1978.

Meanwhile, Japan remained under US occupation from 1945 to 1952, with little contact with China after 1949. This political separation of the two major Second World War belligerents in Asia led to a clear divergence in their circuits of memory. In Japan, the legacy of the war in Asia shaped historiography inexorably in the decades that followed. In China, the desire to burnish the revolution of 1949 became the dominant historical narrative, but the story of the war against Japan disappeared and reappeared over time in public consciousness, becoming (ironically) much more important in the years since the 1980s, rather than in the immediate post-war decades.

In Japan, modernisation became a key theme of the post-war settlement. The dominant political narrative implied that Japan was an almost purely economic actor, which had essentially started from zero in 1945 and was now making immense strides as its GDP grew. The historical narrative changed to reflect this: the Meiji Restoration of the 1880s, when Japan's first modernisation began, became the starting point of the story, and the turn to dictatorship in the 1930s became characterised as a *kurai tanima* ('dark valley') that was, overall, an anomaly in the rise of Japan to economic dominance (the second-biggest economy in the world by the 1980s).

Yet in practice, this bland, economistic story of modernisation with hiccups inevitably became intertwined with the unresolved trauma of the war and the end of the Japanese Empire. Unlike France and Britain, which saw their empires unwind over two decades after 1945, Japan's period as a coloniser came to a sudden end in August 1945 as its 'Greater East Asia Co-Prosperity Sphere' crashed into ruins. Japanese historians would spend the next few decades debating the causes of the disastrous war, with historians on the left, such as Ienaga Saburo, spending much of that time battling the conservative government with demands that Japan do more to face up to its war guilt (for instance, in the way that the war was described in school textbooks). Yet a caricature sometimes heard from outside – that Japan simply refused point-blank to acknowledge its war guilt – was never simplistically true; for instance, one of the most appalling war crimes, the Nanjing Massacre ('Rape of Nanking') of 1937–8, was actually forced into public attention by Japanese journalists such as Honda Katsuichi in the 1970s. In contrast, it was a decade or more before the subject was openly discussed in China: prior to the 1980s, the Beijing government had felt that excessive attention to Japanese war crimes would not help in the task of re-establishing diplomatic relations with Japan (which finally happened in 1972).

Even now, in the 2010s and 2020s, the legacy of the devastating war in Asia has continued to shape Japanese politics, education and culture. Films about the wartime years are still popular, but they tend to hew to very particular sorts of interpretation. Notably, very few such films deal with the China war that broke out in 1937; the 'real' war, it is implied, only seems to begin at Pearl Harbor in 1941, when the US, a Western enemy, joined the conflict. Furthermore, much of the popular culture in Japan surrounding the war deals with experience on the home front, rather than the invasion by Japan of other countries. The hit manga movie by Sunao Katabuchi, *In this Corner of the World* (2016), is a story of great power about a young woman who enters married life during the war years in a small village near Hiroshima (giving a clue to the eventual plot outcome). The story is a moving one, and shows the real suffering of the Japanese population in the final years of the war, but it stands as an example of a wide range of films in which the Japanese army in China, South East Asia or in other places invaded by Japan do not figure in any very explicit onscreen discussion. That is very different in the other major East Asian country whose wartime history shapes its present: China.

China and war

In the Mao era, China's historians were heavily constrained as to what they could write about. Worthwhile if limited work was done in the first decade of Mao's rule, mostly seeking cherry-picked history to underpin the narrative of an inexorable rise to power by the CCP. Then, the Cultural Revolution (1966–76) made it impossible for any intellectuals, including historians, to carry out any kind of meaningful writing. Only with the beginning of the reform era in 1978 did it become possible for historians to widen the scope of their research. One area which became much more widely visible was research on the period of the War of Resistance against Japanese Aggression, as the China Theatre of the Second World War has become known. For decades, discussion of the topic was limited to Chinese historical scholarship. This was largely because such a major part of the resistance to the Japanese was undertaken by the Nationalists (Guomindang or Kuomintang) under Chiang Kai-shek, with the Communists playing an important but essentially secondary role. After the Communist victory on the mainland in 1949, it became near-impossible for the CCP to give any sort of positive assessment of the anti-Japanese record of the enemies they had recently defeated in the civil war.

However, from the 1980s, a variety of factors changed the relative invisibility of the history of the war in China. In particular, historians pushed for a more nuanced approach to understanding the positive as well as the negative contributions that the Nationalists had made to defeating the Japanese, and succeeded in doing so with the perhaps surprising assistance of senior figures within the CCP such as the hardline 'conservative' former personal secretary to Mao, Hu Qiaomu. There were reasons for the Party's willingness to widen the angle of interpretation. Pragmatically, the CCP wanted to improve relations with Taiwan, and felt that being more complimentary about the Nationalists' wartime contribution would help that cause. In a wider sense, the 1980s saw China still recovering from the Cultural Revolution. The ideological rubble left behind at the end of those events had soured the population on the idea of class struggle. Leaders sought a more unifying narrative, and the shared struggle of the Chinese against the invaders during the Second World War fitted the bill well. (Wartime collaboration with the enemy, which was extensive, was not mentioned in this version of events.)

Over the past four decades, the narrative of the Second World War as a shaping event in Chinese history has become much more prominent. The analogy can be confrontational. The Chinese government declared that it would launch a 'people's war' against the COVID-19 virus at the start of the pandemic in early 2020; later that year, State Counsellor Yang Jiechi declared that the PRC would have to follow a 'protracted war' to create connections in its foreign policy. Both expressions are taken directly from Mao's writing on fighting the Japanese in the 1930s. Other uses of the period were more cooperative-sounding, including frequent reminders by Chinese leaders and diplomats that China had been the first signatory to the UN Charter in 1945 (at the San Francisco Conference of that year). By making this point, China was arguing that it was 'present at the creation' of the 1945 world order, and that just as the US has used its status as a maker of the post-war world to make claims in the present era, so China should be entitled to do so as well.

The plausibility of this claim can certainly be contested. But to understand it, Westerners need to know something about the place that China's wartime experience has had in its consciousness of its own recent history (just as one would do for Britain, Poland, Russia and other countries that still draw from the well of that long-ago conflict). It is widely known that China is one of the five permanent members of the UN Security Council, and a good number of people are aware that Beijing was only able to regain the China seat at the UN from Taiwan as late as 1971. However, without some awareness of the Chinese contribution to the war, and the significance that President Roosevelt placed on incorporating (Nationalist) China into the post-war global order, it is hard to make sense of the seemingly sudden appearance of China at the very highest levels of international society. In fact, the rise of China to global status is a narrative that has been underway since at least 1945, but via a path much more circuitous than that of, say, the United States.

Global narratives

China's more remote history has also been put to work in recent years, making claims to bolster a contemporary phenomenon, the increasingly global nature of China's overseas presence. There has been a new enthusiasm to tell the story of Zheng He, the Chinese Muslim admiral who sailed numerous times from China to destinations including South East Asia, India and East Africa in the early Ming dynasty, between 1405 and 1433. Zheng He was a remarkable figure, who led immense 'treasure ships' rowed by hundreds of sailors on expeditions that included trade and cultural exchange, as well as some conflict. Among the more extraordinary events of the voyages happened when the sailors were presented with a giraffe, which they brought back to China. The version of this story approved by the CCP tends to be saccharine: a core idea is that China's expeditions, unlike those of the Western powers in Africa and Asia, were purely about trade and not conquest or violence. The analogy is meant to be obvious: that just as it was the West, not China, that committed major violence in the early modern era, so the world today should be less fearful of China than of the West. In fact, historians have shown that Zheng He often used violence when he found it useful – for instance, in subduing a recalcitrant ruler during his voyage to Sri Lanka. It is, however, true that China did not use its imperial power to establish major overseas possessions as the European empires did (although it was happy to expand its land borders on many occasions).

Yet overall, despite distortions, it is still helpful to place stories like the voyages of Zheng He into the public domain in the West. The idea that the 'age of discovery' was a purely Western venture is long outmoded. Ideally, the understanding of Chinese and South East Asian navigation in the era before Western colonisation would go beyond the story of Zheng He. Chinese navigation techniques were sophisticated and extensive long before his voyages and, in the centuries that followed, we know that Chinese and South East Asian societies were engaged in complex trading relationships with each other. However, Zheng He has provided an approachable starting point to tell the wider story of maritime exploration by East Asian societies in which the West is not the centre of attention.

So far, I have chosen to concentrate on history as it appears in Chinese and Japanese eyes. This is deliberate; in the West, we spend too little time thinking about important strands of history where European actors are not the key players. Yet when it comes to global issues, as other essays in this collection show, the European imperial presence has shaped the modern era, and that was true also for East and South East Asia. For some states in the region, such as Singapore, the long-standing British connection is still evident in many ways. Singapore still sends many of its elites to Britain's top universities, when they don't go to the Ivy League, and the city-state is likely to play a larger role in British engagement with South East Asia in the Brexit era. However, the long history of this outpost, with its complex tale of trade, opium processing, economic exploitation and (failed) defence is little known in Britain, even in comparison with the story of Indian independence.

Yet China provides an even better example of a long-standing relationship with Britain that has almost no visibility in general histories. Trade is a topic much in the news these days, including the idea that Brexit Britain should trade more with East Asia. This should surely be a cue to find out more about the Imperial Maritime Customs Service, an extraordinary institution that lasted for a century. The Service was an agency staffed by Britons to collect taxes on behalf of the Chinese government. Although it was a product of imperialism, established in the aftermath of the Opium Wars, its first inspector-general, the Ulsterman Sir Robert Hart, always made it clear that he saw himself in the service of the Chinese government, rather than an agent of the British Empire. The institution – one in which China gave up parts of its sovereignty on tariffs to achieve a more effective and lucrative tax regime – has both parallels and profound differences with Britain's half-century in the EU.

There are also British connections to the story of China's rise. When people write about the cities of empire, they frequently have Calcutta or Cape Town in mind. It's far less common for them to think of Shanghai. Yet the city was also one of the major creations of settler colonialism, with its heart in a

British-dominated International Settlement for a century from 1843 until Pearl Harbor. Today, the former Settlement area has an ambiguous relationship with that era. Chinese historiography condemns British imperialism as a violation of sovereignty. Nonetheless, the heritage of the colonial era, in particular the Art Deco buildings that mark the famous Bund, or waterfront, is lovingly preserved and thought of as a cultural treasure in its own right. Yet if the impact of the foreign on Shanghai is regarded as an ambiguous legacy in today's entirely Chinese Shanghai, it is essentially absent from any Western historical consideration: outside a coterie of specialists, the significance of Shanghai's British heritage in shaping the modern city is hardly considered in the wider story of empire.

The story of Hong Kong has perhaps been more visible in recent years, because one of the most profoundly important stories of our own era is the erosion of the freedoms of residents of Hong Kong, in particular after the imposition of a draconian National Security Law by Beijing in July 2020. For the historically informed, however, what is intriguing and disturbing is the combination of English common law – the right to habeas corpus and applications for bail, along with barristers in horsehair wigs – with Chinese Communist authoritarianism in the way that the authorities in the city have cracked down on its democrats. Of course, this combination is not unique to Hong Kong: Singapore, Kenya and South Africa have historically been three states which combined the practice of English common law with highly repressive domestic politics. But Hong Kong's case is unique in terms of the direct clash and combination of two systems with profoundly different historical roots at the same time. Understanding how the city came to be in such a position in the 2020s can only come with an understanding of its unique history.

I use the term 'freedom' rather than just 'democracy' because, while the destruction of democratic norms in Hong Kong by its own rulers in 2020 is important, it is the product of a relatively short period of democracy in the colony. India was given elements of self-government from the early twentieth century onward. Hong Kong's first moves toward a very limited democracy took place only in 1952, although they were accelerated in later years. The Hong Kong of the 1960s and 1970s still suffered from major police corruption. The British period, in other words, was not one of unalloyed progress. However, many of the elements that made Hong Kong distinctive – judicial independence, economic freedom, and press and academic freedom – were also very much products of the British presence.

A greater and more nuanced understanding of Hong Kong's history would inform the discussion in two different areas. In Britain, and the West more generally, the discourse on the city's freedoms rightly concentrates on the loss of freedoms in the 2010s and 2020s, but is based on very little understanding of the complexities of Hong Kong's past. China, in turn, seeks to impose a new 'patriotic' history curriculum on the city, approved by Beijing, in which Hong Kong's history is made purely part of a wider Chinese history and, furthermore, a history in which the rise to power of the CCP is the most important and transformative element. Both narratives omit a profoundly important story about the relationship between imperial power and domination and equal treatment of sovereign states.

Why does it matter? History in East Asia is not just the past; it's very much current affairs. Yet the lack of attention to East

Asian history in the Western, and specifically British, perception is causing an increasingly problematic distortion in British and Western understandings of the contemporary world. Because of its economic and geopolitical weight, and because of the dangerous tensions inherent within it, East Asia will matter to the world in the 2020s more than it has for perhaps two hundred years. Today, some of the world's most dangerous potential clashes are in the Asia–Pacific region: the nuclear threat from North Korea, maritime clashes in the South and East China Seas, the possibility of a war over Chinese reunification with Taiwan, the China–India clash in the Himalayas, or the military coup of 2021 in Myanmar. Every single one of these very contemporary flashpoints has its origins in modern East Asian history. Understanding the region's history, both where it interacts with that of the West and where it does not, is an urgent task.

Selected Further Reading

Ian Buruma, *The Wages of Guilt: Memories of War in Germany and Japan* (London: Atlantic Books, 1994)

Paul Cohen, *Discovering History in China: American Historical Writing on the Recent Chinese Past* (New York: Columbia University Press, 1985)

Alexis Dudden, *Troubled Apologies Among Japan, Korea, and the United States* (New York: Columbia University Press, 2008)

Christopher Harding, *The Japanese: A History in Twenty Lives* (London: Penguin, 2020)

Sheila Jager and Rana Mitter (eds.), *Ruptured Histories: War, Memory and the Post-Cold War in Asia* (Cambridge, MA:

Harvard University Press, 2007)

Sheila Miyoshi Jager, *Brothers at War: The Unending Conflict in Korea* (London: Profile Books, 2013)

Rana Mitter, *China's Good War: How World War II is Shaping a New Nationalism* (Cambridge, MA: Harvard University Press, 2020)

Rana Mitter, *Chinese Characters: A History in Twenty Characters*: BBC Sounds Free download at https://www.bbc.co.uk/programmes/b09zgd6y/episodes/downloads

David Pilling, *Bending Adversity: Japan and the Art of Survival* (London: Penguin, 2014)

Tony Saich, *From Rebel to Ruler: One Hundred Years of the Chinese Communist Party* (Cambridge, MA: Harvard University Press, 2021)

Franziska Seraphim, *War Memory and Social Politics in Japan, 1945–2005* (Cambridge, MA: Harvard East Asian Monographs, 2006)

Chapter 17

Why history should always be rewritten

Charlotte Lydia Riley

Rewriting history might sound like a dangerous thing for a historian to espouse. Rewriting history reminds us of the Soviet state airbrushing Leon Trotsky, Lev Kamenev and Alexander Malchenko from photographs after they had been executed and their presence at key historical events became a difficult story to explain. It reminds us of the Turkish government refusing to recognise the Armenian genocide, the Communist Party of China forbidding discussion of the Tiananmen Square protests, the Polish government's refusal to acknowledge their nation's complicity in the Holocaust. This rewriting is framed around denial, and it is dangerous. It limits knowledge and understanding of the past, and it is used to shape contemporary political regimes that are opposed to democracy and openness, and committed to controlling information, to refusing clarity, to taking stories and twisting them to exercise ever more power over their citizens. The denial of historical events – airbrushing pictures, burning books, writing outright lies that aim to obfuscate and obliterate the past – must be resisted by historians and citizens.

But not all rewriting of history is wrong. Some rewriting is necessary. In fact, history cannot exist without being rewritten. This essay makes a case for rewriting history: in fact, it argues that history can only exist through the process of being written and rewritten.

History should be rewritten because history is not the past

Rewriting history is not airbrushing the past, because 'history' and 'the past' are fundamentally different things. The past is everything that has already happened, everywhere, to anyone. The past cannot be revisited or rewound – if you missed something that happened, tough luck! – and it cannot be rewritten. What we can do is research and write histories, which are at their heart stories about the past. These histories are partial and subjective, a single version of many different stories about the past that the historian could have chosen to tell.

This process of reconstructing the past in order to tell a story is not unique to historians. We all imagine the past all of the time, whether we are historians or not; even historians think about the past differently inside and outside of their work. We all have our family histories and the dense thickets of family trees that we construct in our head to imagine our relations, how they fit together, and what they each did, who they loved, how their lives intersected – even people we never met and can never know. All of this information fits into our imagination, although it might be captured only in a few pencil lines, held between two dates on a family tree, or caught in a few black-and-white stiffly posed photographs, or albums full of technicolour family snapshots. We have our personal histories, too, in which we chronicle the year we finished school, passed exams, got jobs, fell in love, fell out of love, married, divorced, had children, or lost people whom we loved. And the more prosaic histories, too: the day we missed a bus after a bad day at the office and cried (and the spot where it happened), the day we went to the seaside on a perfect hot day (and who we went with), the memories that come to mind whenever we get onto a particular train, or walk past a specific house. These are creative imaginations of the past, not just chronicles of events, and they are as constructed and as narrated as a monograph written by an academic historian, and they are as important, too. These histories are rewritten, and written over, as our lives move on, as our memories shift, and as the things that are important to us change over time.

We also all have a relationship to a wider, more encompassing past – the sense of our national history, our international history, the story of how our communities and nations existed in the past. History is, to some extent, a part of 'general knowledge', and we all have a set of touchstones that relate to our understanding of the past. In modern Britain, the Second World War seems to loom large over all contemporary political culture. This includes our communal chronology, which slices the twentieth century into chunks of 'post-war', or 'interwar'. To varying degrees, our collective imagination of the past might also include the First World War, the Easter Rising, the Industrial Revolution, the Napoleonic Wars, the Act of Union and so on further back in time: Glorious Revolution, Magna Carta, 1066. Every nation has a collective sense of the past and of the moments that make it up.

But if there is the Past, which is everything that Really Happened, 'history' is something more slippery. Historians turn their attention to a moment in the past, and worry away at it; they read the sources and go down dead ends and make copious notes and eventually they come away with something that we call History. And all through this process, the historian is making choices – what to include, what to avoid, what to write about and how to write and rewrite it.

This is not always welcomed by everyone. Historians can make themselves deeply unpopular by rewriting histories, by selecting what others believe to be the *wrong* stories, highlighting the *wrong* moments: by picking people understood as heroes and turning them into villains, or vice versa, or by revisiting events that should be familiar and comforting, and turning them upside down and inside out. But this rewriting of comforting myth is fundamental to the historian's role.

Of course, the comforting myth spun from tales of past national glories often resists the historian's red pen. The cultural memory of the Second World War that is so central to British national identity is built around the Blitz Spirit, the Dunkirk Spirit, the British pulling together, united. This story is invoked repeatedly at other points of national crisis, as an intrinsic truth about British identity, a blueprint for how to approach the modern world, or a yardstick against which the modern British should be measured. That historians now refer to the 'myth' of the Blitz, because the image of Britons mustn't-grumbling their way through the conflict is so inaccurate, or that the famous red 'Keep Calm and Carry On' posters were never actually used because they were such a misreading of the national mood, does not seem to matter. Myths are comforting and useful; that is why they survive. But historians will continue to worry away at them, all the same.

History should be rewritten because rewriting history is a historian's job

In this telling, if nations and communities collectively imagine the past, then a historian's job is to upend the ideas that are so comforting and unknit the stories that construct the Past and make something new, called history. But the historian's narrative is itself not the end of the story. The practice of writing and rewriting historical narratives is vital to historians' collective identity. When historians type their final sentence, when they publish their book, that is the start of a conversation, not the end.

After the history is written, we historians argue among ourselves over which version of the story is most compelling, and we look at the work done by historians of generations before us and we pick holes in it, pull it apart, and write it all again from a different perspective, including different people or using different archives or theories or schools. And then we present our history to the world – or at least, to each other – as a rewritten history. History would be a very different discipline if each topic were ticked off as finished whenever a new book appeared. If we could not rewrite history, then bad histories would stand as facts, and contentious interpretations – or worse, intentional untruths – would go unchallenged and unappealed.

Even if history were simply about finding new facts, then this process would take a little longer – historians would gradually fill in the story as we turned over new stones and found new documents underneath them (or, more likely, as archivists pointed us towards these documents in the catalogues that they had painstakingly compiled). Eventually, history would be finished – every fact would be known. But this is not how history works, and historians are not merely chroniclers of facts, compilers of top-ten lists or authors of almanacs.

Finding new sources is important – but not always because it brings to light new facts. Rather, new sources help us to write better histories because they can help us to change the stories and the focus of those narratives. Historians' writing is based on their interpretation of the past. But their work is not really based on the past itself, or certainly not the past as it *actually happened* – historians are not time-travellers, after all, and cannot visit their subject to check for certain what was actually going on. Instead, historians turn to primary sources to find the characters, events and ideas that they will write about, and they chase down rabbit holes to track individuals or moments or concepts across time or space.

What's more, the historian can never find every single primary source about a topic. Modern historians in particular often suffer from a surfeit of sources. Carolyn Steedman has written about a form of 'archive fever' at the end of a research trip that is not the anxiety of never reading all of the possible sources – even this would be impossible for most topics – but of not getting to the end of the single box file that remains on the to-do list. One historian might return to a topic over and over again during their career, and look at new sources every time: turning over new stones, finding new angles, hearing new voices and writing new narratives. So on the one hand, rewriting history is inherent to the life cycle of being a historian; careers are long, and there is always one more box file, one more manuscript, that pushes insistently against what you have written before.

On the other hand, many sources never make their way into the archive at all. So many sources are lost, or hidden, or destroyed, or never existed. Archives are another space for re-telling the past, with their own processes of selection, and the politics of whose story makes it into the archive are important to hold in our minds whilst we write. This might be because of the power politics at play in what we are writing about, itself. When the British Empire was decolonised in the early 1960s, the government issued strict instructions to colonial administrators. Controversial or incriminating files were to be burned (and the ashes broken up), or packed in weighted crates and dropped at the bottom of deep and current-free water. Some were marked either 'personal' (in the Gold Coast) or 'DG' (for 'deputy gover-nor', in Uganda) or 'W' (for 'watch files', in Kenya); all of these classifications were chosen as deliberately bland and unlikely to attract attention, as the files were carefully, hastily removed to England. The process was so secret that officials were warned to keep their 'W' stamps hidden safe in their offices; and, of course, to destroy the circular which gave them these instructions. The files removed to England were hidden in Hanslope Park and not uncovered until 2011 when they came to light during a court case brought against the British government over their respon-sibility for the detainment and torture of suspected Mau Mau fighters in Kenya (and among the folders were some of the very instructions that officials had been told so strictly to destroy). These files are, very gradually, being opened to historians through the National Archives. Colonial histories are being rewritten to include the details within them – details that the British colonial government had gone to such pains to hide from historians.

Sources aren't always hidden through conspiracy and violence, however. Sources get lost all the time. People have their own reasons to tear up a letter, or they lose it or spill tea on it or they decide never to send it in the first place. For every love letter carefully treasured, there is one that has been burned because the affair ended in betrayal, or the contents are now too embarrassing, or for deeper reasons, too; love affairs that could not speak their name in public, such as those of the many same-sex couples who were forced to hide their love from families and the state or whose letters are often undocumented because they were simply too dangerous to preserve.

Ordinary people have no requirement to create and maintain a personal archive (although so many of us do, in shoeboxes and on dusty hard-drives), and their stories can therefore be hard to unpick. Even formal archives don't have space for everything: what they choose to keep is shaped by their own institutional politics (which may not, in the past, have reflected our politics today) as well as broader ideas about what must be saved as the historical record and what can, reluctantly or cheerfully, be lost. So historians always write their histories based on partial sources, and they rewrite them as they come across narratives that show up those stories as partial, with the absences of people and perspectives suddenly made visible.

History should be rewritten because we need to add new voices and new stories

History was, for a long time, the story of dead white men. History was kings, and occasionally queens; it was generals and prime ministers and inventors and explorers. Their subjects, their soldiers, their citizens, the people who benefited from or were hurt by these inventions, the people already living in the places newly 'discovered' – these people were not important to historical narratives. History was the story of Great Men who Made History through their choices and their actions. Then, one day, historians discovered social structures, and started to think about how history might be shaped by forces beyond one person's control, and it turned out that there were other people existing in the past, and those people caused history, and they experienced it too.

This is a massive simplification, of course. The crowd, the mass, the mob has always been a presence in historical writing, and historians still care about top-down histories as well as the bottom-up ones. But the big rewriting of history that came when social history encouraged us to think more about ordinary people, their lives and their experiences (and perhaps even their thoughts and feelings and hopes and dreams) should not be understated. History now is different to history when it was first established in university departments, and it has been rewritten to reflect those new realities.

History departments are different places, too. Lilian Penson was the first woman (in fact, the first person) to receive a PhD from the University of London, in 1921; she became a lecturer at Birkbeck in 1925 and went on to be appointed the first ever female vice chancellor of a university in the United Kingdom and Commonwealth. Between 1921 and 1990, only a fifth of PhD students in history were women; as more women entered the profession, the notion of who had the right to write and rewrite histories shifted. The profession has a long way to go before it will be properly representative, and history departments remain disproportionately white in their composition; it was not until 2018 that Olivette Otele became the first Black female history professor in Britain. People of colour face numerous barriers to becoming academic historians, including racism in the school system, disproportionate levels of poverty and inability to fund graduate studies, and the fact that for too long their voices, their perspectives and their histories have been systematically excluded from curriculums and research projects. Rewriting history is necessary as part of a reparative project to address these inequalities, and it should be led by the voices that have been previously ignored or silenced.

More broadly, it is important to consider who is given the privilege of rewriting history. Whose stories about the past are accepted as history, and whose are seen as myth, lies or polemic? When the National Trust released a report in September 2020 that sought to explore the connections between National Trust properties and the history of colonialism, it was lambasted by right-wing critics as a sop to 'wokeness', an act of political correctness gone mad, an attempt to rewrite history through contemporary values and (bizarrely, specifically) an attack on Winston Churchill (who was mentioned only twice in a report of 115 pages). That such a venerable and often conservative institution should come under such attack shows the extent to which some topics are not considered appropriate subjects for rewriting. But if these stories can never be rewritten, or supplemented, or enhanced, then they are dead history; they do not speak to us today and they will languish and wither, and eventually be forgotten.

History should be rewritten because rewriting is not erasure

When President Donald Trump hosted the very first White House Conference on American History in September 2020, he did so to celebrate a spotless American past, 'the fulfilment of a thousand years of Western civilisation'. But in making these confident claims, the conference also revealed a distinct anxiety about American identity, explicitly motivated as it was by the concern that left-wing historians were seeking to undermine American history with a 'twisted web of lies in our schools and classrooms'. Trump explicitly talked about the need to 'defend' American history against such initiatives as the *New York Times'* 1619 Project, which he believed 'rewrites American history to teach our children that we were founded on the principle of op-pression, not freedom'; the clear fact that America represented the opposite of 'freedom' for millions of enslaved Black people is of course entirely absent from Trump's narrative. But Trump cannot accept that his understanding of American history is partial and political, and for him and his supporters, the 1619 Project attacks not only history but also the very foundations of American nationhood. In defending history against this re-writing, he argued, he and his supporters were ensuring that 'the legacy of 1776 will never be erased'.

The idea that rewriting history is akin to erasing history is pervasive. In the summer of 2020, Black Lives Matter protes-tors succeeded in toppling the statue of Edward Colston that was on display in Bristol and throwing it to the bottom of the harbour. They, too, were accused of trying to 'erase' history – by removing Colston from the streets of Bristol, it was argued, they were preventing people from learning about his role both in the transatlantic slave trade and in philanthropy in the British metropole. But removing a statue is not the same as scrubbing someone from the historical record. Instead, it is a creative re-sponse to the way that history is embedded in our towns and cities. People do not learn much history from statues – not least because statues by their nature are impressive, imposing and valorising objects. Communities erect statues to people whom they wish to celebrate; putting a small, explanatory plaque on the plinth to explain that they also did terrible things does not effectively counterbalance that cultural meaning. Colston remains in the history books; nobody is trying to erase him. In fact, as his statue was toppled, far more people heard his name for the first time, learned something about his life and about the wider history of Bristol, the transatlantic slave trade, and the politics of commemoration.

Making history should be a collaborative, creative act. Pulling down a statue is not erasing history – it's an act of historiography, the process by which historians critically evaluate ideas about the past. Pulling down a statue is the act of challenging a previous generation's interpretation of the past. Communities have the right to think about how their histories are being told, and to think about who is being represented and celebrated, but also which people or groups are absent. And we have no requirement to accept the stories that were told by our forebears. The statues that were erected in the past – like the books that were written by previous generations – can be revisited, updated, debated and yes: rewritten. This is how history can be a live discipline, not a set of dead facts on a page or stuck behind a glass case in a dimly lit room.

History should be rewritten because history tells us as much about who we are *now* as about what happened *then*

The idea of the past as something which has to be rewritten builds on one of the fundamentals of historical practice, which is that history and histories are subjective. When E.H. Carr told the history student that every historian had a bee in their bonnet, and told them to listen out for the buzzing, he was telling the history student to be aware that every historian has their own way of thinking about the histories that they write, and their own identity that shapes the choices that they make about the work that they do. The buzzing is the historian's subjectivities, her opinions, her context, and – as any A level student would tell you – her biases. Of course, Carr actually warns the student to listen out for the bee in *his* bonnet; the fact that he could casually refer to historians as male despite being married to Betty Behrens, an internationally renowned historian of the *ancien régime*, is quite a buzzing in itself. These subjectivities can shape historians' work in problematic ways, then, but they are also what powers our historical research and writing. History is not a series of facts – again, as Carr says, it's not simply fish on a slab. So the past is rewritten because historians are working with their subjectivities and their imagination as much as with what Really Happened.

If this sounds dangerous, it can be. The writing of history is a powerful political act. It is also an act of contemporary importance; history is frequently invoked not just as a set of events that happened in the past but as something more than this, something that has stories or narratives or even lessons built into it. The idea that if you don't understand history you are condemned to repeat it – or that if you do understand history, you are condemned to watch other people repeat it, or that history is repeated once as tragedy, then as farce – is commonplace. Journalists and politicians like to talk about the necessity of learning lessons from history, as if the past were merely a trial run for the world around us today. Journalists and politicians also like to think about what historians of the future will say about *this* moment (and about them): their understanding of the world around them is at least partly contingent on historians being able to look back on us now and make a judgement.

We can learn about the past, but we rarely learn *from* the past; there are no simple lessons from history waiting to be applied. But whilst historians do not write histories only to understand the world around them, reading histories does tell us a lot about the concerns and complaints of the historian and the society in which they were writing. And so rewriting history is necessary as the world around us shifts, and our concerns change; in the future, in turn, the histories that we write now will be rewritten.

History is framed by the moment in which historians are working – their material conditions, their political perspective, their experiences and identities, everything around them as they sit down at their desk and begin to write. And so historians work to reclaim the past, to rewrite the past, to reimagine what the past was and is and how it might be told today. But ordinary people – people who are not historians – have a role too, because history is a collaborative process that involves many different constituencies: professional historians, archivists, museum curators, family historians, local history societies, but also everybody who thinks or talks about the past, and all the places and spaces and objects and artworks that prompt them to do so. The past needs to be imagined, for historians to reimagine it. And ordinary people are not remembering, or simply repeating stories they have been told; they are making choices too, in what they decide to leave in, what they choose to leave out. Ordinary people have agency in prioritising certain historical narratives over others; if historians want to rewrite wider understandings of history, they need to recognise and work with this agency.

We think about our own pasts differently as our lives change. Distance from the past does not always change the way that we feel about it – some memories and emotions stay with people forever. But for most people, even if they don't do this consciously, the past is always being reimagined, just as the future is continuously invented and reinvented, everything being rewritten over and over again. As historians, in our work, part of what we should try to do is capture this sense of fluidity, and contingency, and precarity – the past and the future, as creative endeavours. Imagining the past is a creative endeavour, and it is something that everybody does, all of the time. Historians do it for a living, maybe, but we are not the only ones. History can be comforting, or it can be challenging, but it is always only one of many possible stories. History must be rewritten, over and over again, to reflect this.

Selected Further Reading

Hakim Adi, *Black British History: New Perspectives from Roman Times to Present Day* (London: Zed Books, 2019)

Svetlana Alexievich, *The Unwomanly Face of War* (London: Penguin, 2018)

Catherine Hall, *White, Male and Middle Class: Explorations in Feminism and History* (Cambridge: Polity, 1992)

Saidiya Hartman, *Wayward Lives, Beautiful Experiments* (London: Serpent's Tail, 2019)

Ludmilla Jordanova, *History in Practice* (London: Bloomsbury, 2017)

Jill Lepore, *These Truths: A History of the United States* (New York: W.W. Norton, 2018)

Gerda Lerner, *Why History Matters: Life and Thought* (Oxford: Oxford University Press, 1998)

Alison Light, *A Radical Romance: A Memoir of Grief, Love and Consolation* (London: Penguin, 2018)

Carolyn Steedman, *Landscape for a Good Woman* (London: Virago, 1986)

Carolyn Steedman, *Dust: The Archive and Cultural History* (Manchester: Manchester University Press, 2002)

Chapter 18

How literature shapes history

Islam Issa

Blurred boundaries

That literature is a key facet of culture is beyond doubt. The role of literature is not just to entertain or inform. In fact, literature – both writing and reading – has changed the world and will continue to do so.

To consider how we read literature and history alongside one another is to consider something of a chicken-and-egg situation. What comes first? Does literature shape our understanding of history? Or is it history that shapes the literature we read and write? In a way, these questions don't need an answer. They do, though, point to a dynamic relationship that confirms the importance of both literature and history to the formation of our ideas and the perceptions we have of ourselves and the world around us.

In the sixth and seventh centuries, on the first day of the eleventh month of the ancient South Arabian calendar, thousands of people from all around the region arrived in their caravans for the annual Suq Ukaz (Ukaz Market). The city (in modern-day Saudi Arabia) was located right in the middle of the Spice Route, an industrial voyage so central to Arabs that it inspired the legend of Sinbad the Sailor. Though the market did indeed sell an array of fragrant, colourful spices, key items included clothes and camels, as well as dates, honey and wine – this was primarily a time for different tribes to catch up. Before printing technology or telecommunication, everyone gathered eagerly to find out just what had been happening that year in the world around them. So, one after another, dressed in their tribe's most distinguished garments and colours, a nominated spokesperson would stand up to tell everyone the latest news from their land. And they would do so through the magic and flow of Arabic poetry.

As an ambassador of sorts, the poetry was not only expected to be informative in its content, but grandly impressive in its style. History was essentially being written and reported through these verses, one poem after another. As an alternative to writing books devoted to history, almost everything we know today of pre-Islamic Arabia is a result of the period's poetry, regarded as both the finest verse in the language and a reliable, detailed historical record of the lives and events of that time. These poems constitute resilient oral history, memorised meticulously and passed on with high regard from one generation to the next until recorded. It's also thought that when the King of Ukaz heard a poem he liked, he asked for it to be written. In the eighth century, seven key poems were gathered and transcribed onto the most special linen cloths – the ink used to write them was real gold. So important were these poems that they were hung on the Kaaba in

Mecca, the holiest site of pilgrimage, earning their name Mu'al-laqat, or the Hanging Poems. For the Arabs of that time and even today, history and poetry aren't just related, they are practically one and the same.

It is no surprise that oral history, through its reliance on the spoken word, often has literary qualities. In Ancient Greece, a rhapsode was a full-time professional reciter of the epic poems, most famously Homer's *Iliad* and *Odyssey*. Dressed in a long cloak and holding a staff, the rhapsode moved from town to town, stopping in public places to read the literature aloud. Helen, one would narrate, was the most beautiful woman in the world. When Paris of Troy took her from her husband Menelaus, King of Sparta, the Trojan War ensued. Like Homer's epics, the Greek poems forming the Epic Cycle and the tragedies of such dramatists as Sophocles centred on the Trojan War: simultaneously one of the best-known wars ever and one of the least likely to have ever taken place. In Greek antiquity and for centuries thereafter, these legendary events were assumed to be factual. Naturally, fact and fiction can become convoluted. But in the process, such myths become a part of the historical makeup of places and people. Walking through the streets of a city can be as much about its literary and apocryphal events as the ones we cannot doubt. It is the feeling you get turning every corner of a city like Jerusalem or Rome. In Britain, it's the reason why the road sign into Nottinghamshire reads 'Robin Hood's County'. Within a few decades of the twentieth century, myth and fiction – that we almost find ourselves believing – came to define locations like Scotland's Loch Ness and London's Baker Street. Literature and mythology become part of everyday history and its development, affecting such factors as national identity and a place's architectural and economic landscape. Literature itself becomes part of history, not least cultural history.

But literature also carves and responds to its own historical moment. In William Shakespeare's *The Tempest*, the only humans Miranda has ever met on the remote island are her father and the Native Caliban. When she sees Ferdinand (whom she'll eventually wed), she emits the easiest of phrases: 'What is it?' These three monosyllabic words show Miranda's simplicity and naivety, but also her desire and wonderment. After all, her name originates from the Latin verb 'to wonder', and in turn when Ferdinand sees her, his reaction is 'O, you wonder!' But Miranda's question, 'What is it?', is more than just characterisation: essentially, it's the question of the entire Renaissance. What is life? What is doctrine? What is art?

Even beyond a text itself, literary theories and movements give us insight into historical patterns of thought. At the turn of the nineteenth century, William Wordsworth, attempting to write in accessible language about ordinary subjects, spoke of 'revolutions, not of literature alone, but likewise of society itself'. Responding to the Enlightenment's emphasis on neoclassical literature's serious topics and methodical styles, the Romantic poets moved away from standard, classical modes of writing. The Enlightenment's neoclassical approach to literature signified, for instance, its emphasis on science and order; the Romantic poets responded by writing about nature and innocence. That neoclassical literary position also indicated a wider Enlightenment desire for 'rationality' over 'superstition' which, among other things, helped justify its colonial projects intended to 'save' the Natives. As such, the literary context can elucidate how ideas progress, or better yet, make us question 'progress'.

*

When an ominous skeleton found under a Leicester car park in 2012 was confirmed to be that of fifteenth-century monarch Richard III, a procession was arranged to ensure a reburial fit for a king. As the unusual protagonist of one of Shakespeare's most famous histories, *Richard III*, many eyes turned inevitably to the gripping hero of the play to seek answers about the real-life royal. Shakespeare's Richard is a complex character, so insecure about his appearance and relationships that within seconds of the curtains being raised, he declares: 'I am determined to prove a villain.' He hogs the stage and kills anybody who comes in the way of the throne, including his two innocent nephews. When the real-life procession was confirmed, one tabloid's screaming headline read: 'QUEEN TO PAY TRIBUTE TO "EVIL" KING'. In another, a columnist anguished 'with mounting stupefaction' that 'the world had gone stark staring bonkers' as it watched the 'grotesque televised travesty' of 'without question one of the most evil, detestable tyrants ever to walk this earth', adding that 'Shakespeare's portrayal had a genuine basis in fact'. Like a movie based on a true story, having a basis in fact is very different to historical evidence. We do not even have a portrait of Richard from his own lifetime. There is no clear-cut evidence that he killed key rivals as he does in the play, or indeed his nephews. Shakespeare's sources told him that Richard had a hunched back, a withered arm and a visible limp. Analysis of the bones confirmed that he did have severe scoliosis (curvature of the spine), but evidence of a withered arm and limp couldn't be confirmed. On this occasion, literature had been embedding ideas into the popular imagination, thus informing and even dominating our understanding of a historical past. And, in turn, by affecting reactions to current events, it was also play-ing a part in carving the narrative of present and future history, in this case a brand-new chapter in the history of an English monarch.

The constantly reciprocating process is even clearer if we re-member that this literature was itself based on history writing. Shakespeare read histories before writing his plays, in this case using Sir Thomas More's *History of King Richard III* (1519) and *Holinshed's Chronicles* (1577). Both sources were affected by their political contexts and served as accounts that legitimised Tudor rule at the expense of Richard's House of York. Indeed, the very subjectivity of history means that it is itself a genre of literature. What is more, Shakespeare was a creative writer and businessman whose aims included creating dramatic effect and putting backsides on seats. As a result of his success, Shakespeare became part of the establishment and wrote plays performed for the royals. But in setting up the Globe, he also helped to create a more inclusive public theatre that anyone could enjoy (you could pay a penny to stand in the pit). The reliance on certain sources, the careful business model and the artistic licence all confirm that the historicity of Shakespeare's plays should be treated with a pinch of salt. Add to that how Shakespeare has become so integral to British identity that he is part of British history too – so we might approach him differently to other writ-ers because we assume authority and universality. Nonetheless, history certainly informs literature, while literature affects both our reading of past history and our creation of new history: a perpetual pendulum.

The power of the reader

Literature is not a straightforward phenomenon. There are multiple steps and processes at play involving both the writer and the reader. Think of a novel, poem or play as a contract – first signed by its writer then counter-signed by the reader or audience member. In most cases, the writer is effectively allowing their text to be read and interpreted; the work ceases to be theirs alone and becomes something of a public property. The reader's end of the deal is that they will read and in turn, whether they realise it or not, provide an interpretation. In doing so, while the text itself remains unchanged, its meanings change depending on who the reader happens to be, where they are, and when and how they are reading it. I refer to this, quite simply, as *the power of the reader*. It is the power that makes literature able to morph across space and time. But it is also what confirms a crossover with a key characteristic of history: both history and literature are subjective.

Writers are readers too. This can be clearer on some occasions than others. For instance, writers might use what they read as source or inspiration, or they might provide allusions or inter-texts from previous works. More generally, though, what we read can shape aspects of our personal or collective identities: this might be a bedtime story we heard, something we were forced to read in school, the local newspaper, or even the social media feed.

That different readers can take different things from a single text is obvious but overlooked. As with the theory of intersectionality – our identities intersect lots of different categories to form our own individual identity – can we expect people of different genders, races, abilities, classes, sexualities and faiths to read in the same way? Might not a Black woman at the intersection of sexism and racism respond to a poem (about anything) differently to a white man? Or to give a simple example, wouldn't a Holocaust survivor read lines from *The Merchant of Venice* – 'If you prick us do we not bleed? If you tickle us do we not laugh?' – in a distinctive way? Or should we be surprised that the Nazis put on over fifty anti-Semitic performances of the play between 1933 and 1939, twenty in Adolf Hitler's first year as chancellor? The way people and societies respond to literature, then, tells us about their particular moment of history.

During South Africa's institutional apartheid (1948–94), Robben Island's maximum-security jail held key political prisoners. Confined to religious texts, the prisoners sneaked in Shakespeare's *Complete Works* in the disguise of a sacred Hindu book. As the edition was passed around, the inmates agreed to annotate the passages that spoke to them. On 16 December 1979, one of them, a revolutionary by the name of Nelson Mandela, signed his name next to a speech by Julius Caesar:

> Cowards die many times before their deaths,
> The valiant never taste of death but once.
> Of all the wonders that I yet have heard,
> It seems to me most strange that men should fear,
> Seeing that death, a necessary end,
> Will come when it will come.
>
> *Julius Caesar* 2.2.33–8

These words spoke to a man seventeen years into his life sentence on death row. His act of reading and interpreting gave yet more meaning to these words. They made Apartheid and Mandela part of Shakespearean history and Shakespeare part of their history.

In *Richard II*, Shakespeare presents a key scene that brings to life the hot potato of that period: succession. Based on events in the fourteenth century, the deposition scene sees Richard relinquish his crown to Henry Bolingbroke, later Henry IV. Deposition was serious, so this scene was constantly censored from early printed editions of the play. At the turn of the seventeenth century, the Earl of Essex's London residence had become a focal point for people angry with the government. In 1601, conspirators including the Earl planned the deposition of Queen Elizabeth I. By this time, *Richard II* had become less popular and was not performed regularly, so the Earl paid 40 shillings to Shakespeare's company – a higher than usual fee – to put on a special performance of the play. They did so on the eve of the rebellion as a way of inspiring the conspirators, not least through the deposition scene. When the rebellion failed and the conspirators were executed, one of them, Sir Gilly Meyrick, had commissioning this performance listed as one of his charges. Shakespeare's company was in trouble but managed to convince the court that they knew nothing of the plot and had not done this for ideological purposes but for money. They got away with a warning.

More recently, when Salman Rushdie wrote *The Satanic Verses* in 1988, it was not so much the text as the reaction that made it a phenomenon. Due to perceived blasphemy, Muslims protested globally while Iran's Ayatollah Khomeini ordered for Rushdie to be killed. Until these events, book sales were rather low, but afterwards they understandably increased worldwide. Perhaps the best way to get people to read a text is to ban it. Rushdie is now taught at most universities, not so much because of the text but because of its reception. More generally, the literature opened a series of discussions about real world issues that continue today, like freedom of speech or, in the UK, the development of a seemingly collective British-Muslim identity.

Whether we notice it or not, reading literature is about looking for clues, excavating the world of the text, piecing together different pieces of its jigsaw. The text itself, a product of the context in which it's written, gives insight into people and society, into public and private spaces, into moods and sensibilities, into likes and dislikes – and the activity of reading does that too. Much as E.H. Carr noted how the historian is an important part of history, the writer and the reader of literature are also part of shaping history. Literature defines how we see our present and the decisions we make with it become the essence of history.

There can come a point when reception turns into convention. This doesn't just relate to myths but to real people and events. One such example is the Egyptian queen Cleopatra. Her native Ptolemaic Alexandria was partly under water and the Great Library of Alexandria had been burnt, likely by Julius Caesar's army. As such, we know little about how she presented herself and how her people perceived her. In particular, when she attempted to put her son Caesarion on the throne after his father Caesar was assassinated, the heir apparent, Octavian, unleashed an attack to defeat her. It is writing from that moment – which the influential Plutarch then used as his source – that led to the image of Cleopatra that we have today. One could go as far as calling it propaganda or a smear campaign. Indeed, Roman sources had to present a worthy enemy and justify how a woman was able to divert two of their most prominent men, Caesar and Marc

Antony, both of whom were heroes. Cleopatra's superpower became none other than her sexy seduction. The second-century note that she was capable of 'insatiable passion and avarice' was written by Cassius Dio, a Roman politician turned historian. The gendered writings presented her as a drunk, a temptress, and erotically irresistible. In the few rarely discussed Egyptian and Arabic sources, however, we find a different Cleopatra: a powerful leader and intellectual. For example, tenth-century traveller al-Masudi calls her a sage and philosopher, without any unnecessary reference to her appearance.

Take Cleopatra's well-known suicide in 30 BC. The Romans knew the power of spectacle and, had she been captured, Cleopatra would likely have been paraded humiliatingly around Rome as a prisoner. If it did take place, then, the suicide was not because she was head over heels for a Roman, but because she wanted to die on her own terms. In that way, it can be interpreted as a political act and even an act of pride and resistance. We also have a common perception of how she committed suicide: a snake biting her breast. But Cleopatra's doctor didn't cite a reason for the death. A few decades after she died, Greek historian Strabo described it as suicide either by asp bite or poisonous ointment. In the second century, decades after Cleopatra, Plutarch's account of her death offered the possibility that she pierced her arm with a hairpin before inserting poison, adding that she smuggled an asp in a fig basket before getting it to bite her arm. This has since been regarded as the most authentic account of the suicide despite being doubted by some historians from Plutarch's time through today. But the image of a snake is by no means a coincidence. In fact, there is a chance that Cleopatra herself approved this narrative. The asp would likely have been an Egyptian cobra, which was used to depict female deities and held an important position in Egyptian culture as a symbol of royal divinity and protection. As such, to Egyptians, its symbolism served as a confirmation of Cleopatra's divine and royal status.

Since then, Judaeo-Christian influences, not least the story of Adam and Eve, have helped normalise the image of the woman as seductress (in the company of a phallic serpent). Cleopatra's death has therefore helped cement her image as a femme fatale – an attractive character archetype in literature and art. It is no surprise, then, that she finds her way into canonical English literature. In *The Legend of Good Women*, Geoffrey Chaucer has Mark Antony stab himself to save his reputation before a lovelorn, mourning Cleopatra fills a grave with serpents, strips naked, and slips into it. Chaucer ends the story as follows:

> And she hir deeth receyveth, with good chere,
> For love of Antony, that was hir so dere: –
> And this is storial sooth, hit is no fable.
>
> (700–2)

The last line here, almost serving as an addendum to the more expected rhyming couplet finale, is as fascinating as the story itself. This 'is no fable', the reader is told, but 'storial sooth', meaning historical truth.

More famously, Shakespeare's *Antony and Cleopatra* is one of the primary ways in which people in the West have engaged with Cleopatra over the last four centuries. Aside from creating a complicated character with 'infinite variety', Shakespeare too emphasises her suicide. In the play, she uses an asp, but it doesn't bite her arm, as Plutarch wrote, instead biting her breast. This sexualised version of Cleopatra's suicide has had lasting effects on popular cultural perceptions of the queen. It is also an example of literature becoming a means through which history is received. In fact, the subjectivity of those biased Roman histories became coupled with the subjectivity of the literature that came after it – and indeed with the reception of that literature, which has led to yet more popular cultural notions through artistic paintings and Hollywood movies.

The case of Cleopatra's exotic, orientalised image is also an indication of how important sources can be and the ripple effect they can have. If our source of knowledge for her character is popular culture, like Shakespeare, and his source was Plutarch, it is no wonder that the accuracy of historical accounts can differ. De-historicising this queen – or seeing her as a mere literary character, as Harold Bloom contended – offers her as a shifting conduit for different agendas (like being painted as a blonde woman in the Middle Ages to show beauty ideals, or as a passive woman that needs saving, during colonialism). One solution is to diversify our sources of knowledge, whether history or literature, in order to develop a more representative range of outlooks and opinions. For instance, in Egypt, the renowned poet laureate Ahmad Shawqi wrote an Arabic play entitled *The Death of Cleopatra* (1927). Here, Cleopatra is a confident orator and poet, is spiritually grounded, values the institution of marriage, and puts Egypt's interests above everything else. In an essay appended to the play, the author, possibly Shawqi, laments the 'fictive style' and 'suspect history' of the Roman sources. In direct response to the English canon, they add that 'Cleopatra, whether in Shakespeare, Dryden, or Shaw, does seem the creation of a man's imagination', before asking, 'should not the Egyptian author do justice to this falsely accused Egyptian?' Shawqi is also a reader: his writing is itself a type of reception. He also confirms that literature, as a dramatic form, does not have to abide by historical fact – but that it certainly does influence what we perceive to be historical fact about events, figures and societies. Many Egyptians encounter Shawqi well before Shakespeare, so Shawqi's literary activity serves as their dominant version of history and popular culture.

His response to Shakespeare came during the *nahdah*, or Arab renaissance, in the late nineteenth and early twentieth centuries. At this time, the region was under European colonisation, in Egypt's case, by Britain. This literary renaissance was direct resistance to colonialism. The canonical literature of the coloniser was often introduced into the culture and education systems – not least Shakespeare. The *nahdah* involved elevating Arabic literature through experimentation, for the purpose of renewal and autonomy. In doing so, it engaged with foreign literature to show that it was more than capable of responding to it, learning from it and exceeding it. Since much of the literature was patriotic, it helped create a sense of national identity and anti-colonial sentiment that eventually resulted in independence. Here, the historical context was reshaping the country's literature, before literature itself was used to reshape history.

Moving on from the pendulum, we here see a cyclical process: the past can shape literature, and literature can shape the future.

The future

When European settlers colonised the Americas, the British ones took Shakespeare with them: a cultural symbol of their patriotism. By retaining and claiming Shakespeare as their own despite being on the other side of the world, the settlers – and eventually the Founding Fathers – were able to push English as the predominant emigrant language in the United States. Literature is a key facet in the politics of language and culture, and in turn, identity. In this case, it affected the future of what would become the most influential nation on earth today.

But can literature predict historical events that have yet to take place? In the same way that during its renaissance Arab literature became autonomous, so too did the countries: they achieved independence on the back of the literary developments. Even through today, seventh-century Bedouin poet Qays al-Mullawah's *Layla and Majnun* has consistently been called 'the *Romeo and Juliet* of the east' despite the fact the Arab story came generations before Shakespeare, thus confirming cultural and indeed political hierarchies. The way in which many readers in the United Kingdom are conscious of their own iconic writers but less aware of their European counterparts certainly says something about the country's position towards its continental neighbours (and how we might have expected Brexit). That there are no Black writers clearly embedded into the literary canon (Linton Kwesi Johnson became the first Black poet in the Penguin Classics series as recently as 2002) says something about the imminent need to address racial inequalities.

I would argue that our responses to literature are even more likely to shape the future. Today, for example, taking Shakespeare to the world can risk perpetuating a model of cultural imperialism or neo-colonialism. Literature teaches us that globalisation can be a factor in the invisibility of supposed 'periphery' cultures. While democratised, globalised approaches have begun to exist, they almost always either respond to the normalised narrative or are based on Shakespeare's mythically universal status. Instead, our response to Shakespeare should include an appreciation of how different cultures around the world have read and performed his works. The capital of Shakespeare is no longer just Stratford-upon-Avon or London: it's everywhere. Much as Shakespeare spread from England to the world, Shakespeare can now feed back to England, from the world. These different responses to literature don't falsify one another but are part of an ongoing struggle for interpretation. Inclusivity of interpretation is part of global citizenship. So long as some readers are being neglected, though, populism will continue to rise. After all, the allure of populism is its call for power to be taken from the establishment into the hands of the supposedly relatable everyman. Current structures favour mainstream interpretations: we are often told what to read and how to read it, not least by the education system and the popular outlets. The current structures are therefore biased from the very outset.

While we expect to be empowered as consumers (particularly in the digital age), are we empowered as readers? And with ideological battle lines these days blurred – there is no longer a common enemy as there was, for example, during wartime or colonisation – this kind of hierarchy doesn't look as obvious or harmful as it should.

So, first, I contend that we must consider how we approach culture and arts: I call this the *entry point*. It relates to any artistic medium, from literature to paintings to television shows. To consider the entry point, we should ask ourselves some questions. Are we approaching what we receive and how we receive it from an independent perspective? Are we passively accepting the normalised narratives? Are we basing the work and its afterlife on nonchalant historical myths about popularity and canonicity? For historians and literary critics, the entry point also needs to give validity to the lesser-known viewpoints.

Second, I believe that in order to truly reflect our global citizenship and desire for equality, we must appreciate how diverse *the power of the reader* can be. As mentioned, the text itself only changes through reception, and writers are also readers.

The term *periphery neglect* refers to the way in which some readers, seemingly on the peripheries, are ignored in favour of apparently mainstream readers. To appreciate different readers, we should give a voice to periphery readers and writers, not only mainstream readers and writers (often white, English-speaking males, mostly affiliated to traditional institutions and publishers). Practically, there are a variety of actions and steps that can help to facilitate this, from encouraging under-represented groups to enter and excel in such fields as journalism, writing, publishing and academia (where they may bring new perspectives to what we read), to ensuring that the classroom is always a safe space in which a student's identity enhances rather than hinders their contributions. More personal endeavours are also possible: they can be as simple as diversifying our own friends so that we can be exposed to more opinions when we sit in the coffee shop. By giving this voice to periphery readers and writers, different perspectives come to the fore. Of course, intersectionality is pivotal here: different identity categories coincide in order to form a more precise life experience, and one change can be repercussive overall – all the way to the text, and in turn, to our understanding of history.

Like history, literature is not static. Both are fluid, ever-changing phenomena, especially since our own ideas and ideals are always developing. The role of the writer, reader and literary critic shares a fundamental requirement with that of the historian: to ask *why*? Maintaining the chicken-and-egg analogy with which this essay began, we might remember that literature and history are in many senses one and the same. Life imitates art and art imitates life – or history imitates literature and literature imitates history. History and literature are interchanging phenomena: a series of interpretations by writers and readers that give individuals and societies a lens into the past, inform the present, and frame the future.

Selected Further Reading

M.H. Abrams and Geoffrey Harpham, *A Glossary of Literary Terms* (Stamford, CT: Nelson Education, 2014)

Aristotle, *Poetics* (London: Penguin, 1996)

John Carey, *What Good Are the Arts?* (London: Faber and Faber, 2005)

Kimberlé Crenshaw, *On Intersectionality: Essential Writings* (New York: New Press, 2022)

Ewan Fernie, *Shakespeare for Freedom: Why the Plays Matter* (Cambridge: Cambridge University Press, 2017)

Islam Issa, *Milton in the Arab-Muslim World* (London: Routledge, 2016)

Islam Issa, *Shakespeare and Terrorism* (London: Routledge, 2021)

Edward W. Said, *Orientalism* (London: Penguin, 2003)

Ika Willis, *Reception* (London: Routledge, 2018)

Chapter 19

History, naturally

Simon Schama

Is natural history history? How could it not be, when the epic of the earth circumscribes everything else historians write about? Beware writing history backwards, so the commonplace goes, lest projecting the concerns of today into the past rob it of its contingency, its defiance of *telos*. But the imagined independence of history from the preoccupations of the present is, as Benedetto Croce famously insisted, an illusion. Thucydides, the stern critic of subjectivity, was also an alienated protagonist in the wars he narrated. So the most important issue of our times, pandemics notwithstanding, the fate of the habitable planet; the long story of the interaction of humanity and nature, can hardly help but be a spur to historical thinking and writing, even if it has sought permission from the academy to establish a subdiscipline under the unlovely rubric of 'environmental history'. The reason why this would not have occurred to E.H. Carr – or many of his contemporaries – preoccupied, as they were, by wars and revolutions, class struggle and the conflicts of states – would have been, I imagine, the operational truism that all history is, by definition, human history; nature relegated to the passive matrix upon which human action stamps its seal. In that anthropocentric view, nature's presence is the record of human use: an inventory of resources and commodities to be extracted, monetised, traded, converted into various forms of energy or status value, accumulated, made over for recreation and aesthetic pleasure, contested as territory. The corollary to that assumption is that inanimate nature is incapable of documenting itself, being mute, textless, and thus empty of all the source materials on which historians must habitually depend.

All those working assumptions are mistaken. Every year brings chastening confirmation that nature shapes history quite as much as vice versa. Over half a century ago, Emmanuel Le Roy Ladurie in an essay on climate and history suggested the explanatory richness of natural history data such as tree rings, fossil pollen, geological sedimentation, and meteorological reporting in the wake of volcanic eruptions. But research on the historical impact of natural phenomena goes back much further, and was often the work of scientists come to history, rather than vice versa, discovering their new vocation as a second strand. Andrew Ellicott Douglass, the Arizonan who became the first to teach dendrochronology, was originally an astronomer who, in the 1920s, collaborated with the Museum of Natural History on an archaeological project to date the ruins of Indigenous buildings in New Mexico. Tree-ring evidence allowed him to identify those structures as twelfth century: America's medieval culture. Even earlier, in the late nineteenth century, the Swedish chemist and physicist Otto Pettersson, whose family had built its mercantile fortune partly on herring, trained himself in oceanography, and built a private marine research institute on his own land in the west coastal region of Bohuslän where herring shoals had mysteriously reappeared after going missing for centuries. Pettersson's research work, organised from his Hydrographic Institute, led him to believe in the existence of powerful subsurface waves, and to identify the flow of particular salinity favoured by herring shoals. A disruptive change in those submarine currents in the late medieval period, he believed, had dislocated the shoals from Bohuslän and the Kattegat straits out into the North Sea, allowing Dutch fleets to replace their Swedish predecessors as hegemons of the herring: a major shift in the balance of maritime power.

Once historians came to interest themselves in the ways in which natural phenomena could affect the flows of power and wealth, the records of natural history were scrutinised for what answers they could provide to questions shaped by the traditional agenda of social and political history: the incidence of dearths; the rhythms of popular discontent; the pecking order of powers. This was the approach taken by Emmanuel Le Roy Ladurie, Fernand Braudel and their influential colleagues of the Annales school. But over the past few decades the literature of environmental history has featured works in which the record of nature itself calls the shots and sets many of the questions. The turn has been from nature as a passive, auxiliary field, to nature as an active force; with its own intrinsic complexities, evolutionary patterns, shifting qualities and radical revolutions. These new approaches have implications for the whole discipline, for as Bathsheba Demuth, the historian of the Bering Strait and one of the most impressive of this new generation of environmental writers, aptly puts it in *The Floating Coast* (2019), 'what is the nature of history when nature is part of what makes history?'

In fact, this particular branch of 'history now' has always been present, buried in our pre-professional archive. The functional indivisibility of history and geography stretches back, at least, to Pliny the Elder whose *Natural History*, that stupendous *omnium gatherum* of every conceivable scrap of knowledge about the earth (and beyond into the cosmos), was in turn indebted for much of its zoology to Aristotle's morphological resistance to Platonic universalism, in particular his acute observations at the lagoon on Lesbos, and, for its botany, to Aristotle's friend and successor, Theophrastus. The major part of Pliny's volumes is, as per the title, concerned with physical elements, both organic and inorganic, but throughout and especially in Book VII Pliny added, wherever he felt like it, anecdotes, fragments from legend and mythology, about the manners and mores of nations and the 'genius' of rulers (including Caesar), all with the implication that the natural and the human worlds – and their histories – were inseparably bound together, each contributing to the formation of the other. Printed Renaissance histories of nations – Sebastian Münster's *Cosmographia*, for instance, or Camden's *Britannia*, written in the new age of printed cartography – likewise were as much geographies as histories and assumed topography to be the trigger and repository of collective memory. In such chronicles, events were embedded in sites: fields of battle, outcroppings of fortified defence. But unbuilt landscape began to be seen as the matrix, the motherly womb, in which shared identity gestated.

The Romantics went much further. In their writing, painting and music, nature became not just a set of signifiers of eventful human action, nor merely the passive field of man's dominion, but an organic system invested with its own independent agency; obliviousness to the fundamental datum of the world's

317

vitality – that humanity and nature lived in necessary reciproc-
ity – would, at some point, the Romantics believed, incur the
law of diminishing returns. Complacency about industrialising
nature, Ruskin and Wordsworth both prophesied, would end
up sabotaging the human well-being it had been engineered to
advance. This was not just a matter of pastoral regret. Though
conventional cultural periodisation has Romanticism yielding to
positivist science somewhere around the mid-nineteenth century,
the Romantics themselves saw no contradiction between their
poetic expressiveness and the rigour of scientific inquiry. In their
belief that both were needed to explain the world, in particular
the natural world, some of them took their cue from Erasmus
Darwin's startling, eroticised verse on botany – *The Loves of the
Plants*; and all of them were steeped in Alexander von Humboldt's
Kosmos, passages which proceeded, unembarrassed, from scientific morphology to poetic threnody. Thus it was that in order
to write about Turner's images of mountains, Ruskin devoted
almost an entire volume (and one of the most memorable) of
Modern Painters to the geology of the Alps and in particular its
glaciers. The operatically high-pitched chapters on 'Slaty Crys-
tallines', for instance, are both hard geological analysis and prose
rapture, seeking above all to give the stones a *history* – of their
origin in volcanic fire, the great heavings and shakings of the
earth miraculously preserved and inscribed as surface striation.
Inanimate rocks could yet deliver geological eloquence about the
drama of their making. Fossils were primordial archives.

But the writer who most explicitly insisted that the morphology of nature was indeed a kind of history was the prodigious
Jules Michelet. After being expelled from the Collège de France
and dismissed as director of the Archives Nationales, both for

being an unrepentant public critic of Louis Napoleon, Michelet, nailed to the rock face of his nineteen-volume *Histoire de France,* produced, at the same time, a series of short densely poetic and highly personal books, a number of them on nature. *L'Oiseau* (1856) was followed by *L'Insecte* (1858), *La Mer* (1861) and *La Montagne* (1868). Interspersed between them were effusions on *L'Amour* and *La Femme.* Published in the format of a Railway Travellers' Companion, the nature books, unlike *L'Histoire de France,* were a commercial success, selling tens of thousands of copies. And they were also a collaboration between Michelet and his much younger second wife, Athénaïs Mialaret, known in her own right as a nature writer. At the time of Michelet's death in 1874 husband and wife were collaborating on a general work, *La Nature,* which Athénaïs subsequently published under her own name. Conjugal and natural histories were psychologically wired together. The couple had lost their infant child in 1850, and five years later Michelet's daughter, Adèle, estranged from her father and married to the historian Alfred Dumesnil, died as well. Michelet himself explained that his response to a succession of losses – children, friends, the scholarly jobs that had sustained him and made him celebrated – was to immerse himself in what he called the source of the world's vitality. And so, among other startling qualities (not least his compulsive, sometimes egregious, gendering of natural species and phenomena – hence the homonymic equation of *la mer/la mère*), the books are impassioned testimonies to the interdependence of human and natural history. Commenting on a friend's work on the domestication of animals, Michelet insisted that it should be justified not by 'the usefulness that the animals have for man but the usefulness that man can have for the animals'.

As Linda Orr convincingly argued many years ago, echoed more recently by Lionel Gossman, the process of writing his natural histories radically altered Michelet's view of the relationship between human and natural history. He had begun with a sense of flora and fauna as the primitive matrix of ancestral life out of which humanity had liberated itself, much as the French Revolution had pried loose the people from the carapace of the *ancien régime*. And there were aspects of the animal world – what he characterised as war and murder, and the phenomenon which really horrified him in the insect and marine world – infinitely teeming fecundity: seventy million codfish eggs in one hatch – that represented a brutal universe. But as he went along, Michelet, an ardent pantheist, came to see humanity and its history as an extension of, not an opposition to, the natural world. All animate creatures existed, both in the present and the immemorial past, linked by a great chain of organic connection. Sometimes Michelet gave way to sentimental anthropomorphising, idealising, as had Bernard de Lacépède before him, baleen whales as exemplars of conjugal and maternal devotion. He was struck by the gestation of whale offspring taking the same nine-month period as humans, and the spectacle of eight pairs of right whales lying beside each other beached at the estuary of the River Elbe in 1723 spoke to him of tender mutuality. Modern ethological studies may make those emotively loaded observations less ingenuous than they once seemed. And if Michelet was so moved by the plight of a medusa jellyfish in danger of expiring in a drying rock pool that he picked it up and, unstung, deposited the medusa back in the water, it was because he was convinced that animal life was to be located on the extended spectrum of existence where humans too were unmistakably located.

No matter how ostensibly simple the sponge and the sea anemone, they were, somehow, our remote ancestry. There's no evidence that Michelet knew of Darwin's *Expression of Emotions in Animals* published in 1872, though he had read his much earlier work on coral, and corresponded with him about the behaviour of cats, but equally no doubt that he would have agreed with its arguments and examples.

Not many people read Michelet any longer, even in France, except perhaps from literary curiosity (in which case they are richly rewarded), and if they do it's unlikely to be the natural histories. Should you try it, do so in the original. In English translation, the literary hot air ascents may come with tonal altitude sickness. But the nature books ought not to be written off as giddy flights of Romantic self-indulgence. Exiled from Paris, Michelet – like the other two contemporary maritime lyricists, Hugo and Melville – was profoundly immersed in the worlds he wrote about, whether smelling the sea winds in Brittany where he went after the loss of his positions, in warming Liguria or at Hyères on the Côte d'Azur where he died. His winter at Hyères in 1858 which produced much of the material for *La Mer* is in many ways reminiscent of the two years at the lagoon on Lesbos spent by Aristotle, scrupulously observing the species that would fill the pages of his pioneering zoology. And like Aristotle, Michelet's evolving methodology strove to find coherence and even unity in the patterning and ramifications of nature, while never compromising the particularity of individual species. Without formal knowledge of evolution, the trunk, the ramifying branches and leafy outcroppings were all familiar to his understanding of natural development. The acuteness of his observations, however poetically embroidered, seem in places to anticipate the early marine books of Rachel Carson, especially *The Sea Around Us* which made her name and fortune in the 1950s and which also viewed the formation and filling of the teeming marine world as essentially a historical process, narrated moreover in a Humboldtian style that was immediately read as marrying scientific rigour with poetic vividness.

None of this meant that Michelet took his eye off the presence of humans at the edge of the sea, as well as plumbing its depths. Mostly – born of personal experience – he thought of the seaside beach as innocent and even therapeutic, though he deplored the furious velocity (only twenty hours!) with which the railways rushed their pallid travellers from Paris to the Mediterranean. The sea – *mer/mère* – would enfold and heal. There was no hint, as yet, of the pollution of crowds, though Michelet did hate the flimsy structure of bathing booths and houses built of 'boxes'. Though he canvasses the human engagement with the sea from the beginnings of harpooning to the advent of marine therapy, there's no sense in *La Mer* of the baleful consequences of man's arrival on the strand. Of the commerce of the seas, he has no interest whatsoever, seeing it as just watery roadway, surface traffic.

But such roadways, the connecting paths of cultures as well as economies, and the theatres of conflict, are, of course the principal focus of the modern encyclopaedic histories of the oceans, from Fernand Braudel's *The Mediterranean and the Mediterranean World in the Reign of Philip II* – the methodological lodestar of our generation of historians coming into our own in the 1960s and 70s – to the magisterially immense volumes of David Abulafia covering nothing less than the entire history of four of the world's oceans. Or, rather as Abulafia makes clear, the *human* history of those four; in other words, the history of commercial contact, and military conflict. *The Boundless Sea* is, by any standards, an extraordinary and definitive achievement, but what sometimes feels missing from it is the salty matter itself, other than as a route for connecting otherwise distanced and often mutually uncomprehending cultures. That is itself a huge achievement for the grateful reader. At the outset Abulafia declares clearly what his book is not, in particular not a natural history; though this presupposes that natural and human history are, in fact, disconnected stories; an assumption belied by what we now know about the impact of oceanic circulation on climatic change, to say nothing of shifting herring shoals. Abulafia also concedes he's not much interested in fishing; which is a little disappointing to this writer who half a century ago, before tourists arrived in any numbers on the Algarve, witnessed the ancient *Al-madrava* netting and violent dispatch of bluefin tuna, a method, as its Moorish-Arabic name suggests, going back, uninterrupted, to the medieval centuries but which remains the most sustainable alternative to industrial harvesting of endangered bluefins.

The disconnect between the geophysical and human histories also explains the omission, in *The Boundless Sea*, of Antarctica, which although for the most part empty of human presence, turns out, calving by calving, to be the ocean (together with Greenland's seas) on which the imminent fate of the world, especially its low-lying population centres – including Miami, Mumbai, New York, Bangkok and Djakarta – now depends. (To say nothing of *Addio Venezia!*) As one of the great classics of environmental history (and something of a literary masterpiece in its own right) Stephen J. Pyne's *The Ice: A Journey into Antarctica* (1986) made clear more than thirty years ago, the absence of trade and settlement ought never to be confused with the absence of human history.

The structure of Pyne's book is itself something of a template for deep environmental history of the kind that marries natural and human history. He begins with an astonishing lexicon of more than a hundred terms for different kinds of polar ice – for bergs: 'bergy bits . . . growlers, brashers, dirty ice . . .', for sea ices: 'pancake ice, frazil ice, grease ice . . .', for coastal ices: 'fast ice, glacial ice tongues, ice cakes, rime ice, ice haycocks . . .' and so on. You don't have to be a post-structuralist to know that naming is meaning. Except in its pure construction from water, the ice is anything but uniform. Then, in Pyne's artful ordering, chapters follow in which geophysical descriptions of, respectively, the berg, the pack, the shelf, the dome, lead to their respective human histories: the psychodrama of exploration, from Cook's 'negative discovery' (a place unfit for people), to the crucial International Geophysical Year work of 1957–8; chapters on the literary and painterly-photographic response to the Antarctic, and at the end, the politics of this last arena of imperial competition from the eighteenth century through the Cold War.

Antarctica is not, in fact, as Pyne shows, devoid of life: a glacial desert. The pack is a platform for marine mammals and birds, rafts to carry penguins and seals, but within it are contained multitudes of micro-organisms – 'algae, ciliates and flagellates within a crystalline scaffolding'. The biota colonies then generate a prodigious production of krill which in turn feed all kinds of marine life including of course baleen whales, which in their turn drew whalers, until inhibited by enforced conservation. Pyne's work – as in his many, equally essential, works on fire (read his chapter on fire and the eucalypt in *Burning Bush. A Fire History of Australia* and you will never dare to assume again that vegetation doesn't have historical narrative) – has for years been the perfect model of the necessary interconnectedness of natural and human history. He has also written a fine text, *Voice and Vision,* on writing all kinds of history.

Of course with an uninhabited continent comes the imaginative freedom to wander off-piste from the dominant narrative of much environmental history writing. You can guess how it goes. A pristine auto-sustaining ecology, tended by the light footprint of Indigenous peoples, gives way, sometimes by force, to intensive arable cultivation and the introduction of non-native species grown for the market. Absolute property rights, oblivious both to natural boundaries and traditionally shared usufruct, inevitably follow, allowing for the intensive exploitation that is the inevitable herald of habitat exhaustion and economic depletion.

Never mind! Onward march the ecocides to pastures and forests new, leaving behind them a wasteland. Today's deforested terrain converted to livestock-feed production, the Great Chain of Hamburger, is tomorrow's field of windblown plastic. Repetitive though the story may be, it is all too often the bitter truth. One of the great paradigmatic classics of environmental history – which is also, and this is strikingly true of so much of the genre, most beautifully written – is Donald Worster's *The Dust Bowl* (1979), which hews closely to this tragic dialectic. Worster describes the native grasses of the American Great Plains: tall, big blue stem, Indian grass, and switchgrass, sometimes eight foot tall and rooted six feet below the surface; southwest in what would become the Dust Bowl, tenacious short wire grass, buffalo grass, the only varieties suited to survive the extremes of midwest climate swinging between extended drought and cataclysmic storms. Into this habitat, originally grazed by twenty million bison until hunted to near-extinction along with their Indigenous hunters who had, as Worster put it, fitted into the ecology of the prairies as just 'another predator', further decimated by invasive infections, came immigrant cattle men. When the herd-drivers failed to make a go of it, their place was, in turn, taken by sod-busting, steam-driven, mechanised machinery tearing up the soil that had been bound together for thousands of years with tenaciously rooted native grasses. For a time, driven by market demand from swollen city populations, arable farming harvested dizzying profits. But when the next inevitable period of extended drought arrived, the fatefully loosened topsoil turned to blown dirt, and the dirt built into titanic dust storms (especially in the black year of 1935), blinding livestock where they stood, bury-ing poultry alive and drowning an entire rural world in heaving mounds of dirt. The journalist Robert Geiger described what was left in 1935 as 'a vast desert with miniature, shifting dunes of sand'. *Collier's* magazine called the region the 'Land where our children die', a place where there was only 'famine, violent death, private and public futility, insanity and lost generations'. The catastrophe produced the great migration west of 'Okies', memorably narrated in Steinbeck's *Grapes of Wrath*, along with whole populations of the Plains states, all victims of the unsus-tainable cult of industrialised agriculture. But under the auspices of the New Deal, the disaster also led to a better ecological un-derstanding of what nature could and could not tolerate.

The narratives of environmental history may seem as though they turn, almost invariably, on such falls from ecological grace: a counter-scripture to the hubris of human 'conquest' of the earth. But this is not because environmental historians are in-dulging themselves in prelapsarian idealism, but rather because the evidence from natural data is undeniably chastening. The transformation of rural New England described in William Cronon's classic, *Changes in the Land* (1983), from the hunting and gathering practices of Native villages to the intensive agriculture of European settlers, is not so much morally loaded as the result of incommensurable attitudes to property rights and land use; assumptions which all too often backfired on the 'civilised'. The same is true of the mass destruction of the population of bowhead whales in Beringia described in Bathsheba Demuth's *Floating Coast* (2019), driven first by the demand for lighting-oil rendered from blubber; and when that was made obsolete by gas lighting, the market for whalebone-stiffened corsets. For a while, in the first half of the nineteenth century, the bowheads evaded their killers through intelligently acquired information, diving beneath the sea ice, aware that further pursuit by the harpoon boats would risk their being crushed by unstable blocks of that ice, as indeed they often were. 'Their culture', Demuth writes of the bowheads themselves, 'became one of not choosing to die for the commercial market.' Coal-powered steam engines and armoured ice-breaking ships in the last quarter of the century changed all that, and the inexorable hunt to near-extinction followed. Commerce arrived, temporarily, as Demuth argues, while sinking civilisation.

Sobering but impassioned, moved by what one of my own research mentors, Richard Cobb, called 'the archive of the feet', environmental history should not be assumed to be suffocated under a mantle of righteous fatalism. Because it engages with complex changes over long periods of time, it actually leaves room for under-determined outcomes, not just fateful dead ends but roads sometimes not taken but which might still be open. One of those outcomes includes the repair of the planet not least through recovering past attitudes to, and practices in, natural habitats. Understanding, as past cultures have, the nature of fire as regenerative rather than purely destructive, and engaged with rather than warred against, is historical experience made fit for the present and the future. The same is true about a less barricaded approach to inundation in flood zones, which are expanding with every year of accelerating climate change. Of all our histories, that of the environment is perhaps the one where past and future most hopefully seed each other.

It is a little over a quarter of a century since I published the book I felt most compelled to set down for the future: *Landscape and Memory*. It was, and is, emphatically not a work which sets the natural and human worlds at odds with each other. It is intended, at least, to be something like the very opposite: a history of a profound and inescapable entanglement which has produced much fruitfulness alongside barren waste. I still believe deep environmental history to be loaded with one of the great drivers of historical research and writing: the instinct of hope that acts as the salve of despair.

Hudson Valley
February 2021

Selected Further Reading

General introductions and surveys

David Armitage, Alison Bashford and Sujit Sivasundaram (eds.), *Oceanic History* (Cambridge: Cambridge University Press, 2017)

William Cronon, *Uncommon Ground. Rethinking the Human Place in Nature* (New York: W.W. Norton, 1993)

J. Donald Hughes, *An Environmental History of the World*
(London: Routledge, 2nd ed., 2009)

Andrew C. Isenberg (ed.), *The Oxford Handbook of
Environmental History* (Oxford: Oxford University Press,
2014)

Carolyn Merchant, *The Death of Nature: Women, Ecology
and the Scientific Revolution* (New York and London:
HarperCollins, 1990)

Carolyn Merchant, *The Columbia Guide to American
Environmental History* (New York: Columbia University
Press, 2002)

Climate

Wolfgang Behringer, *A Cultural History of Climate*
(Cambridge: Polity Press, 2010)

Emmanuel Le Roy Ladurie, *Times of Feast, Times of Famine.
A History of Climate since the Year 1000* (London:
Doubleday, 1971)

Geoffrey Parker, *Global Crisis: War, Climate Change and
Catastrophe in the Seventeenth Century* (New Haven and
London: Yale University Press 2013) (a great tour de force of
scholarship and ideas)

Some classics

David Abulafia, *The Boundless Sea: A Human History* (Oxford:
Oxford University Press, 2019)

William Cronon, *Changes in the Land: Indians, Colonists and
the Ecology of New England* (New York: Farrar, Straus and
Giroux, 1983)

Robert Macfarlane – anything by him – especially *The Old Ways:*

A Journey on Foot (London and New York: Penguin, 2012),
Underland: A Deep Time Journey (London and New York:
Penguin, 2019)

Stephen J. Pyne, *Burning Bush: A Fire History of Australia*
(Seattle: University of Washington Press, 1988)

Stephen J. Pyne, *Vestal Fire: An Environmental History, Told
through Fire, of Europe and Europe's Encounter with the
World* (Seattle: University of Washington Press, 2000)

Stephen J. Pyne, *The Ice: A Journey to Antarctica* (Seattle:
University of Washington Press, 2006)

Donald Worster, *The Dust Bowl. The Southern Plains in the
1930s* (Oxford: Oxford University Press, 1979)

Recent approaches

Jakobina Arch, *Bringing Whales Ashore: Oceans and the
Environment of Early Modern Japan* (Seattle: University of
Washington Press, 2018)

Bathsheba Demuth, *Floating Coast: An Environmental History
of the Bering Strait* (New York: W.W. Norton, 2019)

Jon Gertner, *The Ice at the End of the World: An Epic Journey
into Greenland's Buried Past and our Perilous Future* (New
York: Penguin, 2019)

Daegan Miller, *This Radical Land. A Natural History of American
Dissent* (Chicago: University of Chicago Press, 2018)

Richard Ravalli, *Sea Otters: A History* (Lincoln, Nebraska:
University of Nebraska Press, 2018)

and not so recent

Simon Schama, *Landscape and Memory* (New York and
London: Knopf, 1995)

ACKNOWLEDGEMENTS

HC: Thank you Liz Altwasser and David Carr for giving the nod to this book and for your trust and encouragement throughout.

Thank you, Maddy Price, for taking a chance on this idea, it has been a joy to work with you. Thank you to Rachel Mills for your constant support (as ever!) and to Carrie Plitt. You have both dedicated so much time and thoughtful consideration.

Thank you to Professor Thomas Dixon for your time and thoughts on the history of emotions, and how I might discuss them in a relative nutshell. I am grateful and I look forward to further enjoyable conversations.

Thank you to my mother for giving me a psychologist's perspective behind our emotions.

Enormous thanks to our wonderful contributors, who also took a chance. Without your brilliance, this book literally would not be: what a community you are!

To Suzie, who shared the vision for this book from the outset. This would never have materialised without you, and in the process you have taught me innumerable lessons without ever being in the same room. I am proud to have my name beside yours on the cover of this book and thank you for sharing it with me.

Finally, to Henry, to whom I owe the most thanks. For giving up the precious little time you have to yourself between working, parenting, cooking and cleaning to read my scribbles or listen to me orate them. Thank you for encouraging this project from the outset and above all, for being my greatest support.

SL: Thank you to Maddy Price for taking a chance on the book, and to Carrie Plitt and Rachel Mills for backing us so completely.

Thank you to Dr Hilary Davidson for thoughts on Richard Lipscomb's clothing, and to Professor Sarah Knott for steering me towards some wonderful historiography. Thank you to Alan Scadding for first introducing me to E.H. Carr and to Robin Briggs for his generous intellectual support – as ever.

Thank you to each and every one of the essayists in this book for writing so powerfully about what they know. Thank you to those who responded, astonishingly, with favour to an email from the blue, and to those who have suffered me taking advantage of years of friendship.

Thank you to my mother for always being my first reader.

Thank you to Dan Jones for lovingly (though you'll probably think that an empty adverb) savaging my essay to its betterment.

Thank you to Helen for responding enthusiastically to my impertinent suggestion that I clamber aboard your nascent project to edit a book based on your great-grandfather's crucial text.

It has, throughout, been a great joy to work with you, and it has been a privilege to become your friend. Sisterhood feels good.

Thank you, always and forever, to my dear husband, for everything.

CONTRIBUTORS

Justin Bengry

Dr Justin Bengry is a cultural historian of sexualities and the queer past focusing on twentieth-century Britain at Goldsmiths, University of London, where he is Director of the Centre for Queer History and leads the world's first MA in Queer History.

Leila K. Blackbird

Leila K. Blackbird is an adoptee of Mescalero Apache and Eastern Cherokee descent. She is the Pozen Family Human Rights Doctoral Fellow of History at the University of Chicago and a Research Associate at the American Historical Association (AHA), working at the intersection of Black and Indigenous US and Atlantic histories.

Emily Brand

Emily Brand is a historian, author and genealogist with a special interest in the Georgian era. Her book *The Fall of the House of Byron* is a sweeping history of the eighteenth century through the eyes of one notorious family.

Helen Carr

Helen Carr is a historian, author of the bestselling book *The Red Prince: John of Gaunt, Duke of Lancaster*, and a TV producer. Helen is working on a doctorate in the history of medieval emotions at Queen Mary University London.

Gus Casely-Hayford

Dr Gus Casely-Hayford is the inaugural Director of V&A East, Professor of Practice, SOAS, and was previously Director of the Smithsonian National Museum of African Art, Washington DC.

Sarah Churchwell

Sarah Churchwell is Professor in American Literature and Chair of Public Understanding of the Humanities at the School of Advanced Study, University of London. Her most recent book is *Behold, America: A History of America First and the American Dream*.

Caroline Dodds Pennock

Dr Caroline Dodds Pennock is Senior Lecturer in International History at the University of Sheffield. She is the author of *Bonds of Blood: Gender, Lifecycle and Sacrifice in Aztec Culture* and is currently writing a book on early Indigenous travellers to Europe entitled *On Savage Shores: The American Discovery of Europe*.

Peter Frankopan

Peter Frankopan is Professor of Global History at the University of Oxford. He is the author of the internationally bestselling *The Silk Roads: A New History of the World* and *The New Silk Roads: The Present and Future of the World*.

Dan Hicks

Dan Hicks is Professor of Contemporary Archaeology at the University of Oxford, Curator of World Archaeology at the Pitt Rivers Museum and a Fellow of St Cross College, Oxford. His book *The Brutish Museums: the Benin Bronzes, Colonial Violence and Cultural Restitution* is published by Pluto Press.

Bettany Hughes

Professor Bettany Hughes is an award-winning historian, author and broadcaster. Her latest book is *Venus & Aphrodite: History of a Goddess*.

Islam Issa

Dr Islam Issa is an award-winning writer, curator and broadcaster. He is Reader in Literature and History at Birmingham City University. The author of *Milton in the Arab-Muslim World* and *Shakespeare and Terrorism*, he has also presented television and radio programmes including *Cleopatra and Me: In Search of a Lost Queen* and *The Balcony*.

Maya Jasanoff

Maya Jasanoff is the Coolidge Professor of History at Harvard University. She is the author of three acclaimed books of imperial and global history, including *The Dawn Watch*, winner of the Cundill Prize in History, and *Liberty's Exiles*, winner of the National Book Critics Circle Award and finalist for the Baillie Gifford Prize.

Suzannah Lipscomb

Suzannah Lipscomb is Professor Emerita of History at the University of Roehampton and the author of five books: most recently, *The Voices of Nîmes: Women, Sex, and Marriage in Reformation Languedoc*. She is the writer-presenter of more than forty hours of history documentaries and a columnist for *History Today*.

Rana Mitter

Rana Mitter is Professor of the History and Politics of Modern China at the University of Oxford. His books include *China's War with Japan: The Struggle for Survival, 1937–1945* (US title: *Forgotten Ally*), which was named a Book of the Year in the *Financial Times* and the *Economist*.

Onyeka Nubia

Dr Onyeka Nubia is a historian, writer and presenter, and lecturer at Nottingham University. He is reinventing our perceptions of the Renaissance, British history and Black Studies.

Charlotte Lydia Riley

Charlotte Lydia Riley is lecturer in twentieth-century British history at the University of Southampton. She is the editor of *Free Speech Wars: How did we get here and why does it matter?* She is currently writing *Imperial Island*, which tells an alternative history of Britain's relationship with its empire.

Miri Rubin

Miri Rubin is Professor of Medieval and Early Modern History at Queen Mary University of London. Her research explores

European religious and social relations with special interest in the operation of gender, in material and visual cultures, and in relations between Christians and Jews. Her most recent book is *Cities of Strangers*.

Simon Schama

Sir Simon Schama is University Professor of Art History and History at Columbia University. He is the author of nineteen books and the writer-presenter of fifty documentaries on art, literature and history for the BBC. His work has been translated into fifteen languages and he is Contributing Editor at the *Financial Times*.

Alex von Tunzelmann

Alex von Tunzelmann is a historian and screenwriter. She is the author of five books: most recently *Fallen Idols: Twelve Statues That Made History*. Her first feature film, *Churchill* (2017), starred Brian Cox and Miranda Richardson. She has also written episodes of *Medici* on Netflix.

Jaipreet Virdi

Jaipreet Virdi is a scholar-activist and historian of medicine, technology and disability. She is Assistant Professor at the University of Delaware and author of *Hearing Happiness: Deafness Cures in History*. Her work has appeared in *The Atlantic, Slate, Aeon, Wellcome Collection* and *New Internationalist*.